A Culture of Corruption

A Culture of Corruption

EVERYDAY DECEPTION AND POPULAR

DISCONTENT IN NIGERIA

Daniel Jordan Smith

PRINCETON UNIVERSITY PRESS

PRINCETON AND OXFORD

Copyright © 2007 by Princeton University Press
Published by Princeton University Press, 41 William Street,
Princeton, New Jersey 08540
In the United Kingdom: Princeton University Press, 3 Market Place,
Woodstock, Oxfordshire OX20 1SY

All Rights Reserved

Library of Congress Cataloging-in-Publication Data

Smith, Daniel Jordan, 1961–
A culture of corruption: everyday deception and popular discontent in Nigeria /
Daniel Jordan Smith.
p. cm.
Includes bibliographical references and index.
ISBN-13: 978-0-691-12722-4 (hardcover: alk. paper)
ISBN-10: 0-691-12722-0 (hardcover: alk. paper)
1. Corruption—Nigeria. 2. Nigeria—Moral conditions. I. Title.
HV7165.5.S65 2006
364.1'32309669—dc22   2006006620

British Library Cataloging-in-Publication Data is available

This book has been composed in Galliard

Printed on acid-free paper. ∞

pup.princeton.edu

Printed in the United States of America

10   9   8   7   6   5   4   3   2

In memory of
Claus Gustav Jordan and Charlotte Backus Jordan

Contents

Illustrations

Preface

IT IS EASY TO FEEL ambivalent about Nigeria. In my experience, the people are outgoing, warm, and welcoming. They exude confidence and pride. For scholars and other friends of Africa who sometimes feel compelled to combat misguided stereotypes that the continent and its people are helpless and hopeless, nothing could serve as a stronger counter than witnessing ambitious, vibrant, and entrepreneurial Nigerians going about their daily lives. Against seemingly insurmountable obstacles, people exhibit fortitude and persevere with great resilience. As big as Nigeria is, it sometimes seems too small to contain its astonishing fury of human activity. More than any place I have ever been, there is never a dull moment. Maybe the only thing more striking than Nigerians' extraordinary efforts to fulfill their aspirations is the critical collective awareness they possess regarding the problems in their own society—a national self-consciousness perhaps most evident in Nigerians' biting, unrestrained, and frequently self-mocking humor. Nigeria is an exciting place to live, work, and of course study. For these reasons and many others, it is impossible not to love Africa's giant.

But Nigeria can be a very difficult place as well. The same characteristics that make Nigeria appealing can also make it loathsome. As an anthropologist, it is usually considered impolitic to say you dislike the place you work, even if you love it too. In published representations of our research, anthropologists generally err on the side of empathy for our subjects. Part of the beauty of our craft is that immersion in another society and culture offers insights and perspectives not available through other methods of social science. Getting to know something about real people and their everyday lives by working, living, and being with them over a relatively long period of time is at the core of our contribution to scholarship, and to any larger idealistic ambitions we may have for making the world a better place. For all that we celebrate cultural difference, we also affirm that in many crucial ways, "they" are just like "us."

While it might seem odd to emphasize my ambivalence about Nigeria up front, ironically it is a sentiment I share with many, if not most, Nigerians. Part of their collective self-consciousness is an unsurpassed capacity for self-criticism. So when I say that in addition to being gregarious and hospitable, Nigerians can be aggressive and intimidating, or that even as they are proud and self-assured, they are also frequently arrogant and unyielding, I suspect that many Nigerians will recognize these traits in their compatriots, and maybe even in themselves. I have frequently described Nigeria to colleagues who work in other West African countries by saying that they would find many similarities, but that in Nigeria the volume is turned up—sometimes too high. The country's huge population and a process of rapid urbanization contribute to a sense that life is hectic, hurried, and stressful—a perception often voiced by Nigerians in the ubiquitous pidgin English phrase "Nigeria na war-o," which translates literally as "Nigeria is a war." For ordinary Nigerians, and certainly sometimes for me, getting ready for each day in Nigeria is a bit like preparing for the tension of battle. Life is hard, but what is more, Nigerians almost seem to take pleasure in making it harder for themselves and others.

Anyone who has experienced a Nigerian "go slow," the local slang for a traffic jam, has seen some of these dynamics at work. Drivers aggressively attempt to circumnavigate the traffic, maneuvering between lanes, cutting off competing vehicles, driving on the shoulders, and frequently even racing between oncoming vehicles in the opposite lane—all the while loudly cursing and condemning other drivers who resort to the same tactics. On public transportation, passengers exhort their drivers to take drastic measures to get them where they are going as fast as possible, even as they lament the whole spectacle. All involved appear to know that bad driving only worsens the traffic, but once others are doing it everyone feels compelled to participate or risk being overtaken, left behind, and even squashed.

The parallels to corruption, the topic of this book, are striking. While corruption is obviously much more complex than a traffic jam, in each phenomenon ordinary Nigerians are participants in a process wherein they are simultaneously the main victims and the loudest critics. Traffic jams, like corruption, contribute to making Nigeria such a stressful place. In moments of frustration, it is easy to attribute these problems to some kind of shared national flaw. Nigerians themselves often lead the bandwagon in this regard. Debating and analyzing the country's woes is a popular obsession, from the ranks of the intellectual elite to the poorest of the poor. No other national issue so riles Nigerians as corruption. They are acutely aware of its consequences and ambivalent about their own role in its perpetuation. Discontents about corruption dominate the national discourse. This book is about understanding corruption and its discontents, and showing how corruption and the discourses of complaint it generates are at the core of contemporary events, shaping collective imagination and driving social action.

For a long time, my affection for Nigeria, attachment to people there, and intellectual orientation as an anthropologist prevented me from approaching corruption as an object of scholarship. From a personal point of view, I felt that focusing on corruption stereotyped and oversimplified the lives of people I knew and cared about. From an intellectual point of view, I thought that writing about corruption ran the risk of perpetuating common Western misrepresentations of Africa.

My inclination over the years has been to play down corruption in my accounts of Nigeria to friends, students, and professional colleagues in the United States. When U.S. friends and colleagues would ask me about the infamous harassment at the airport in Lagos, I usually replied that the reality was not nearly as bad as perceived and that the situation had improved a lot over the years—both true. In response to more general questions about corruption, I always tried to emphasize that Nigerians are good people, like people everywhere. When I thought someone might actually listen, I often added that we would do well not to exaggerate the differences in corruption between Nigeria and our society, a warning that resonated in Providence, Rhode Island, the city where I currently reside, where a long-time and very popular mayor ran a notoriously corrupt city government for many years. Recent U.S. corporate corruption scandals like Enron and news media accounts of shady government contracts awarded to companies such as Halliburton, which has extensive dealings in Nigeria as well as Iraq, have also reinforced a degree of caution in seeing corruption as a problem primarily in so-called Third World countries. Nevertheless, the popular and global association of Nigeria with corruption produced a particularly bad image, and my inclination was to combat it.

Although my most common response to inquiries about Nigerian corruption has been to try to correct overly negative images of the country, it would be disingenuous if I did not admit that I sometimes take a certain pride in the fact that I have lived, worked, and studied for so long in a place that has a reputation for being so difficult. Anthropologists are perversely fond of celebrating the hardships of our trade, whether they are the deprivations of rural life, the exposure to tropical diseases, or the adjustments to strange foods and "exotic" cultural practices. When other anthropologists or Africans in other countries in which I have spent a lot of time, such as Sierra Leone and Ghana, say things like, "You must be strong to live all those years in Nigeria," I have perhaps enjoyed this response too much. I must admit that at times, Nigeria's corruption has served as my symbol of its exoticness.

My effort to avoid portraying Nigeria's corruption as exotic, but also to sidestep confronting my own perverse enjoyment of that image, prevented me from addressing corruption head-on. The intense preoccupation that Nigerians themselves exhibit regarding corruption in their society, however, always left me with a nagging feeling that simply countering negative images obscured important questions. Nigeria *is* rife with corruption, and no one is more aware of it than ordinary Nigerians. In various ways that I will describe and explain in this book, Nigerians are fixated on and passionate about corruption. Navigating corruption preoccupies people in all kinds of everyday endeavors, and talk about corruption dominates popular discourse. Much as I would like to be able to wipe the stigma of corruption from Nigeria's global reputation, Nigerians themselves regularly reminded me that corruption is one of their most pressing problems. Increasingly, instead of trying to minimize the significance of Nigeria's notorious corruption, I realize that explaining it is central to understanding the very fabric of Nigerian society.

I began working in Nigeria more than fifteen years ago, first as a public health adviser for an international development organization and then for the last decade as an anthropologist. I met my wife in 1989, not long after I arrived in the country, and my relationship to Nigeria became even more personal when we married in 1992. Being an in-law became a central part of my identity in Nigeria, not only among my wife's kin and community members, but in much larger social networks. Over the years, being an in-law has proved to be a great advantage, not only as an anthropologist, but in navigating daily life in Nigeria. Nigerians almost universally become even more welcoming, helpful, and outgoing when they learn I am married to a Nigerian, even in settings that are seemingly impersonal, such as in government offices, at police checkpoints, or during airport customs searches. Indeed, being an in-law has illuminated how the interpenetration of personal networks and the bureaucratic offices of the state are integral to the mechanisms of corruption.

I would like to think that being an in-law has mostly added to my capacity to get the anthropologist's much sought-after "insider's perspective." But I do not mean to exaggerate these advantages or suggest that this book would have been impossible without them. Further, I do not want to minimize some of the obstacles created by being an in-law, perhaps especially in Ubakala, my wife's natal community, where I have lived much the time during my research. In some cases, people have proven less willing to trust me precisely because I am an in-law, and am therefore perceived to have vested interests that they need to consider in deciding what to say to me. Yet this is not a book about me or the impact of being both an in-law and anthropologist in Nigeria. In the chapters that follow, when my in-law status seems relevant to explaining something that occurred in my interactions with people or I think it influenced what they said, I mention it, in the same way that I try to explain other salient contextual issues. But I deal with it here mostly to acknowledge it up front so that the book can focus on corruption and its discontents as they are experienced by Nigerians.

The fact that I have spent most of my years in Nigeria in the Southeast, and almost all of them among Igbo-speaking people certainly affects the version of "Nigeria" that comes across here. I have little doubt that many readers who are intimately familiar with Nigeria will read this book and recognize that it is particularly influenced by the Igbo perspective. Such an observation is almost certainly true. A few years ago, I traveled with an Igbo colleague from a university in southeastern Nigeria to Kano, the largest city in Hausa-dominated northern Nigeria. Our car broke down in the northern state of Kaduna and we were stranded for two days in a small village while a local mechanic rebuilt the engine. On the second day, we were joined by a Hausa man from Kaduna whose car also broke down. Inevitably our conversations turned to Nigerian politics. At a point, my Igbo colleague and the Hausa man were discussing the issue of ethnicity. They were debating the relative contributions and difficulties posed by their respective ethnic groups to the future of Nigeria. After extolling the Igbos' ingenuity and work ethic, the Hausa man said, "The problem with the Igbo man is that he has an 'exaggerated personality.'" My Igbo friend laughed uproariously, accepting his Hausa interlocutor's characterization, even if it was a criticism. I remember thinking that most people from neighboring African countries would probably apply the Hausa man's critique of the Igbo to Nigerians as a whole, but it was a useful reminder of the diversity and nuances of culture within Africa's most populous country.

Almost all of my ethnographic examples of corruption as well as the contemporary events and popular discourses that corruption generates come from southeastern Nigeria. That is where I have lived for more than six years, and it is the place I have visited in all but two years since 1989. While my experiences and evidence have an Igbo slant, the kinds of everyday corruption I describe are not unique to the Igbo or the Southeast. Further, a good deal of the book focuses on local and popular understandings of corruption in the world of politics and the machinery of the Nigerian state, particularly in the arenas of development and democracy. Although Igbo interpretations are certainly colored by their history and cultural context, I believe Nigerians of all ethnic groups along with scholars and students more conversant with other parts of Nigeria will find much that is familiar. Indeed, part of my argument is that corruption and the discourses of complaint it produces are central to the way all Nigerians experience and understand the relationship between state and society.

In showing how discontents about corruption drive contemporary events and explain important social trends, I rely on local examples about which I have concrete ethnographic evidence. My analysis of resurgent ethnic nationalism focuses on Igbo nationalism, but I believe that similar arguments hold in other regions of the country. My explanation of the burgeoning popularity of born-again Christianity in southeastern Nigeria surely has parallels in the Muslim North. The vigilantes I describe in southeastern cities, and the rumors and accusations about the occult that circulate in

Igbo communities, are found in their own vernacular forms elsewhere in Nigeria. The most persuasive evidence that I present is local and specific, but I contend that this strengthens rather than weakens the larger theoretical assertions I wish to pursue. At the very least, I hope it gives other scholars rich material to compare to their own findings and conclusions.

The research for this project has occurred over all the years I have lived and worked in Nigeria. I gathered some of my material before I even knew I was studying corruption. Only later did I realize what a large corpus of "data" on the subject I had accumulated over time. Even during my dissertation research, from 1995 to 1997, corruption was not my topic of study. I was interested in the effects of social change on population processes such as marriage, family organization, and fertility. But as is inevitably the case in Nigeria, corruption figured prominently in everyday experience and the common conversations of daily life. It was only in 2000 (the first time I returned to Nigeria following its transition to civilian rule in 1999) that I decided corruption was something I wanted to write about, perhaps spurred by the extra intensity of national discourses about corruption in the wake of Nigerians' rising expectations about democracy. Since 2000, I have spent every summer in Nigeria, and in 2004 I was there from June to December. Gathering ethnographic data about corruption meant being more attentive to media stories about the subject, interviewing people about their experiences with everyday forms of corruption and their interpretations of national corruption-related scandals, and trying to be even more diligent about observing and documenting the instances of corruption and the plethora of common narratives and complaints about corruption that are the stuff of daily life in Nigeria. It also meant paying attention to a wide range of contemporary events with the intention of pursuing their connections to corruption and its discontents. The book uses the experiences of particular people to understand and explain phenomena that have broad social and theoretical implications. By focusing on corruption ethnographically, I hope to show the kinds of insights that can be produced by taking this approach to studying a major contemporary problem.

Writing about corruption involves important ethical issues, including protecting people's confidentiality and anonymity. Although many people have told me that I have their permission to use their names in the stories I tell, in most cases I have chosen to protect people's identities by disguising their names, and in some instances slightly altering the context of their cases. Obviously I cannot do this where the people involved are public figures, but in almost all instances, what I write about public figures is available in the media or is in regard to what ordinary Nigerians say about them. When I utilize quotations from newspapers and other publicly circulated documents, including e-mail scam letters, I reproduce them verbatim, without grammatical or spelling corrections.

Many people have asked me whether I think I will be banned from Nigeria once this book is published. I have always said that I do not think so, because I have forever found Nigeria to be a place of remarkable freedom of expression. The stories I tell about corruption in Nigeria are no more inflammatory or revealing than what circulates in everyday discourse, including in the media. Further, I do not try to document high-level corruption in this book. I am much more interested in how typical Nigerians experience corruption and what they have to say about it. Finally, and most important, I intend the book to be empathetic as well as critical. I certainly hope it is read that way, for that is surely the Nigerian spirit.

Acknowledgments

As I TRAVELED DOWN the long road of completing this book, I developed a new appreciation for the depth of debts that authors must acknowledge. I now read others' acknowledgments with a much greater appreciation, and hope my readers will realize that the gratitude and thanks I express here are much more than a formality.

This study would not have been possible without financial support from a number of sources. Though my dissertation ostensibly had nothing to do with corruption, in retrospect, many of the first ideas for this book were kindled during my dissertation research, and much of the evidence for the book was gathered during that initial long period of fieldwork from 1995 to 1997. I thank the Institute for International Education–Fulbright Program, the Population Council, the Wenner-Gren Foundation for Anthropological Research, and the National Science Foundation for funding my dissertation research.

I have continued to conduct fieldwork in Nigeria in every year since 1999. Although I have been funded to study a variety of topics, being in Nigeria inevitably enabled me to advance my research on corruption. I gratefully acknowledge the National Institutes of Health (3 P30 HD28251–10S1 and 1 R01 41724–01A1), the National Science Foundation (BCS–0075764), and the Wenner-Gren Foundation for Anthropological Research (6636) for their generous support of my research in Nigeria, without which this book would not have been possible. I also thank the Watson Institute for International Studies and the Department of Anthropology at Brown University for funding portions of my summer research. I owe particular gratitude to the Andrew W. Mellon Foundation, which not only funded my two-year postdoctoral fellowship at the Population Studies and Training Center at Brown University from 1999 to 2001 but also supported half of my salary for my first four years as an assistant professor of anthropology. Without this support, this book—and much else for which I am grateful—would not have been possible.

Two chapters in the book are adaptations of previously published articles. Chapter 5 is a revised and expanded version of "Ritual Killing, '419,' and Fast Wealth: Inequality and the Popular Imagination in Southeastern Nigeria," which appeared in *American Ethnologist* (28, no. 4:803–26) in 2001, and was copyrighted by the American Anthropological Association. Chapter 6 is a revised and expanded version of "The Bakassi Boys: Vigilantism, Violence, and Political Imagination in Nigeria," which appeared in

Cultural Anthropology in (19, no. 3:429–55) 2004, and was copyrighted by the American Anthropological Association and the University of California Press. I thank the American Anthropological Association and the University of California Press for permission to use versions of these articles in this book.

I owe an incalculable debt to my supportive colleagues at Brown University. In the Department of Anthropology, my work has been encouraged, constructively criticized, and improved by a group of generous and engaged colleagues. They have all made me feel like they want me to succeed, and have always been willing to advise and assist. Douglas Anderson, William Beeman, Lina Fruzzetti, Richard Gould, Matthew Gutmann, Marida Hollos, Stephen Houston, David Kertzer, Shepard Krech III, Philip Leis, Catherine Lutz, Patricia Rubertone, William Simmons, Patricia Symonds, Nicholas Townsend, and Kay Warren have all acted at one time or another as adviser, cheerleader, critic, and teacher. In particular, I thank Philip Leis and David Kertzer for serving as mentors, reading and critiquing my work, and providing invaluable career counsel. I am especially grateful to David Kertzer, not only because I owe him a great professional debt, but because he continually shows the goodwill to do the little things to support and encourage his junior colleague.

A large number of anthropology graduate students have challenged my thinking and enhanced my scholarship through comments on my work, but particularly through their own work. I am especially grateful to Caroline Archambault, Lacey Andrews, Katie Rhine, and Bruce Whitehouse. Also, since 2001, I have taken one or two Brown undergraduates to Nigeria each summer, and their fresh eyes have enabled me to see familiar things in new ways. Heather Clark, Sora Chung, Bathsheba Demuth, Rahul Kamath, Sarah Kimball, Nayla Khoury, Emily Timm, and Rachel Weston share in experiences that have created a special bond.

The Population Studies and Training Center has been my interdisciplinary home at Brown. A second office there in a wonderful new building during a semester of sabbatical provided an environment that enabled me to complete the book manuscript. I am especially grateful to Mark Pitt, the director, not only for accommodating me while I wrote the book, but for providing material support and enthusiastic encouragement ever since I arrived at Brown. A number of colleagues at the Population Studies and Training Center and in the Department of Sociology have encouraged and enhanced this project, including Francis Goldscheider, Patrick Heller, and Susan Short. I particularly want to thank Calvin Goldscheider and Michael White for their keen interest and tireless encouragement. Both exemplify the concept of collegiality.

I also owe thanks to a large number of colleagues outside Brown. Several faculty members who were at Emory University when I did my doctorate provided and continue to offer invaluable support, and they pushed me in ways that enriched this book. In particular, I must thank Peggy Barlett, Peter Brown, Donald Donham, Marcia Inhorn, Ivan Karp, and Cory Kratz. I am especially grateful to Ivan Karp and Cory Kratz for their advice and encouragement about the book, and to Peter Brown, not only for his constructive suggestions about the book, but also for his wise counsel and trusted friendship. In addition, former fellow graduate students John Bing, Andrew Cousins, Joanna Davidson, Jessica Gregg, Gayatri Reddy, Malcolm Shelley, Holly Wardlow, and John Wood contributed to my thinking, and to the joy of being an anthropologist, both in graduate school and since.

Numerous colleagues and mentors across the academy have supported this project and enhanced it directly and indirectly through their encouragement, suggestions, and critical intellectual contributions. Misty Bastian, David Pratten, and Elisha Renne have shared both a love for Nigeria and a willingness to read, criticize, and improve my work. Andrew Apter, Giorgio Blundo, Pamela Feldman-Savelsberg, James Ferguson, and Jane Guyer have provided ideas and encouragement for which I am very grateful. Akhil Gupta graciously shared some of his not yet published manuscripts on similar topics in India, which helped refine my thinking. Giorgio Blundo generously shared his unpublished papers, which supplemented an impressive and stimulating corpus of his published work on corruption in West Africa. Bruce Knauft, who I did not know well when I was at Emory, has become a generous and helpful adviser, infectious in his enthusiasm. Caroline Bledsoe and Peter Geschiere have proven to be amazing mentors, always responsive for requests for advice, and providing wonderfully constructive feedback on anything I sent their way. My current research collaborators, Jennifer Hirsch, Shanti Parikh, Harriet Phinney, and Holly Wardlow, remind me all the time what a great job this is. Their incredible minds always challenge my thinking. Several of my colleagues read the entire manuscript and offered invaluable constructive critiques and advice, including Peter Brown, Peter Geschiere, Jennifer Hirsch, Stephen Houston, David Kertzer, Philip Leis and David Pratten. In addition, two anonymous reviewers provided extensive and insightful criticism, advice, and suggestions, which aided me immensely in revising the manuscript. Fred Appel, my editor at Princeton University Press, expressed unfailing enthusiasm and provided expert guidance throughout the entire process. His professionalism, expeditious work, and patience with all my questions are much appreciated. I am also grateful to Cindy Milstein, whose meticulous and clear copyediting made the writing much better.

My old friend Scott Auwarter, with whom I shared my first Africa experience in the Peace Corps in Sierra Leone over twenty years ago, has always stayed interested in my academic work, pushing me to make it readable to people outside the ivory tower. Kelley Smith provided a fantastic editorial eye and warm-spirited encouragement. Ever since we have known each other, some people have asked whether we are related. We are not, but I would be proud if we were. Maggie Friedfeld helped immensely getting the illustrations ready when I was in the most hectic final stages, and managed to reinsert humor into the whole process.

In Nigeria, my academic debts are wide, but I must especially thank P. J. Ezeh, Patrick Ngoddy, and Pat Ngwu at the University of Nigeria, Nsukka. At the University of Ibadan, I salute and say thank you to my friend and colleague Oka Obono, whose sharp mind and wonderful sense of humor embody the best of Nigeria. At Abia State University, which has served as my primary institutional base in Nigeria, I thank the former vice chancellor, Professor Ogwo E. Ogwo, David Chidi Imo, and Blessing Mberu. Most of all, I must thank my colleague and close friend Igwe Aja-Nwachuku. When I think of who I would seek out in a pinch in Nigeria, Igwe is at the very top of the list.

Over the years, a number of people at various other institutions have assisted with one or another aspect of living and working in Nigeria, including Jay Taylor and Bene Uche at United States Information Service in Lagos, and Lillie Kamanu and Noelle Wright-Young at the U.S. Consulate in Lagos. In addition, Alan Alemian, Jack Marrkand, Dewitt Webster, and the late Bekki Johnson all taught me that the difficulties and contradictions in development programs would be far worse were it not for people of their caliber and commitment.

A number of other friends and professional colleagues in Nigeria have been instrumental in teaching me about Nigeria, and making my many years there joyous and rewarding. Chibuzo Oriuwa has been a valued colleague and trusted friend since the beginning, as has Bishop M. N. Nkemakolam, whose goodwill for his fellow human beings seems to know no bounds. Jane Ibeaja never fails to impress me with her intelligence, hard work, and kindness. Ukay Wachuku has been the best of friends, and never fails to challenge my assumptions. Benjamin Mbakwem has proven to be both a good friend and a source of inspiration. He is the keenest observer of Nigeria I know, and almost every word that comes out his mouth is an ethnographic gem. All of these people, and many more I cannot name, have taught me much.

Everyone who knows me in Nigeria knows the joy I experience playing tennis and spending time with my friends at the various tennis clubs in Owerri and Umuahia. I am not sure, however, that everyone knows how much I owe my friends and fellow clubbers for my intellectual fulfillment in Nigeria. Their stories, observations, and experiences permeate this book. I cannot thank all of them by name, but I must mention Emma

Anosike, James Anukam, Emma Chijioke, James Ifediora, Goddy Nwogu, Chudi Ofodike, Ike Ogbokiri, Levinus Okeh, Sam Okonkwo, B.C.B. Okoro, S. K. Okpi, Ferguson Onuoha, Goddy Onuoha, Odi Onwudiwe, and Lawrence Ukattah. To them and all my other friends I say "*Ahi* Club!"

In Ubakala, my wife's community and my home in Nigeria, my debts are many. Fortunately, Igbo people are fond of saying that a debt never dies, so I have a lifetime to repay mine. I am especially grateful to Eze Raphael Mbagwu, Chief Israel Iroabuchi, Prince Udo Ogbuehi, Chief Ufomba Ihenacho, Sir Samuel and Lady Chinkata Nwachukwu, Mr. and Mrs. Okwuchukwu Amuzie, and Mrs. Elizabeth Uhuegbu. Thank you all for welcoming me as your *ogonwoke*. I owe an especially great debt to Chidozie Amuzie, who always pointed me in the right direction and asked just the right challenging question.

I cannot thank enough my late father-in-law, Joshua Agoha, my mother-in-law, Jemmaimah Agoha, my brother-in-law Christian Agoha and his wife, Ulunma, my brother-in-law Moses Agoha, and my sister-in-law, Elizabeth Ogbonna, for accepting me as one of the family. It is all of them who make me feel that when I go to Nigeria, I am going home.

My father, William C. Smith, my mother, Gretchen McKnew, and my stepfather, Donald McKnew, have given me more than any son should rightly expect. My brother, Derek, and sister, Story, and their families direct my attention outside academia just often enough to keep things in perspective. My debt to them goes well beyond anything to do with this book.

Finally, I must thank Ada, my wife and life partner, who continually reminds me what really matters and why.

To the extent that this book offers something useful, I am obliged and pleased to acknowledge all of the above. Of course, any errors, mistakes, and other shortcomings are solely my responsibility.

A Culture of Corruption

BY THE TIME I ARRIVED in Nigeria in 1989 as an employee of an international development organization, I was well aware of the country's reputation for corruption. I had heard the common stories of immigration and customs officers who shake down arriving passengers at the airport, police looking for money who harass motorists, taxi drivers who collude with criminals to rob customers, and government officials who do nothing without a bribe. Further, I had read that the government-controlled oil industry was riddled with graft, and that beginning in the 1980s, Nigeria was believed to be a transit hub in the international narcotics trade, with widespread allegations of official collusion. The U.S. Department of State issued bold warnings about fraud in its advice to travelers and businesspeople contemplating visits to Nigeria. The country's image as a bastion of bribery, venality, and deceit has remained constant over the years. Most recently, the global expansion of the Internet delivered evidence of Nigerian fraud to the e-mail in-boxes of millions of people around the world, in the form of scam letters seeking bank account numbers and advance fees in schemes that are premised on Nigeria's worldwide reputation for corruption.

In one of my first letters home in 1989, I recounted a story I heard as I met new friends over beers after a game of tennis:

Last night, AC, who is a businessman, told the most amazing story about how some Nigerians in Lagos duped a Texas oil executive out of one hundred thousand dollars. I don't know if you have heard of it, but apparently Nigerians commonly send letters and faxes to U.S. and European businesses looking for partners in fantastic deals where the foreigner is asked to provide money up front against the assurance that the initial investment will secure the payment of millions of dollars of ill-gotten wealth that can somehow only be released to a foreigner. The foreigner is offered a large cut of the millions in exchange for providing access to their bank account where the millions will be remitted. The fraudsters make their money by convincing the dupe that advance funds are necessary in order to get the money released. Once they lure the person in, they keep increasing the amounts necessary to get the bigger payoff, until eventually the victim realizes the whole thing was a scam. By then the dupe has lost lots of money.

Apparently these schemes can get remarkably elaborate, as AC's story last night attests. My new friends and I had finished playing tennis, and we were sitting down to share beers when AC began his story. He had just come back from Lagos and said that during his visit some of his colleagues had told him of the most recent case of "419"— 419 is what Nigerians call fraud, apparently after a section in the Nigerian criminal code that describes these crimes. AC's account was stunning.

He said that these 419 guys had snared this Texas oil executive with a series of letters, faxes, and phone calls, and had convinced him that thirty-five million dollars remained in an NNPC (Nigerian National Petroleum Corporation) account from a huge contract for an oil-industry-related construction project. The 419 guys pretended they were high-level managers at NNPC. They told the oil executive that the money was leftover from the project, and that they needed a foreign partner and a foreign bank account in order to pay out the remaining thirty-five million dollars. All the correspondence they sent the oil executive was on official NNPC stationery. The oil executive was apparently interested but skeptical. At a point, the 419 guys who spoke with him on the phone arranged for him to call an NNPC office in London to try to assure him that the whole thing was real. When the guy seemed primed but still had not completely swallowed the bait, they invited him to come to Lagos and meet with top NNPC officials. They told him that if he came to Nigeria, they would pay all his expenses once he arrived, and that if after the visit he still was not convinced, no problem. They sweetened the offer by stressing that even if the money transfer proposal did not work out, they might be able to arrange some legitimate contracts between NNPC and the oil executive's Texas-based business.

The guy agreed to come to Lagos. The 419 guys told him not to bother to get a visa. As a guest of NNPC, they would handle everything. Sure enough, when the oil executive arrived at the airport in Lagos, he was met at the gate by a Nigerian in an expensive suit who held an NNPC placard with the executive's name. The visitor was whisked through immigration and customs without even having his passport checked or his bags opened. Each immigration and customs official he passed simply greeted him: "Welcome to Nigeria!" The oil executive had heard plenty of stories about the hassles at Murtala Muhammad Airport and he was impressed by the clout of his NNPC hosts. Outside the airport, he was ushered into an air-conditioned Toyota Land Cruiser with the NNPC logo emblazoned on the doors. He was taken to the Sheraton Hotel, the fanciest and most expensive hotel in Lagos, where he was told that all of his bills were "taken care of." In the morning, he was picked up by the same vehicle and taken to an NNPC office on Victoria Island, the most upscale area in Lagos. The guard, receptionist, and secretaries all greeted him: "Welcome to Nigeria!"

After a short wait, he was escorted into a large and expensively furnished office. Over the door the placard read, "Deputy Managing Director: Foreign Investment." Behind an impressive desk sat Ibu Onye Biribe, who greeted the executive with the now-familiar words, "Welcome to Nigeria!" Mr. Biribe immediately handed the executive his business card, carefully pronouncing his name for the visitor's untrained ears.

At this point my other friends who were listening to the story laughed uproariously because the supposed deputy manager's name, Ibu Onye Biribe, translates into "you are a fool" in the Igbo language. When the laughter died down, AC continued the story.

After a brief exchange of pleasantries, Mr. Biribe's secretary buzzed to inform him that "the minister" was on the line. Mr. Biribe had a brief and cryptic conversation in which his side of the call consisted of mainly, "Yes sir, I will do that, sir." After dropping the phone, Mr. Biribe apologized to his Texas guest, saying that it was the federal minister for petroleum resources on the line and he had no choice but to take the call.

The NNPC's deputy manager for foreign investment then proceeded to explain again to the oil executive how this thirty-five million dollars had become available and why they needed a foreign partner, and particularly someone who was in the oil business in order to pay out the money. Paying the money to the Texas oil executive, he explained, would make it appear that the payment was related to the completion of the initial contract. The only problem, he continued, was that one hundred thousand dollars was necessary to secure the release of the funds because various officials would need to be paid off to facilitate the release of the money to the executive's account. "Unfortunately, so many of our bureaucrats are greedy and corrupt," the deputy manager lamented. He suggested that his guest transfer one hundred thousand dollars to an NNPC account in London rather than in Nigeria, so that he might feel more secure. As he suggested this, he buzzed his secretary and asked her to get the London office on the line. He put the call on speakerphone and the call was answered by a woman with a very British-sounding accent, who said, "This is the London office of the Nigerian National Petroleum Corporation, how may I direct your call?" Mr. Biribe then asked for the appropriate official, and when he answered Mr. Biribe explained to him that one of their U.S. partners needed to transfer money to the NNPC's London account. He handed the phone to the oil executive. The man took the phone, and wrote down the NNPC bank account number and the instructions for how to transfer the money. The deputy manager then told his visitor that once he transferred the one hundred thousand dollars, the thirty-five million dollars would be released in forty-eight hours. The Texan's share would be 25 percent, or almost nine million dollars. Once the money was in the oil executive's account, he would then transfer his Nigerian partners' share to another account and all of this could be taken care of before the Texan departed Nigeria in three days. The deputy manager then handed his guest the phone and told him that it was an international line. He left the room while the oil executive dialed the United States. When the deputy manager came back, the Texan informed him that he had transferred the money. "Very well," Mr. Biribe said, "the driver can take you back to the hotel and I will come join you for dinner tonight. Then tomorrow and next, we can complete the transfer of money to your account in the United States and talk about other business."

That evening, the deputy manager never showed up at the Sheraton. The Texas oil executive was worried, but figured the money went to a London account and if there were any problem the whole thing could be reversed. The next morning, no one came to pick him up. When he inquired at the desk whether anyone had looked for him, he was told no one had. The receptionist then asked whether he would be staying another night. When he said that he would, she informed him that he would need to present his credit card. When he protested that his bill was being covered by NNPC, the receptionist told him that whoever had paid his bill had only paid for two nights. Now the man really panicked. He quickly hired a car to the address on Victoria Island where he had met with Mr. Biribe the previous day. When he arrived, all the evidence of an NNPC office had disappeared. AC said, "He turned even whiter than a white man"—again drawing uproarious laughter from my friends. There was no sign-board, no placard over the deputy manager's door, no receptionist, nobody. When he asked a person who appeared to be cleaning the stairwell what hap-pened to the NNPC office, the cleaner replied, "There's no NNPC office here. This office was vacated at the end of last month and the landlord is still looking for new tenants."

The panicked oil executive then asked where he could find the nearest police station. When he found a police station, the first thing they asked for was his passport. When the police looked at his passport and saw that he had no visa, they informed him that he was in Nigeria illegally. His protest and his story seemed to get him nowhere. In the end, the man had to arrange for his Texas office to wire him three thousand dollars to pay the police and immigration officials to allow him to exit the country. When he got home, he discovered that the London account to which he had transferred the one hundred thousand dollars was empty and closed. It had never belonged to NNPC.

As AC closed his story, my friends at the tennis club exclaimed variously, "Nigeria na war-o!" "We are in trouble," and "These guys are too much," expressing a combination of resignation, unease, and lament about cor-ruption as well as a sort of admiration for the audacity and ingenuity of the 419 men. When I asked AC whether the 419 perpetrators had received assistance from real officials in NNPC in order to pull off their plot or had concocted everything themselves, he answered simply: "In this country anything is possible."

AC's story and the reception it received illustrate a profound critical collective self-consciousness that Nigerians share about corruption in their society. Ordinary citizens are ambivalent about corruption. They recog-nize that it undermines the country's democratic political institutions, economic development, and global reputation, yet they also realize that wealth, power, and prestige in Nigeria are commonly achieved through practices that can easily be labeled as corrupt. People frequently condemn corruption and its consequences as immoral and socially ruinous, yet they also participate in seemingly contradictory behaviors that enable, encourage, and even glorify corruption.

This book examines the relationship between corruption and culture in Africa's most populous country. It offers an answer to the question of how ordinary Nigerians can be, paradoxically, active participants in the social reproduction of corruption even as they are also its primary victims and principal critics. Taking its cue from Nigerians, who see corruption at work in every corner of social life, the book presents an ethnographic study of corruption, demonstrating that there is much to be learned about social action, collective imagination, and cultural production when they are seen through the lens of an anthropological account of corruption. The book takes readers into the everyday world of Nigerian citizens as they encounter a society plagued by corruption. From police checkpoints where motorists offer banknotes in exchange for safe passage, to Internet cafés where thousands of young Nigerians craft their notorious e-mail scam letters, to local nongovernmental organizations (NGOs) created to siphon international donor dollars into individual hands, the book provides a detailed portrait of the social organization of corruption. It examines not only the mechanisms and contexts that explain corruption but also how the intense discontent that Nigerians feel about corruption propels contemporary events and stimulates Nigerians' collective cultural imagination.

When Nigerians talk about corruption, they refer not only to the abuse of state offices for some kind of private gain but also to a whole range of social behaviors in which various forms of morally questionable deception enable the achievement of wealth, power, or prestige as well as much more mundane ambitions. Nigerian notions of corruption encompass everything from government bribery and graft, rigged elections, and fraudulent business deals, to the diabolical abuse of occult powers, medical quackery, cheating in school, and even deceiving a lover. Although the use of the term corruption risks privileging a seemingly Western concept, my aim is to examine the Nigerian experience of corruption. I argue that it is empirically justified and theoretically important to study this spectrum of ideas and behaviors under the rubric of corruption, not only because Nigerians connect them in their collective conceptualizations, but also because together they reveal the complex intertwining of popular morality, contemporary social processes, and postcolonial statecraft.

Corruption, in its many valences in Nigeria, is a potent stimulus for cultural production, both as a means for corruption's pursuit and a method to combat its consequences. Stories about corruption dominate political and symbolic discourse in Nigeria. Everyday practices of corruption and the narratives of complaint they generate are primary vehicles through which Nigerians imagine and create the relationship between state and society. The contradictions of corruption both mirror and explain Nigerians' growing expectations and frustrated aspirations for democracy and development. Further, I contend that understanding corruption and its discontents is central to explaining and connecting a wide range of important contemporary social phenomena, such as resurgent ethnic nationalism, the rising popularity of born-again Christianity, violent vigilantism, and a range of common yet seemingly bizarre fears and accusations regarding witchcraft, cannibalism, and other occult practices. It is in these cultural responses to corruption that the relationship between political-economic transformation, social imagination, and the intimate sphere of interpersonal relationships is revealed. Unraveling the connections between corruption and culture is integral to understanding not only contemporary Nigeria but also the broader dynamics of culture, politics, and social change in a world marked by enormous inequality.

Writing about the relationship between corruption and culture runs the risk of blaming Nigerian culture and, by extension, Nigerian people for the corruption that plagues their society. Oscar Lewis's (1959) seminal work on the everyday lives of poor people in Mexico gave rise to the notion of a "culture of poverty," in which the habits, values, and behaviors of the poor were elevated to the level of an explanation for their predicament. The culture of poverty perspective obscured the historical and social structural dimensions of poverty—factors largely beyond the control of individual people. It also reinforced a misguided view of culture as timeless, static, and somehow unbound from the economic and political forces of society and history. I reject this view of culture, and try to show how even as ordinary Nigerians are participants in perpetuating corruption in their society, they do so in circumstances that are partly beyond their control. The explanation for corruption in Nigeria requires understanding the intersection of local culture and larger systems of inequality, and in ways that refute a simplistic scenario that blames the victims. Further, as the evidence presented in this book will make clear, to the extent that it is reasonable to talk at all about a "Nigerian culture" (a country as vast and diverse as Nigeria is, of course, characterized by considerable cultural heterogeneity), it is as much a "culture *against* corruption" as it is a "culture *of* corruption." Yet it would be misleading to dismiss entirely Nigerians' sense of culpability for the extent of corruption in their society. In many instances, ordinary Nigerians see themselves as complicit in corruption, and indeed it is this awareness of collective responsibility for corruption that fuels hopes for change, even as it paradoxically perpetuates cynicism and a sense of intractability.

The Nigerian Factor: Corruption as a National Discourse

Throughout the 1990s, Amibo struggled to become the last of eleven villages in Ubakala to be connected to Nigeria's national electricity grid. Many families in Amibo had wired their houses for electricity over a decade ago, and the community had contributed money to erect poles in order to induce the National Electric Power Authority (NEPA) to extend service. Numerous village delegations had been sent to NEPA and to a series of military administrators and civilian governors. On each visit, these delegations deposited money with state officials as an incentive to mobilize assistance for their dream of electrification. Yet electricity was never provided. Community frustration frequently boiled into accusations of corruption targeted at the government, but also directed inward. Politicians and bureaucrats who had collected the community's money were condemned for their venality. But many villagers who had contributed funds as part of collectively imposed levies suspected that perhaps their own kin had pocketed some of the community money, leaving too little for the payoffs to government and NEPA officials. When I asked one of my most trusted friends where he thought the problem really lay, he said, "Who can tell? In any case, it is 'the Nigerian factor.'" Suspicions of corruption span the social spectrum, potentially implicating not only elite politicians but also relatives in village communities.

In 2003, Nigeria conducted its first successful national elections managed by a civilian government. Since the country achieved independence from Great Britain in 1960, no democratically elected government had previously managed a national election that did not result in a military coup. The transition from one civilian government to another—even though incumbents handed over power to themselves—was widely represented as another step toward the consolidation of democracy. Yet in many localities, most people believed that the election results were rigged. In one local government area in Imo State, a close friend's younger brother was heavily involved in organizing young men, to both vote and intimidate other voters, and even stuff and carry away ballot boxes. When we talked about the elections just a couple months after they occurred, he assured me that the outcome in Imo State was predetermined. The result, he said, was not a reflection of the will of the people but rather the inevitable product of the Nigerian factor. He cautioned me, "If you don't understand the Nigerian factor, you won't understand anything about politics in this country."

In 2004, as crude oil prices hit record highs, my friends at a local tennis club in Umuahia began calculating how much extra revenue was being generated for the federal government. Because the 2004 national budget was based on a reference price of twenty-five dollars per barrel, the surge in oil prices beyond fifty dollars per barrel meant that government revenues would far exceed projections. Recalling that over twelve billion dollars in excess oil revenue generated in the wake of the 1990s' Gulf War had never been accounted for (Apter 2005, 247), my tennis pals speculated about the vast amounts of new money that would never even enter government ledgers. When club member and local businessperson Goddy Nwogu said, "Our national thieves may have changed from khaki to *agbada* (from military to civilian dress), but that has not changed the Nigerian factor," his statement provoked gestures and sounds of assent, ranging from laughter and resignation to anger and dismay.

Nigerians routinely complain about corruption. It is not an exaggeration to say that it is the national pastime. Stories range from the large scale to the mundane, but the archetypal narrative focuses on how the country has squandered its rich natural and human resources. I could not possibly count the number of times I have heard this classic story of complaint, beginning with an emphatic statement like, "This country has resources!" Knowing that their country is the world's seventh-biggest oil exporter and the largest producer in Africa, and that it is Africa's most populous nation, with over 130 million people, most Nigerians believe that the country is rich, and that their own poverty is purely a consequence of corruption. Indeed, many people's perceptions of the magnitude of oil wealth far exceed the reality. Even at my tennis club, where members are obviously educated and elite, some people spoke as if individual Nigerians would all be wealthy if only the government gave each citizen an equal share of the annual oil revenue—a fantasy belied by the numbers. But Nigerians are surely correct to believe that their country would be, could be, and should be better off were it not for corruption.

In his trenchant book *The Trouble with Nigeria*, the renowned author Chinua Achebe (1983, 2) notes Nigerians' penchant for complaining: "Whenever two Nigerians meet, their conversation will sooner or later slide into a litany of our national deficiencies." Achebe laments this national inclination as a sign of resignation and says his book aims to challenge such complacency. Corruption is indeed so prevalent in Nigeria that ordinary citizens experience and express some degree of resignation. The very expression "the Nigerian factor" suggests that Nigerians have concluded that corruption is so endemic that it defines the nation. Yet resignation is only one of the meanings of Nigerian narratives of complaint. Even as Nigerians feel compelled, enticed, trapped, and resigned to participate in Nigeria's ubiquitous corruption, they also feel angry, frustrated, dismayed, and betrayed.

Popular anger about corruption is common not only in Nigeria but across Africa, and in many countries around the globe. In an excellent analysis of the dynamics of corruption in sub-Saharan Africa generally, Jean-Pierre Olivier de Sardan (1999, 29) notes the extent of discontent about corruption: "At the everyday level, there is scarcely a conversation without hostile or disgusted references to corruption." In many ways, corruption has become the dominant discourse of complaint in the postcolonial world, symbolizing people's disappointments with democracy and development, and their frustrations with continuing social inequality.

In this book, as mentioned earlier, I aim to understand the mechanisms of everyday corruption in Nigeria. Further, I document, interpret, and analyze Nigerians' multiple responses to corruption. These responses are signaled in overt narratives of complaint, but extend to diverse arenas of social imagination and cultural production. Complaints about corruption reveal a rich popular consciousness, and trigger complex cultural responses that are both complicit in and challenging to the status quo. Recognizing the seriousness of Nigerians' discontents, including ambivalence regarding their own roles, and examining the range of social and cultural phenomena that are produced in response to corruption, are essential to explaining the multiple meanings implied when Nigerians attribute their predicament to the Nigerian factor.

ANTHROPOLOGY AND CORRUPTION

Anthropologists have undertaken very few studies that explicitly examine corruption.[1] The anthropological inattention to corruption is probably due to several factors. First, for a long time anthropology focused most of its attention on smaller-scale societies and institutions. Both theoretically and methodologically, the discipline was oriented toward studying relatively bounded communities, often characterized by face-to-face social relations, where breaches of law and morality are not normally glossed as "corruption." Anthropological investigations and expertise centered on social and political institutions such as marriage, kinship, and customary law, and economic systems such as foraging, pastoralism, horticulture, and regional trading networks. Modern nation-states, global capitalism, and transnational cultural flows have become objects of anthropological interest only much more recently (Appadurai 1996; Hannerz 1996; Taussig 1997; Comaroff and Comaroff 2001).

Second, because most anthropologists aim to understand human motives and behavior at least in part from the perspectives of the people they study, those processes that political scientists typically describe as corruption often appear in the anthropological literature under rubrics such as gift exchange, moral economies, reciprocity, and patronage. Anthropology's emphasis on local rationalities and cultural logics, and the largely sympathetic sensibility of anthropologists regarding their subjects, produces a disinclination to attach a seemingly derogatory Western label like corruption to the behavior of non-Western peoples. Indeed, as this book will illustrate, there is much to be gained by examining corruption from local perspectives, and recognizing that what might look to an outsider like pure venality is often undertaken for very different reasons that can be discovered by studying local social institutions and cultural logics.

Finally, the relative barrenness of the ethnographic literature on corruption is due partly to the fact that it takes some time for anthropological interests to catch up to the changing realities in the places we study. Corruption, I suggest, has become an increasingly important issue for ordinary people in the postcolonial places where anthropologists typically work. This is certainly the case in Nigeria. Popular awareness and discontent about corruption extends at least back to the colonial period (Smith 1964; Afigbo 1972; Tignor 1993; Pratten 2000; Guyer 2004). But collective fascination and frustration with what Nigerians themselves call corruption has escalated throughout the country's postcolonial history, reaching an unprecedented peak since the transition from military to civilian rule in 1999, a trend reflected in Nigerian scholars' growing attention to corruption (Lame and Adekunle 2001; Akani 2002; Ugwu 2002; Aku 2003). Just as increasing anthropological interest in phenomena such as globalization and transnationalism was catalyzed by observable changes in the communities and lives of people anthropologists study, so too I suspect that anthropological interests in corruption will likely grow considerably, as researchers realize they can no longer ignore the salience of corruption as an organizing force in the lives of people in many contemporary societies. There is already some evidence to suggest that the anthropological awareness of corruption is growing (Gupta 1995; Olivier de Sardan 1999; Sissener 2001; Ezeh 2002; Haller and Shore 2005), and this book aims to engage and advance that trend.

Perhaps not surprisingly, some of the initial contributions of anthropology to understanding corruption have built on the discipline's theoretical strengths regarding the social and symbolic dimensions of economics, politics, and power. For example, several anthropologists have utilized Marcel Mauss's seminal work on gift exchange to explain how interactions that look like corruption to outside observers frequently serve crucial social and symbolic functions in local contexts (Yang 1989, 1994; Yan 1996; Werner 2000). Other anthropologists have emphasized the importance of solidarity networks and the logics of patron-clientism through which power and prestige depend on the conspicuous redistribution of accumulated wealth in a logic that encourages corruption (Olivier de Sardan

1999; Smith 2001b). Such perspectives are represented in some of the more compelling political science analyses of corruption, including scholarship focusing on Nigeria and, more generally, Africa (Joseph 1987; Bayart 1993).

For example, in his book on politics in Nigeria, Richard Joseph (1987, 54) emphasizes the importance of various kinds of vertically organized solidarity networks in Nigerians' relationship to the state, and argues that corruption hinges partly on the inseparability of individual and collective interests: "The fundamental social process in Nigeria is one in which these two propositions—(a) I want to get ahead and prosper and (b) my group (ethnic, regional, linguistic) must get ahead and prosper—cannot logically be separated, whether in the context of behavior, action, or consciousness." Patrick Chabal and Jean-Pascal Daloz (1999, 107n14) capture concisely the significance of such solidarity networks by citing the African proverb "Whoever does not rob the state robs his kith and kin." One of the most important contributions of Africanist political science and the emergent anthropology of corruption has been explaining how so-called corruption frequently occurs as the result of social strategies, cultural logics, and moral economies that assign values different from those assumed in the ideologies of the neoliberal bureaucratic state.

Such perspectives offer insight into the social reproduction of corruption, including ordinary citizens' participation. Nevertheless, as I have come to recognize the intense frustration that average Nigerians feel about corruption, and as I have observed the extent and growth of popular discourses and social movements expressing these discontents, I have come to believe that it is not sufficient to explain corruption in terms of local cultural logics and enduring African social institutions. A dimension of continuity is no doubt part of the story, but just as important, or probably more important, is explaining why corruption has become the dominant discourse of complaint in contemporary Nigeria, and what sorts of changes this reflects.

CORRUPTION, PATRON-CLIENTISM, AND THE POSTCOLONIAL STATE

As we approached a police checkpoint on the road from Port Harcourt to Owerri, the minibus slowed down. Several vehicles had stopped ahead of us. Fellow passengers groaned over the delay that heightened the discomfort of the afternoon sun in our crowded vehicle. A man behind me, who had fallen asleep earlier in the journey, muttered "thieves" under his breath, apparently referring to the heavily armed police officers who blocked our way. When the vehicle just ahead of us seemed to stop for more than the usual few seconds, a woman in the front row said audibly,

"Ah, give them something so we can pass now." As our bus finally reached the head of the queue, our driver gave a police officer a scrunched up banknote in an almost furtive handoff, and we were again on our way. I had seen the transaction so many times over the years that I hardly noticed. But as soon as we passed the checkpoint, my student, who had just arrived for the summer to work on a project with my Nigerian colleagues, asked me in a whisper, "If everyone knows exactly what is happening, why do the driver and the police officer halfheartedly try to conceal it?" In retrospect, this simple question and the events that preceded it raised critical issues about the relationship between ordinary citizens, corruption, and the state.

The half-concealed levy paid to a police officer at a roadside checkpoint in order for a bus to pass represents an example of a transformation in Nigeria's political economy of patron-clientism that characterizes Nigerian citizens' relationship to their postcolonial state. In traditional systems of patronage, or at least as Nigerians romanticize them, exchanges between elites and common people were based on reciprocity and a sense of mutual obligation. Inequality was tempered by a moral economy in which the links between the haves and have-nots created mechanisms for accountability. In contemporary Nigeria, people of all social strata continue to navigate political and economic insecurity and inequality by relying on social networks of patronage rooted in such a system of reciprocity, whereby ties based on kinship, community of origin, and other associations provide access to the resources of the state (Berry 1985, 1989; Smith 2001b; Guyer 2004). Yet many Nigerians believe that elites have hijacked the patronage system and perverted it to serve their own interests. Further, the Nigerian state, with its alternative idiom of accountability based on a social contract between the government and the people, is equally experienced by Nigeria's citizens as corrupt. Indeed, it is the integration of a system of patronage with the facades of bureaucracy and officialdom produced by the postcolonial state that facilitates the corruption that is so ubiquitous in Nigeria. Jean-François Bayart (1993, 87) has suggested that "the postcolonial state thus represents an historical mutation of African societies, taken over the long term: never before, it seems, has the dominant class managed to acquire such marked economic supremacy over its subjects."

The conventional wisdom in Western society, exemplified in many donor-sponsored programs to promote democracy and "good governance" in Africa, opposes the realms of modern neoliberal democracy and traditional systems of kinship and patron-clientism. But in Nigeria, elites and ordinary citizens live simultaneously in both worlds. Although observers and analysts frequently make sense of this complexity by contrasting the two systems (Ekeh 1975), or by describing Africans as "straddling" multiple social worlds (Bayart 1993, 69–70), for most people these contrasting systems are experienced as one reality. The Nigerian state is at once a neoliberal institution claiming the full range of powers and responsibilities typical of modern nation-states and a prize to be captured and shared according to the principles of patronage (Joseph 1987; Nelson 1996; Bayart 1993).

Inherent in a political economy of patronage is the role that ordinary citizens play in the social reproduction of corruption, even as the vast majority of people are acutely aware that the system disproportionately benefits a few at the expense of the many. The most elite politicians, government officials, and economic moguls—federal ministers, state governors, NNPC managers, major construction and petroleum industry contractors, and so on—commonly reap many millions of dollars through corruption. But people at many levels of society participate in corruption in order to survive. In a patron-client system, almost everyone has a stake in corruption, no matter how small. It is almost a cliché to recognize that in African societies, everyone is a patron to a lesser person and a client to a more powerful person (d'Azevedo 1962). As Olivier de Sardan notes (1999, 41), "Woe betide the man who knows no one, either directly or indirectly."

It is important to emphasize that in a country where the World Bank estimates that nearly 60 percent of the population lives below the poverty line of roughly one U.S. dollar per day, most people are not benefiting substantially from either the formal mechanisms of government or the more informal networks of patronage that constitute a significant proportion of the everyday political economy. But even ordinary people have daily experiences with corruption in their efforts to forge better lives for themselves and their families, confronting and participating in everyday forms of corruption in offices, schools, and hospitals, and in a wide range of efforts to obtain basic services from the state. As much of the evidence presented in this book will attest, at the same time that Nigerians in ever larger numbers aspire to modern lifestyles, they become increasingly caught up in the paradoxes of corruption and its discontents. While the millions of very poor people in Nigeria are largely left out of the struggle for resources that occurs at the nexus of the state and the networks of patronage that vie to control it, in my experience even the extremely poor are remarkably aware of the fact that it is through the social connections of patron-clientism, and increasingly corruption, that people control wealth and power in Nigeria.

To be without a patron is to be without access to resources, but to be a patron is to be under great pressure to accumulate and share wealth, including through corruption. Many of my friends in positions of relative power in Nigeria remark on and frequently complain about the pressures from kin, community members, friends, and associates to use the power of their offices or the benefits of their wealth to fulfill requests for help. Whether one is a school principal, a successful businessperson, the director of a development NGO, a customs officer, or a motor vehicle licensing agent, the pressure to use one's position to benefit people in networks of personal association is intense. These expectations are particularly powerful in situations where patrons are in a position to leverage benefits and services from the state. The centrality of the state in the system of corruption should not be surprising given its importance as an employer and provider of services but also given the sheer economic dominance of the state in a country where the principal source of wealth is petroleum, and oil revenues are directly controlled by the government (Watts 1992; Apter 2005).

The significance of the state in Nigeria is intensified by the particular history and current configuration of Nigeria's petroleum-dominated political economy (Watts 1992; Karl 1997; Apter 2005). Oil was discovered in Nigeria in 1958, but it was not until the 1970s, when the country joined the Organization of Petroleum Exporting Countries (OPEC), and the Middle East crisis sent the price of oil skyrocketing, that Nigeria was transformed into a "petro-state" (Watts 1994; Apter 2005; for a similar analysis of Venezuela's petro-state, see Coronil 1997). As the nation became increasingly dependent on oil as a source of revenue, rent-seeking behavior gradually replaced productive agriculture as the primary means to achieving wealth and prestige. The Nigerian state became the locus of competition for resources, a reality captured eloquently in the colloquial expression Nigerians use to describe the state: "the national cake." During the oil boom, the government rapidly consolidated state control over the oil industry and centralized the distribution of revenues to the lower tiers of government and society. The collapse of oil prices in the 1980s exposed the contradictions in Nigeria's largely nonproductive petroleum economy, making control of the state and its increasingly scarce oil revenues the object of even more intense competition, while also feeding corruption and stoking discontent over the consequent poverty and inequality.

For Nigerians, the state and corruption are synonymous. Because they must navigate, indeed participate in, corruption if they are to achieve even their most mundane aspirations and reasonable goals, most Nigerians realize that what Bayart (1993, 89) describes regarding African postcolonial states more generally is particularly true in Africa's giant: "It would be an error to see all these dealings simply as the corruption of the State. They are, conversely, the State's fabric." In Nigeria's petroleum-dominated political economy of patron-clientism, where corruption rules, it makes sense that "strategies adopted by the great majority of the population for survival are identical to the ones adopted by the leaders to accumulate wealth and power" (Bayart 1993, 237). Yet even as ordinary Nigerians participate in corruption and recognize that the trappings and facades of the state are manipulated in a politics of illusion, rising expectations are created regarding the very institutions and ideals that are perceived in Nigeria to be provided only as fakes. In other words, despite the fact that the pretenses of democracy and development are employed to facilitate corruption, Nigerians increasingly judge the performance of their state and the circumstances in their society based on aspirations associated with these ideals.

The dynamics that characterize the relationship between patron-clientism and corruption are certainly not unique to Nigeria or Africa. Akhil Gupta (1995, 397) found exactly the same kind of social expectations in postcolonial India: "For example, a highly placed official who fails to help a close relative or a fellow villager obtain a government position is often roundly criticized by people for not fulfilling his obligations to his kinsmen and village brothers. On the other hand, the same people often roundly condemn any official of another caste or village who has done precisely that as being 'corrupt' and as guilty of 'nepotism.' " The fact that clients judge the behavior of patrons in their own networks by one standard and assess the behavior of patrons outside their networks by another is commonsensical, and probably reflects universal aspects of human social life. Certainly this feature of human social relations accounts for some of the ambivalence Nigerians feel about corruption—it is OK when it benefits me; it is bad when it does not. Yet it is in the diversity of the meanings that people ascribe to corruption—drawing on idioms of accountability that include liberal ideals of development and democracy, kinship-based expectations of reciprocity, notions of the occult and supernatural justice, and promises of divine intervention offered in Pentecostal Christian churches—that the full intricacy of the relationship between corruption, patron-clientism, and the postcolonial state reveals itself.

It would be misleading to claim that this book is about the Nigerian state. But as an ethnographic account of corruption, it is very much about Nigerians' experiences and understandings of the state. In part, the book addresses the discursive construction of the state by examining narratives about corruption. Yet I am more concerned with how concrete experiences of corruption—the ways in which everyday interaction with their government affects Nigerians' material lives—constitute ordinary citizens' relationship to the state. As Joseph notes (1987, 1), "In Nigeria . . . the state has increasingly become a magnet for all facets of political and economic life, consuming the attention of traders, contractors, builders, farmers, traditional rulers, teachers, as much as that of politicians or politically motivated individuals in the usual senses of these terms." Nigerians are fully aware that their state and society are plagued by corruption—to the point where rumors and stories of corruption frequently exceed what could possibly be verified empirically. The other side of popular cynicism, however, is a growing awareness of what could be possible were the facades of democracy and development—so vital to corruption—transformed into more legitimate endeavors. Implicit, and increasingly explicit, in the narratives of complaint about corruption is not only an awareness of a bureaucratic and democratic standard of accountability but a growing expectation that it be adopted and respected (Gore and Pratten 2003).

FORMS OF CORRUPTION

Defining corruption is difficult and has occupied a good deal of space in the social science literature, particularly in political science (Nye 1967; Heidenheimer 1970). Most political science definitions include or imply the existence of the state, and typically emphasize the misuse of public office for private gain. For example, Joseph Nye's (1967, 419) classic definition is widely cited: "Corruption is behavior which deviates from the formal duties of a public role because of private-regarding (personal, close family, private clique) pecuniary or status gains; or violates rules against the exercise of certain private-regarding influence." In formulating his definition, Nye recognized that corruption also has much broader moral meanings, including "a change from good to bad" (419). For a political scientist looking at corruption from the perspective of the state, Nye's definition and its many subsequent variants, which sidestep issues of morality, provide a parsimony that facilitates an appealing clarity.

As an anthropologist looking at corruption ethnographically, from the bottom up, as it were, such parsimonious definitions obscure as much as they reveal. In Nigeria, the question of whether the misuse of public office for private gain constitutes corruption varies significantly depending on the context. The social morality of behavior figures much more prominently in popular assessments of corruption than does any technical definition. Nevertheless, it is certainly the case that rising expectations about the state, as well as democracy and development, are part of a process in which the relationship between social morality and governance is changing. This means that rather than separating corruption and morality, my task is to try to sort out how they fit together in Nigeria.

As an anthropologist, my inclination is not to impose a definition of corruption on the Nigerian situation and then arrange my ethnographic material accordingly. Rather, I examine the multiple ways that Nigerians employ the concept of corruption, and then use local categories and implied definitions to build an analysis that makes sense in light of what Nigerians do and say. Given that Nigerians see corruption at work not only in public offices but also in a wide range of commercial exchanges and interpersonal relations as well as in the realm of the supernatural, tying the definition of corruption too strictly to affairs of the state is overly limiting. Still, even as I provide an ethnographic account and an anthropological analysis of corruption that includes a range of local meanings, it will become clear that the emergence of the postcolonial state is central to Nigerian experiences of corruption, and that the expectations and disappointments generated by the state permeate Nigerians' collective imagination about corruption. Many of the narratives of discontent that appear most obviously moralistic and least directly about official corruption per se are, in fact, heavily influenced by experiences with and expectations regarding the state.

Based on an intensive comparative study of corruption in three West African countries (Benin, Niger, and Senegal), Giorgio Blundo and Jean-Pierre Olivier de Sardan (2001a) have developed a useful typology of forms of corruption that maps reasonably well onto the Nigerian scene. The seven basic forms they identify are: (1) commission for illicit services, (2) unwarranted payment for public services, (3) gratuities, (4) string pulling, (5) levies and tolls, (6) sidelining, and (7) misappropriation. Briefly, commission for illicit services refers to the payment by users to officials who then grant access to unwarranted advantages. For example, a contractor might provide money to a government official to ensure that he receives a job in a process supposedly based on competitive bids, or an importer might pay a customs official to underestimate the value of their goods to reduce a tariff. Unwarranted payment for public services involves an official forcing a user to pay for a service that is ostensibly provided for free, or inflating the cost of a routine service. In Nigeria, people commonly pay extra money for basic services such as the issuance of licenses, passports, and birth certificates. A gratuity is also a kind of payment for services, but usually after the fact, and commonly couched in the idiom of a "thank you." Nigerians typically call such a gratuity a "dash," and do not think of it in the same terms as a bribe. But as Blundo and Olivier de Sardan point out, a dash only makes sense in an environment where officials diligently doing their jobs without the demand for a bribe is an exception and deserves a reward. In fact, many Nigerians recognize that dashes are frequently simply more sociable and socially acceptable ways of paying bribes.

String pulling refers to using social and political influence to promote favoritism, offering preferential access to employment, education, and a whole range of other opportunities, particularly those allocated by the state. From experience, Nigerians commonly believe that resources and opportunities of all kinds are awarded based, above all, on who you know. Levies and tolls are relatively stark forms of tribute that persons in positions of power can extract from ordinary citizens. For example, police who collect illegal tolls from motor vehicle drivers at roadside checkpoints, vigilante groups that demand a security levy from local businesses, or bureaucrats who require pensioners to pay money in order to receive their pensions fall into this category. In most cases, this type of levying is viewed by Nigerians as outright extortion. Sidelining refers to the use of public or company resources for private purposes—for instance, using official vehicles for personal travel, running a private clinic in a public health facility, or using university resources to conduct a private consulting job. Misappropriation extends this practice further, whereby public materials are not simply used for private purposes but expropriated entirely, usually in a manner more concealed than sidelining because it is both more illegitimate and more obviously illegal.

This typology captures and describes a wide range of forms of corruption that are prevalent in Nigeria, but as Blundo and Olivier de Sardan acknowledge, the boundaries between these forms can be fluid, and the perceived legitimacy of particular practices can depend very much on context, and particularly on the position of the people participating in or assessing the behavior. Some forms of corruption are almost always less legitimate than others. For example, the tolls collected by police at checkpoints are widely resented, whereas string pulling by a patron to assist a friend or relative is often seen as highly legitimate and even morally honorable. A number of dimensions are salient in situating particular forms of corruption and understanding their degree of acceptability in Nigeria. Whether a particular behavior is perceived as corrupt and how corrupt a behavior is judged depend on where the behavior falls along a number of intersecting continuums. These continuums include legality and illegality, legitimacy and illegitimacy, and scale (that is, petty and massive) as well as whether one is a beneficiary or a victim. Social distance from acts of corruption is generally predictive of perceived illegitimacy, tapping people's sense of corruption's corrosiveness in society, whereas perceptions in cases of closer proximity depend heavily on whether one is a beneficiary or a victim. While smaller-scale corruption is more widely tolerated, it is also true that it is the biggest forms of corruption that are least likely to be punished because the most egregious forms are undertaken by the most powerful people.

In the many examples of corruption that are described in the chapters to follow, I show how important social context is for explaining when and why Nigerians participate in corruption, but also for understanding what kinds of corruption are acceptable and what kinds produce the popular discontent that fuels so many salient social phenomena in contemporary Nigeria. I argue that over the past couple of decades, new forms of corruption have emerged that Nigerians widely view as illegitimate. This illegitimacy is most pronounced with regard to the deceptions Nigerians associate with the failure of their postcolonial state to deliver the expected benefits of development and democracy, at the same time that more traditional mechanisms of patron-clientism are perceived to be breaking down. In other words, as elites manipulate the intertwining of modern bureaucratic and more traditional kinship-based clientelistic idioms of accountability in order to maximize their wealth and power through corruption, the legitimacy of both idioms is undermined.

A patron-client system—in which people rely on kin, people of the same community of origin, and other hierarchically organized social ties of affection and obligation for assistance—has long served as a buffer against the capriciousness of the state by providing access to resources through familiar mechanisms of reciprocity. This system is widely perceived by ordinary Nigerians to have given way to a much more individualistic pursuit of wealth and power. I show how the deceptive mechanisms of corruption associated with the state are perceived to have diffused throughout society, creating a popular sense of crisis about social morality, wherein Nigerians see the repercussions of corruption in everyday life as both caused by and contributing to the demise of morality. This perception that corruption is rooted in social amorality both obscures the political and economic underpinnings of inequality and creates some hope. At the same time that Nigerians see themselves as complicit in corruption, they also view themselves as the ultimate agents of change.

419: CORRUPTION, DECEPTION, AND SOCIAL MORALITY

If the Nigerian factor is corruption, the primary mode of illegitimate corruption in Nigeria is 419. Named after the number in the Nigerian penal code that deals with a specific form of fraud, as mentioned earlier, 419 (pronounced four-one-nine) first emerged in the 1980s, during Nigeria's economic decline, when the country fell from the heady heights of the worldwide oil boom into a period of political and economic struggle marked by military dictatorships, inflation, a rapidly devaluing currency, and widespread poverty and unemployment (Watts 1984, 1992, 1994; Apter 2005). The original meaning of 419 was linked to a specific practice of fraud, such as that described in AC's story, in which the perpetrators sent letters and faxes that relied on the symbols of Nigeria's petroleum-dominated political economy—official letterhead and signatures, NNPC insignia, lines of credit, government contracts, and so on—to bait mostly foreign targets into providing advance fees against the promise of a larger payoff. The scams relied not only on the trappings of the Nigerian state but also its reputation for corruption, enticing dupes with the expectation that some of the millions of dollars siphoned off by corrupt officials could be obtained simply by providing a foreign bank account and advance fees to enable the funds to be released. Apter (2005, 226–36) has cogently described how 419 emerged as Nigerians became disillusioned with the state at the same time that the state itself, no longer awash in oil money, relied on the politics of illusion to maintain its eroding legitimacy.

The original 419 scams have continued to flourish; if anything, they have increased and expanded as the Internet has democratized access to the technology of 419 during the same period that Nigeria itself has been embarking on its transition to democratic governance after many years of military rule. But even more significant than the continued practice of 419 scams through e-mail is the fact that 419 has become an all-encompassing signifier in Nigerian discourse for any behavior that relies on dissimulation, illusion, or some other manipulation of the truth in order to facilitate gain or advantage. Indeed, nothing illustrates better the Nigerian definition of corruption than the spectrum of activities and behaviors that are described as 419. A few brief examples will suffice to indicate the expansive meaning of 419, an issue that will be developed more thoroughly throughout the book.

During my most recent period of fieldwork in 2004, the Nigerian Labour Congress, an umbrella organization representing many trade unions, called a national strike to protest government efforts to deregulate the price of gasoline, kerosene, and diesel—a policy that would result in significant increases in the cost of Nigeria's highly subsidized domestic fuel. The strike in June was widely observed, and after several days, during which the nation's economy was largely paralyzed, the government was forced to compromise, still raising fuel prices but keeping them well below the deregulated levels that had been proposed. In the period during and after the strike the issue of corruption in Nigeria's oil economy, always a favorite topic, reached peak levels in everyday conversation.

Nigerians commonly believe that cheap domestic fuel is a kind of national birthright, perceived as one of the few benefits that an otherwise corrupt and ineffectual government ought to be able to deliver to the masses in Africa's oil-producing giant. National strikes over fuel prices have been common in Nigeria's recent history (Apter 2005). In one of the great ironies and tragic symbols of Nigerian underdevelopment, for the past several years Nigeria has imported nearly all of its refined fuel from overseas, as the country's four broken-down oil refineries remain nonfunctional, despite numerous huge government contracts awarded to repair them. The popular belief, voiced in the idiom of 419, is that the country's political elite, led by the president, has deliberately kept Nigeria's refineries from being repaired so that they can profit from controlling the importation and distribution of fuel. One account of the do-

Figure 1. To ordinary Nigerians, the country's frequent fuel shortages—in spite of the fact that Nigeria is the largest oil producer in Africa—are an egregious example of the consequences of corruption (photo by author).

mestic fuel situation, provided by a friend during a conversation as we waited in line for fuel at a crowded gas station after the June 2004 strike was called off, illustrates a widely held view:

> [President] Obasanjo is just playing us 419. Government could easily repair the refineries but they leave them failing on purpose. I mean, in this country, with the billions generated from oil revenues, are you telling me that for several years they cannot even repair one refinery? No way. Obasanjo and the ex-military boys, they want it this way. They control the importation of fuel from abroad. They own the ships, the local marketing companies, the petrol stations—I understand some of them have even built refineries abroad. Can you imagine? While our refineries rot, they have built their own abroad to profit from our suffering. It is not enough that they steal the oil revenues. They also sell our oil back to us at a profit. No. It's 419, it's 419.

Whether or not my friend's account is entirely factual, it represents a common awareness that elites are getting rich at the expense of the masses and that 419—illusions created through deception—is the central strategy.

But as much as most people see elites as the biggest perpetrators of 419, people also share a common belief that practices of 419 have filtered throughout Nigerian society—a perception also illustrated in some of the discourse produced around the fuel strike. For example, proprietors of local filling stations were accused of 419 for hoarding fuel as the strike approached and pretending their stocks had run out in anticipation of higher prices after the strike. Even the impoverished urban street urchins who sell black market fuel in plastic jugs at the roadside when gasoline is scarce are accused of 419, because motorists suspect that they mix cheaper kerosene with more expensive gasoline to increase their small profits.

Politics is, of course, a primary arena for 419. Over the years, the Nigerian public has realized that various programs of transition implemented by military governments as part of the promise to return the country to civilian rule were elaborate ruses. No example is more telling then the 1993 presidential election, when then military dictator Ibrahim Babangida annulled the vote after a long and torturous process in which the military directed every step of the transition from above, including the creation of political parties, the writing of their manifestos, and the determination of eligible candidates. Babangida's cancellation of the election just days after the vote, which led to five more years of brutal dictatorship under General Sani Abacha, was viewed by many Nigerians as the ultimate 419, committed by the Nigerian leader most associated with the term (Apter 1999; 2005, 236–48; Diamond, Kirk-Greene, and Oyediran 1997). Political 419 has not been the exclusive province of the military. The most recent election in 2003, conducted by a democratically elected government, was widely viewed as 419 by Nigerians who saw the huge victories for President Obasanjo's ruling People's Democratic Party as a process of elite-driven selection masquerading as a democratic election.

The concept and practices of 419 have extended to multiple spheres of contemporary life in Nigeria. Any new visitor to the country is bound to notice the odd phenomenon that literally thousands of houses and buildings in cities and towns bear the message "THIS HOUSE IS NOT FOR SALE," painted prominently near the front door. Ask any Nigerian the purpose of the message and they will quickly tell you that it is to prevent 419. Apparently, one popular method of 419 is to assume the identity of a real estate agent or simply a property owner trying to sell one's house. In Nigeria's cities and towns, where the real estate market is tight, buyers can be induced to make down payments to secure a later purchase, and in some cases entire transactions have been completed before the buyer discovered that the deal was a scam. By labeling houses as "not for sale," property owners are trying to prevent themselves and their buildings from becoming embroiled in 419 cases—and in Nigeria there is always the added fear

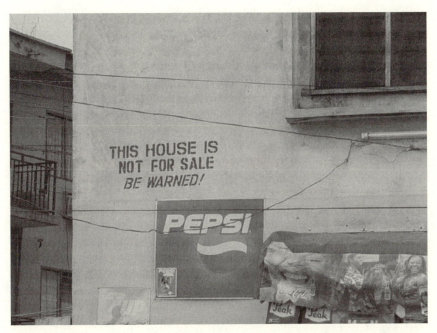

Figure 2. Countless houses and buildings across Nigeria bear the warning "THIS HOUSE IS NOT FOR SALE" to combat a common scam (photo by author).

that even if your house has been sold in a scam, you might still lose it if the buyer has more money or better political connections.

The 419 scams appear in contexts one might not expect them; that is part of the way 419 can be successful. In my first years in Nigeria, young men in Lagos sometimes stood on the side of the road signaling to drivers that something was wrong underneath their cars. If a driver stopped, the young man would offer to check under the car, quickly creating a real problem that only a mechanic—his coconspirator—could fix. On a recent bus ride I took between cities in Nigeria, one of the passengers stood up at the beginning of the trip and asked that we all pray for Jesus's journey mercies, a practice not uncommon in the heavily Christian South. Indeed, buses are a popular venue for evangelism, and I braced myself for proselytizing. But the man quickly shifted from talk of God to talk of illness and medicine, explaining that he was a renowned healer and had brought his medicines on board to help his companions on the journey. He proceeded to describe how his plastic bottles full of red liquid treated malaria and typhoid, and how the ones with yellow liquid treated an assortment of "woman problems" such as irregular menses and infertility; he even had different powders for toothaches and foot odor. Each time he introduced a new medicine a man in the back of the bus shouted that he wanted it and asked the price. He paid enthusiastically and was given his medicines. Eventually, a few other passengers bought some too. After several stops the medicine peddler bid us adieu and disembarked, presumably to continue his sales on a bus going the other way. His main customer, who had purchased so many medicines, also departed at the same stop. Once they exited, the woman sitting beside me turned toward me and said, as I had been thinking, "It's 419. The fellow at the back eagerly buying all the medicine is his partner." She paused and added, with a sigh, "Nigeria."

The popular association of corruption with deception seems almost infinitely expansive. Indeed, even partners in failing romantic relationships occasionally accuse each other of 419, when reality turns out to be different from appearances. The fact that 419 is perceived to be so pervasive is incredibly troubling to most Nigerians. In this ethnographic study of corruption, I take seriously Nigerians' narratives of discontent and the anxiety about social morality that they signify. An immense array of contemporary trends and events can be productively interpreted as a response to popular ambivalence and frustrations regarding corruption. Understanding corruption and its discontents illuminates the intertwining processes of statecraft, moral imagination, and cultural production in postcolonial Nigeria.

CORRUPTION AND ITS DISCONTENTS

Nigerians' sense that their state and society have become increasingly amoral—with elites pursuing wealth and power without regard for the consequences, and ordinary people seeking money by all means available simply to survive—contributes to a popular perception that law and order have given way to rampant corruption at every level. The concept of 419 and the breadth with which it is applied across social domains represents this collective conclusion that the country has spiraled out of control.

Yet implicit in Nigerians' anger and frustration about corruption is the recognition that things could and should be different. In their acute collective self-consciousness about the shortcomings of their society, Nigerians express their awareness of alternatives. The perception of 419 as amoral is rooted in strong expectations about social morality, in part based on a traditional moral economy wherein reciprocity, kinship, and personal allegiance dictated forms of sociability and social obligation in which the welfare of others was privileged over individual interests. Or perhaps more accurately, individual interests were tied to protecting the welfare of others. In many ways, this moral economy remains powerful in contemporary

Nigeria, and even contributes to forms of "corruption" that Nigerians see as more or less legitimate. In some situations, Nigerians' discontents are projected backward to better times, in a sort of nostalgia for an idealized past. But in their frustrations over the current state of affairs, many people also look forward to anticipated transformations. Expectations about social morality are increasingly influenced by the ideals of democracy and development promulgated by the postcolonial state. Concepts of probity and official accountability are fertilized even in a setting where they are frequently deployed duplicitously.

Because this book is about corruption, most of the cases presented in the narrative emphasize this dimension of everyday life and try to explain it. But it is absolutely essential to recognize Nigerians' ambivalence about corruption. Their acute dissatisfaction with the most amoral forms of corruption, commonly glossed as 419, is produced in relation to experiences with institutions and forms of human relationship that are *not* corrupt. Whether it is trusted friendships and family ties, upright and generous religious congregations and fellowship groups, or networks of informal business relationships that cooperate effectively based on high degrees of trust and internal self-regulation, all Nigerians have experiences with social forms that are honest and scrupulous. Even in the realm of formal institutions associated with the state, examples of people and organizations with a reputation for integrity are well-known. Understanding the social currents that push against corruption is as important as explaining those that facilitate it.

While the first four chapters of this book aim to present and explain Nigerians' experiences, understandings, and ambivalent participation in corruption, the last three chapters examine popular responses to it. I show how urban vigilantism, spectacular witchcraft allegations, resurgent ethnic nationalism, and the dramatic rise of born-again Christianity are in part fueled by discontents about corruption. These crucial trends in contemporary Nigerian culture must be understood, in large measure, as *challenging corruption*. In each case, part of the motivation and justification is to combat corruption. But even social movements and arenas of cultural production that can be usefully analyzed in the context of popular discontents about corruption do not necessarily or automatically contribute to its amelioration. The people, institutions, and ideas to which Nigerians resort in their frustrations over corruption can themselves become instruments of 419.

CORRUPTION IN GLOBAL PERSPECTIVE

Corruption has become one of the symbols of popular discontent in the modern world, not only in Nigeria, but across the globe. Stories of corruption dominate the media in both developed and developing countries. In addition, corruption has become the focus of policymakers, watchdog groups, and scholars, most of whom share a more or less explicit assumption that corruption is inimical to good governance and economic productivity. Watchdog groups like Transparency International regularly rank countries in terms of their perceived corruption, and numerous programs to combat corruption have been initiated by multilateral donors such as the United Nations and the World Bank, Western and non-Western governments, and a plethora of NGOs. It seems as if corruption has become the primary culprit in explaining the dysfunctions of government and the inequities of global economics.

The focus on corruption is particularly intense in developing countries. While there is widespread awareness in developed countries that corruption remains a pervasive problem, it is also true that poor nations are portrayed as especially plagued. This spotlight on developing countries, particularly Africa, is worrisome for two reasons. First, as I alluded to already, many accounts of corruption rekindle and reinforce misguided stereotypes that link corruption, and the associated ills of poverty and inequality, with an image of timeless cultural traditions. Such stereotypes perpetuate notions of African backwardness that obscure the extent to which the relationship between corruption and culture in places like Nigeria can only be understood in the context of larger historical patterns of political and economic inequality. Second, as an explanation for the failures of democracy and development, the idea of corruption runs the risk of deflecting responsibility for the injustices of the contemporary world from the haves to the have-nots, whether that means from rich to poor countries or from the elites in poor countries to their largely poor populations. Although ordinary Nigerians frequently implicate themselves in the perpetuation of corruption, it would be a mistake to lose sight of the larger context of inequality.

Whether so much global attention to corruption is really warranted remains an open question. Even if one takes for granted what democracy and development are, and even if one assumes that they offer the best hope for better societies (one need not—perhaps should not—take these issues for granted), it is not clear whether corruption is the primary obstacle to these ideals, or if it is an obstacle, whether it acts as an obstacle in the same way in different places. Many people who have wide experience in a number of other countries have remarked on similarities or resonances with things I describe in Nigeria. The academic literature on corruption is replete with parallels, but also suggests important differences. For example, scholars of Italy note the extensive corruption in that country, and yet Italy is a Group of Eight industrial power with levels of development only dreamed of in contemporary Nigeria. Colleagues working in India have identified discourses of complaint about corruption there that respond to the postcolonial state's self-justification as the engine for development in ways that are similar to Nigeria (Gupta 1995), and yet India has a reputation (at least compared to Nigeria) as a stable democracy. Parallels to other oil-producing states such as Venezuela are intriguing (Coronil 1997), and the similarities of corruption in Nigeria to other African states are striking (Bayart 1993; Olivier de Sardan 1999; Blundo and Olivier de Sardan 2001c).

My experience and expertise are limited to Nigeria. I hope to be able to demonstrate how corruption and the popular discontents it produces are at the center of Nigeria's struggles to develop and democratize, and to show how an ethnographic account can contribute to answering broad questions about the organization, meaning, and consequences of corruption in the case of Africa's most populous country. For ordinary Nigerians, corruption has become the ultimate symbol of modernity and its malcontents (Comaroff and Comaroff 1993). In their popular responses to corruption, Nigerians seem to suggest that corruption is both inimical to democracy and development, and paradoxically, part of a historical process in which these expectations may eventually be achieved. Examining corruption and its discontents offers a revealing window onto processes of social transformation that extend well beyond Nigeria.

CHAPTER 1

"Urgent Business Relationship": Nigerian E-Mail Scams

PERHAPS THE MOST potent international symbol of Nigerian corruption is the notorious fraudulent e-mail scam. Prior to the creation of more sophisticated spam-blocking software, many people using e-mail in the English-speaking world received a regular deluge of messages from Nigerians purporting to be in a position to transfer millions of dollars into the bank accounts of willing foreign collaborators. The writers claim to be high government officials, senior military officers, oil industry executives, bank managers, politicians, and even widows of dead dictators. The scam letters are classic confidence tricks, wherein the writers attempt to lure the recipients into advancing money and bank account information against the promise of much larger payoffs. The infamous Nigerian e-mail scams are emblematic of Nigeria's worldwide reputation for corruption. Yet the focus on these international Internet scams obscures the fact that the primary victims of Nigerian corruption are Nigerians, not foreigners. This is true in two senses. First, the types of fraud for which Nigeria has earned a global reputation, including advance-fee schemes, are also commonly perpetrated in Nigeria by Nigerians against other Nigerians. Foreigners are by no means the only or even the primary targets (although in Nigeria the main mechanism is not the Internet but rather ruses concocted around fake contracts, impostor officials, and the deceptive manipulation of the symbols of state power—much like the scam perpetrated against the Texas oil executive in my friend AC's story). Second, the main losers in all of these schemes are ordinary Nigerians, because national resources are looted and squandered by a relatively small group of criminals, international investors are extremely wary of Nigeria, and Nigeria's global reputation is smeared to the point where many honest Nigerians living, traveling, or doing business abroad are assumed to be criminals until they prove otherwise.

Perhaps the most deceiving aspect of the e-mail scams, however, is the tendency to see them only as a mode of Nigerian corruption. They are certainly that. But they are much better understood if they are also seen as a mode of interpretation, and a Nigerian response to larger systems of inequality and corruption. When one knows, as I will explain below, that the authors and senders of most of these e-mails are rather ordinary young

Nigerians, most of whom have some secondary school or university education, then the style, content, and context of these letters and the motives of the authors must be read differently. The top figures in Nigerian networks of fraud are, no doubt, rightly considered kingpins of international crime. They are criminals by almost any definition, and they should probably be lumped with military dictators, corrupt politicians, venal banking and oil executives, and all of their assorted international collaborators as the chief culprits in Nigeria's continued poverty, inequality, and instability. But an analysis of the history, social organization, and content of Nigerian e-mail scams suggests that these schemes reveal much more about Nigerian corruption and its relationship to systems of global inequality than is apparent in stereotypical understandings. The young people in Nigeria's burgeoning cybercafés who write, reproduce, and re-create the many genres of scam letters that appear in e-mail in-boxes around the world are creating cultural objects that illuminate the authors' interpretations and critical understandings of inequality and corruption, not only in Nigeria, but in the larger world system.

THE HISTORY OF NIGERIAN ADVANCED-FEE FRAUD

Though familiar in law enforcement circles for two decades, Nigerian fraud catapulted to global prominence over the past decade, as the Internet grew into a principal means of international communication. The current notoriety of Nigerian e-mail scams makes it easy to forget that confidence men and their tricks have been an important part of the histories of many societies (Halttunen 1982; Rebhorn 1988). The perpetration of fraud through which somebody obtains something of value by first gaining the trust of the victim and then betraying that person is an ancient game. Further, confidence tricks have by no means disappeared as a means of making money for people in many countries around the world. Nigerians are not the only players in the multiple versions of international financial fraud, many of which continue to depend on some sort of confidence scheme. But at the beginning of the new millennium, Nigerian e-mail fraud is perhaps the most notorious of contemporary confidence tricks.

Nigerian advance-fee fraud, known in Nigeria, and now internationally, as 419, first emerged as a worldwide phenomenon in the 1980s, following the dramatic decline in oil prices that left Nigeria's national economy reeling (Watts 1984; Apter 1999, 2005). The 1980s were also a period in which Nigeria's military retook and retained control of the government through coups, establishing a period of more than fifteen years of uninterrupted military rule. The declining economy and the military's entrenched power contributed to the growth of Nigerian advance-fee fraud in a number of ways. First, the oil boom of the 1970s brought investment in education and other public services and infrastructure to Nigeria's youth-dominated high-fertility population, meaning that by the 1980s, the country had larger numbers of educated young people with higher expectations for their futures than at any time in the past. By the late 1980s, approximately half of Nigeria's nearly one hundred million people were less than fifteen years old. The subsequent economic crash and the return of the military created a situation where this increasingly educated and ambitious young population was frustrated in its attempts to secure gainful employment or other legitimate economic opportunities.

Second, the military governments of the 1980s and 1990s were brazenly corrupt, and they created a climate where ordinary citizens believed that they would have to resort to any means available to achieve their own economic aspirations (Maier 2000; cf. Bayart 1993, 238). Indeed, some of the mechanisms used by Nigeria's longest-serving military ruler, General Ibrahim Babangida (1985–1993), to enrich himself and his cronies presage the kinds of schemes proposed by the 419 letter writers (Apter 1999). Many of the scam writers' seemingly preposterous stories of huge sums of money somehow siphoned from Nigeria's coffers are in fact reminiscent of the actual methods corrupt Nigerian elites have used for years to steal the country's wealth. Both international agencies and internal Nigerian critics have suggested that the Babangida administration not only served as a model for numerous 419 activities but that it also facilitated them (Apter 1999, 2005; Bayart, Ellis, and Hibou 1999). During the Babangida administration, international fax and telephone service became much more widely available in Nigeria. In places like Lagos, entrepreneurs established literally hundreds of so-called business centers; almost every sizable Nigerian city and town had dozens. These enterprises typically provided photocopying and word-processing services, but many specialized in offering international telephone and fax service. Nigerians widely believed that they really specialized in 419—the perpetration of advanced-fee fraud.

In the early 1990s, common stories described the enormous telephone bills these business centers generated. Yet the businesses frequently disappeared overnight when the national telephone company, NITEL, tried to collect its bills. Before the advent of mobile phone technology in Nigeria in 2001, the country had only about half a million telephone lines for over one hundred million people. For an average citizen, obtaining a phone line required paying bribes of tens of thousands of naira (several hundred dollars) on top of the official price. Given the dearth of lines, getting a new phone usually meant that NITEL workers simply transferred an existing line to a higher bidder. Further, individual customers could only get international direct-dial on their private phones with the payment of a huge deposit. Knowing the scarcity and expense of phone lines, especially international lines, many Nigerians believed that the burgeoning business center industry, with its 419 focus, was operated in collaboration with top NITEL officials along with high-level government and military support. The popular consensus was that the Babangida administration not only tolerated 419 but also supported and benefited from these activities (Apter 1999). Regardless of the actual levels of collusion between the ruling military elite and the kingpins of advance-fee fraud, the record of the military's extensive corruption in the 1980s and 1990s, and the fact that Nigerian officialdom has long been open to all kinds of shady deals, contributed to the evolution of Nigeria's advance-fee fraud enterprises. Indeed, the reality of official corruption in Nigeria is one reason why at least some of the people targeted in these confidence tricks take the bait.

Babangida had earned a reputation for skillfully spreading the tentacles of corruption to every sector within the reach of government for the ultimate benefit of himself and his cronies. When General Sani Abacha took the reins of power in 1993 he promised, like every other new Nigerian leader before and after him, to root out corruption. A couple years into the Abacha administration, many Nigerians joked that his strategy to clean up corruption was to make sure that only he and his closest cronies profited from it. Abacha was notorious for clamping down on smaller-scale corruption even as he set up mechanisms to transfer the country's wealth directly to himself. For example, in the mid-1990s, Abacha ordered the closing down of all business centers, ostensibly in an effort to stamp out 419. It became illegal to operate private businesses that offered international phone or fax services. While Abacha justified the new ban as a measure to fight 419, human rights activists in Nigeria criticized the move as a ploy to stifle Nigerian communication with the outside world during a regime that became increasingly brutal in its suppression of dissent. It is not clear what effect Abacha's crackdown on business centers had on the level of 419 scam activity in the mid-1990s. Some of it surely continued on phone and fax lines that could still be obtained with bribes paid to the right people. Other scams moved abroad, handled by Nigerian expatriates who had easier access to phone and fax services in other countries.

Advance-fee fraud certainly did not suffer a fatal blow in Abacha's crackdown on business centers, and the transition to democracy in 1999 was followed swiftly by the proliferation of Internet and cellular phone technology in Nigeria. By 2002, ordinary Nigerians in urban areas experienced remarkably improved access to international communication. Cybercafés and mobile phone call centers replaced, and ultimately far surpassed, the business centers of the early 1990s as the most common form of communications-related small enterprise in Nigeria. With expanding Web access as well as growing numbers of young people who were Internet and e-mail savvy, the World Wide Web quickly became the primary means for dissemi-

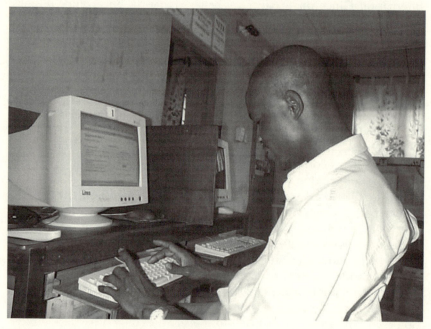

Figure 3. Internet cafés such as this one are ubiquitous in Nigeria's cities, and are patronized mainly by young people, some of whom write and send the notorious e-mail scam letters (photo by Sarah Kimball).

nating 419 scam letters. E-mail technology multiplied exponentially the numbers of potential dupes who could be contacted at little cost. It also opened up the possibility that much larger numbers of young Nigerians could try their hands at 419. While many of the promised dividends of democracy have yet to be realized by ordinary Nigerians, the democratization of 419 has been dramatic, as almost anyone who wants to participate can try.

The U.S. Secret Service Agency estimates that these scams yield the perpetrators hundreds of millions of dollars each year, and that in the 1990s, the total losses associated with Nigerian 419 schemes amounted to five billion dollars (Smith, Holmes, and Kaufmann 1999; Edelson 2003). A recent article in the *United States Attorneys' Bulletin* (Buchanan and Grant 2001) describes several successful prosecutions of Nigerian 419 fraudsters in the United States, with two of the three primary cases centered in Texas. The preeminence of Texas in these fraud stories is not coincidental. Texas has one of the largest populations of Nigerian immigrants in the United States, and the literature suggests that Nigeria-based scam artists frequently have Nigerian expatriate partners who further develop the scam scenarios and hook potential dupes in places like Texas (Smith, Holmes, and Kaufmann 1999; Buchanan and Grant 2001; Edelson 2003). In addition, Texas is the hub of the U.S. oil industry, and legitimate deals between Texas-based U.S. companies and the Nigerian government are common. Sometimes even the official deals are plagued by allegations of corruption. For example, recent contracts between the Nigerian government and firms like Enron and Halliburton have come under scrutiny for alleged fraud.[1] In retrospect, it is no wonder that the victim in my friend AC's classic scam story was a Texas oil executive.

A SERPENT WITHOUT A HEAD: THE SOCIAL ORGANIZATION OF E-MAIL FRAUD

Over the past few years, I have been a regular customer at cybercafés in the southeastern Nigerian cities of Aba, Owerri, and Umuahia as well as in Kano and Lagos. The growth in Nigeria of the Internet café business over the past several years has been dramatic. In Umuahia, a town of perhaps two hundred thousand people, for example, the number of Internet cafés multiplied from just a handful in 2002 to more than forty in 2004. The sizes of the cafés range from those with just four or five computer terminals to one café with almost forty machines. In Umuahia in 2004, it cost slightly less than a dollar for an hour's Internet access, with discounts available for purchasing larger blocks of time. In Owerri, a city perhaps twice as large as Umuahia, but also with four large tertiary educational institutions and a postsecondary student population of close to one hundred thousand, the demand for Internet services was much higher. Owerri had dozens of cybercafés in 2004, including several with well over fifty terminals. Prices were also significantly cheaper, with an hour's access at about seventy cents. In addition, at all the major cafés in Owerri and at a few cafés in Umuahia, customers could pay the equivalent of about two U.S. dollars for the privilege of "night browsing," meaning that one could stay on the Internet uninterrupted from 10:00 p.m. until 7:00 a.m. for one low fee.

Through inadvertent glancing over the shoulders of the hundreds of Nigerian cybercafé customers sitting in neighboring terminals, deliberate efforts to walk around cafés to see what customers were doing on the Internet, and interviews with cybercafé proprietors and a few scam letter senders who agreed to talk, I began to put together an emerging picture of the social organization of Nigerian e-mail scams, at least at the lowest levels of the 419 hierarchy. I have never been able to interview anyone at the higher levels of these scam operations, though I was told stories about the 419 bosses by some of the young people who send scam letters. And of course, I have collected numerous 419 narratives like the one AC told me at the tennis club many years ago.

The Western criminology literature offers a somewhat limited portrait of Nigerian fraud, and I think it is fair to say that little scholarship has been able to penetrate 419 organizations in ways that have generated reliable descriptions and analyses. What I collected in Umuahia and Owerri is partial at best; it is most empirically valid at the lowest rungs of the enterprise. My main interest, and the material about which I have the most information, is the wider popular Nigerian perception of 419, reflecting ordinary Nigerians' critical collective awareness about corruption. Before proceeding to analyze e-mail scam letters as texts that illuminate widespread Nigerian understandings of corruption, I describe what I have been able to learn about the social organization of 419 e-mail scams.

At almost any hour of the day the cybercafés in Umuahia and Owerri are busy, with peak patronage in the late afternoon and evening. In Owerri, the Internet cafés have turned Ikenegbu Layout into one of the busiest sections of the city, with bars, restaurants, video rental stores, pharmacies, hair salons, and a wide range of street hawkers that did not exist before the cafés, and could not survive without them. Cybercafés themselves do not typically offer any services besides Internet access, Internet telephone calls, and occasionally other computer-related services such as word processing, printing, and photocopying. They do not serve food or coffee, and are not in any traditional sense cafés. The bigger operations in Owerri often have televisions with satellite service mounted high on the walls at each end of the café, typically broadcasting CNN or MTV—making it all the less surprising that e-mail scam letters have evolved to include ruses based on the Iraq War, the Asian tsunami, and other recent current events. The most popular cybercafés serve as meeting points for young people. But there is really nowhere to sit except at the computer terminals, so people who meet at the cybercafés usually move elsewhere for their social interactions.

The typical clientele ranges between ages fifteen and thirty-five, with those eighteen to twenty-five years old being by far the most numerous. Although one frequently sees people above forty years old in the cafés, they are more likely to be there to make an international phone call, and if they are on the Internet, it is often with the aid of a younger person who helps them navigate the new technology. Young Nigerians on the Internet are commonly chatting (also known as instant messaging) as well as checking and sending personal e-mail. Instant messaging is wildly popular, and young Nigerians online are often chatting simultaneously with several people while also doing e-mail and other tasks. As in many other countries, instant messaging is a means of communication between friends and relatives, but also between strangers, as online relationships offer opportunities for young people to experiment with new ideas and fantasies about sex and love. In addition to personal e-mail and chatting, other common uses of the Internet in Nigerian cybercafés are searching for jobs, education, and visa opportunities outside Nigeria, viewing online pornography, doing research for a school assignment, reading the latest news or sports, and of course, 419. On several occasions, I also observed cybercafé customers using instant messaging to communicate with people who had responded to 419 messages sent by regular e-mail.

Despite the fact that in nearly every Internet café I have visited in Nigeria large signs are posted warning customers against using the Internet for 419, on any given visit several customers are typically writing and sending scam letters. Most writers looked to be between the ages of twenty and thirty. Although I did not do any scientific measurement, and although the proportion of customers sending 419 e-mails varied considerably each time I consciously tried to observe it, I think it is reasonably accurate to say that in an Internet café of twenty to twenty-five terminals, at any one time at least four to five terminals were being used to send scam letters. Over the course of my most recent six months in Nigeria—when I went to Internet cafés in Umuahia about every other day and one of the major cafés in Owerri about once a week—I was able to identify three young men and one young woman at three different cafés who were frequent Internet café customers regularly sending 419 messages. I eventually approached each of them and asked if they would talk to me.

In each case, the scam writers initially denied they were involved in 419. They were afraid that I was in some way connected with law enforcement. Indeed, I recall numerous instances over the past few years when young people obviously sending scam letters would switch screens when I passed or stood behind them, no doubt concerned about being observed. But just as common were scam writers who seemed absolutely oblivious to my presence, or to any possibility that they might be caught or prosecuted for sending 419 e-mails. Eventually, I managed to convince each of the four scam writers to talk to me. I explained that I was an anthropologist, that I was interested in understanding how 419 actually worked, and that I was not interested in prosecuting anyone. I assured them that I did not even need to know their names. As is always the case, when I told them about myself, and particularly the fact that my wife is Nigerian and Igbo, and that I had lived off and on in Nigeria for the past fifteen years, it changed the whole way they viewed me. Instead of being a foreigner suspected of possible ties to the law, I was seen first and foremost as an in-law, and thus I am fairly confident that what these young people told me is true.

All four young people said they got started sending 419 e-mails after having been Internet café regulars for other reasons. Two of the young men had learned about computers and Internet technology in previous jobs at cybercafés, and it was through those jobs that they became familiar with and eventually part of the somewhat loosely organized bottom tier of Nigeria's e-mail scam industry. The other two, a male and a female, had spent time at cafés doing ordinary e-mail, chatting online, and browsing the Web. Other acquaintances in the cafés who were involved in sending 419 messages introduced them to the enterprise. My questions about where they got the e-mail addresses to send the messages produced predictable answers. Massive numbers of e-mail addresses can be accessed from online company directories, chat rooms, electronic bulletin boards, and personal ad sites. In addition, one can apparently purchase lists of tens of thousands of e-mail addresses on the Internet for as little as a few dollars, though my informants said that only the bigger players do that, as it requires access to a credit card. All four said that they sometimes shared and received lists of e-mail addresses from friends who were also sending 419 messages. Two of the four worked directly with either the proprietor or the manager of the Internet café where they wrote and sent most of their messages. The other two worked more independently, almost like freelancers, and were much more loosely connected to a larger organization. The two who worked with their manager or proprietor had regular access to free Internet time at the cafés where they sent the messages, though they said that the managers or proprietors asked them to work mainly when legitimate business volume was low, especially during the all-night browsing hours. In only one case was it obvious that the café proprietor was directly aware of and involved in 419. In another case, it seemed as if other employees managing the café may have been facilitating the activity behind the back of the proprietor, or perhaps they engaged in 419 with the proprietor's awareness, but the proprietor was not involved in any contact with the scam writers. Many of the owners of cybercafés in southeastern Nigeria are not at their cafés on a regular basis because the cybercafés are often just one of many business ventures they own.

The fact that millions of 419 e-mails in in-boxes around the world fall into a few basic genres is a product of how the scam enterprises are organized. The people sending the e-mails usually begin with copies of other e-mails that have been used in the past. The common genres are those that have been successful previously. Their themes are directly related to the structure of real fraud and corruption in Nigeria, and to the unfolding of current events. For example, overinvoiced (inflated) contracts are a timeless theme in the Nigerian context, while letters from Abacha's widow, Maryam, only emerged after the general's death in 1998. Those working directly within the loose organizational hierarchy send most of their e-mails based on the previously successful prototypes. Those working freelance also begin with the prototypes, but are more likely to try stories that could generate a direct transfer of money, since the freelancers obviously don't have the resources to concoct the elaborate scenarios like the one in my friend AC's story.

When a 419 e-mail gets a reply, the scam writers may follow up with a few more communications in order to further hook the respondent. They are particularly interested in getting personal information like phone numbers, addresses, and of course bank account numbers. The two writers working freelance said that their first aim was to try to get the recipients to send them money—either by Western Union or wire transfer to a bank. If that did not work, they could pass on information about a potential dupe to someone in the more organized sector of the business for a small fee. Those who worked more directly within the loose structure said that they were supposed to pass all responses to their bosses. Nevertheless, one young man admitted that he sometimes tried to solicit direct transfers of money to himself, and that he also sent his own scam e-mails that were somewhat different from the typical inflated contract, dead expatriate, and dictator's widow letters that are the staple of the more organized efforts. He and the two more independent scammers described some of their more creative e-mails, where the writer sometimes presented themself as a victim of persecution for reasons of religion, gender, or disability, or as a young person in need of assistance with education, health, or family problems. Sometimes they simply sent new versions of the more typical advance-fee themes. None of my informants had ever actually received any money directly from a dupe, but they had all received some money from people higher up the hierarchy to whom they passed recipient responses. The two young men who worked directly in the loose organization received fairly regular money. None said they could really support themselves from the effort, though they all repeated stories they had heard about people who had received money directly from a scam victim. The dream of a big payoff seemed to be as much of a motive as the small income they actually earned.

I was curious how they viewed what they were doing, especially in light of the widespread awareness in Nigeria that the country's international reputation was dominated by the stigma of 419. All four expressed a certain amount of ambivalence. Each said they would prefer gainful employment to sending 419 letters. Each blamed the larger system of corruption in Nigeria for leaving them with no choice but to find any means to survive. One said he regretted any harm to the victims of these scams, but the other three said that anyone who would fall for the 419 scams was both greedy and rich enough so that there was no need to feel sorry. The words of one of the young men in the loose 419 organization capture some of the common sentiment:

> For me, I am just struggling. I could not finish university because my parents did not have the money and our government does not care about the people. Obasanjo and his boys are stealing so much money while the rest of the society is falling apart. That's the real 419. What I am doing is just trying to survive. I would not be here sending these e-mails looking for rich, greedy foreigners if there were opportunities in Nigeria. How much do I really get from this anyway? The people getting rich from this are the same people at the top who are stealing our money. I am just a struggle-man.

The volume and style of the e-mails in Western in-boxes suggest that much of what we associate with Nigerian 419 begins with ordinary young Nigerians like my informants. A friend who owns a small cybercafé in Umuahia, and who denies any involvement in 419, says he knows many cybercafé businesses that either participate in or tolerate the 419 scams. He confirmed much of what my scam-writer informants revealed about the loose organizational structure of 419, particularly at the lower levels. Once a writer snags a potential dupe, the information gets passed up a hierarchy, eventually reaching those at the higher levels who are able to employ significant resources in order to make the scam more believable and eventually extract large sums of money from a few victims. When tens of thousands of e-mails are being sent every day by thousands of small-time scammers like my informants in Umuahia and Owerri, the success rate need not be high to make it worthwhile for those who run these operations.

Western government criminal investigations (Buchanan and Grant 2001), the criminology literature (Smith, Holmes, and Kaufmann 1999), and the little research that has been done in the traditional social sciences (Bayart, Ellis, and Hibou 1999) suggest that even at the top, the networks of Nigerian fraud are loosely organized. Nigerian criminal networks purportedly manage these multimillion dollar illegal schemes using ties of kinship, place of origin, ethnicity, and patron-client relationships that cut across the government and the private sector, and link Nigerians at home to the large Nigerian diaspora. The literature indicates that the same networks that run the higher echelons of the 419 e-mail scams are also involved in numerous other criminal activities, including identity theft, bank fraud, and drug trafficking. Although I am not in a position to verify the extent of government involvement in Nigeria's infamous 419 activities, it is undoubtedly the case that the whole 419 enterprise depends on the perception that Nigerians at the highest levels of government, banking, and the oil industry are hopelessly corrupt. This is certainly the reputation of Nigeria abroad, and it is also the view that most ordinary Nigerians have of their government and leaders. Nigeria's global reputation for corruption and local Nigerian interpretations of corruption in their society are reflected in the content of the e-mail messages themselves.

SCAM LETTERS AS CULTURAL COMMENTARY

Once one recognizes that the majority of Nigerian scam letters are written and sent by fairly ordinary young people rather than a few kingpins of fraud, it is clear why analyzing them as popular cultural texts might be a fruitful endeavor. Nigerian 419 e-mails have generated a small industry of web sites in the West, including many that aim to combat e-mail fraud. Others provide comical collections of the scam letters, and examples of hilarious interchanges between creative recipients and the scammers. Many offer some combination of advice and humor.[2] A Google search of "Nigerian 419 scams" produces tens of thousands of hits, and searches with similar terms produce equally large results. Thousands of sample 419 e-mails are available on the Web for perusal. In 2002, I began saving e-mail scam letters that I received on my university e-mail account. In addition, when they remembered, three colleagues, two at my own university and one at another university, forwarded me their scam letters. I saved approximately a hundred scam letters over the past three years, and my colleagues sent me another sixty. Several days of looking through the many anti- and humorous 419 Web sites revealed a diversity of scam-letter stories that is wider than my own collection, but also convinced me that my sample is representative of the main genres. I use the letters I have received to show how Nigerian scam letters can be productively analyzed as a form of popular interpretation and critical cultural commentary regarding corruption in Nigeria.

The following analysis of e-mail scam letters as cultural texts focuses on the common structural formats, the main story lines used to try to hook recipients, the typical rhetorical styles, and perhaps most important the creative innovations that individual writers bring to what appears on the surface to be a fairly narrow range of variation. I use letters that have Nigeria itself as the location where the 419 plot unfolds because I am interested particularly in what the letters reveal about the Nigerian writers' understandings of corruption in their own society. Almost half of the letters I received have other countries as their focus, however. The increasing prevalence of non-Nigerian scam stories is partly due to the fact that con artists in other countries are imitating the Nigerian schemes, but research by information technology specialists who analyze e-mail headers that can reveal the actual place of origin of the e-mails suggests that upwards of two-thirds of scam letters in which stories focus on non-Nigerian locations originate in Nigeria (Edelson 2003). In addition, a large proportion of the remainder come from the Netherlands, South Africa, and other West African countries where law enforcement authorities believe that many of the mushrooming fraud enterprises are being run by Nigerians. Changing the stories to non-Nigerian settings reflects a growing recognition on the part of the scammers that global awareness of the Nigerian scams has become so widespread that letters focused on Nigerian opportunities to make quick money might be less effective. They also reflect the long-standing capacity of scam-letter writers to incorporate current events into their narratives. Nonetheless, Nigeria itself remains a staple location for, and international symbol of, the scam stories, no doubt in part because the premise of most scams still depends on the presumption of large-scale corruption in the place where the easy money is available.

Before proceeding, it is necessary to address the extremely uneven quality of the writing in the many thousands of 419 e-mails that arrive in inboxes around the world. While the general format of 419 letters reflects a template developed and copied over many years and across many thousands of individual scam writers, the variable quality of the written English is further evidence of my contention that most of these letters are not the work of a small group of 419 kingpins but rather are written and rewritten by large numbers of literate yet often poorly educated young people. Though the collective tone of the letters amounts to a common strategy, the frequent appearances of poor grammar, bad spelling, and awkward writing are not part of some grand strategy but rather reflect the outcome of an educational system that has itself been damaged by decades of corruption. Most scam-letter writers adopt a few basic narrative genres that circulate widely among the authors. But the writing styles and the innovations in each letter simultaneously reflect the creativity and stunted potential of the writers.

No doubt many recipients of Nigerian e-mail scam letters recognize them immediately by the subject line. While some scam letters have innocuous subject lines such as "Good Day," "Hello," or "Your Kind Attention," more typical are phrases such as "Urgent and Confidential Business Proposal," "Mutual Business Benefits," "Business Friendship," "Contacting You Urgently," "My Entire Family Needs Your Help," and "In Connection with Our Future." The urgency, confidentiality, and reciprocal benefits emphasized in the subject lines presage many of the themes that are prominent in the body of the letters. While the senders' e-mail addresses range from ordinary Yahoo accounts to addresses designed to appear more official, the format of the letter often includes an inside address indicating the purported official position and organization of the writer. In my sample of Nigeria-focused scam e-mails, the titles of the senders included executives in the NNPC (especially officials who were members of contract award and monitoring committees), bank directors, accountants with foreign oil companies, bank auditors, directors in federal government ministries, and elected politicians. The types of positions that the scammers claim to hold are, of course, meant to convince the recipients that the senders are in a position where they really would have access to the kinds of money the recipient will assist in expatriating. The supposed official titles also reflect popular Nigerian understandings of the main venues of large-scale corruption in their society.

The names of the senders are usually fictitious, but sometimes the scammers use the real names of officials or politicians. Some of the anti-419 Web sites track names that are commonly used in 419 e-mails and post warnings. One of the most popular anti-419 Web sites, called "Scam-O-Rama Presents: The Lads from Lagos" (http://www.scamorama.com), leads its home page with a section called "scammer recognition corner, guys named Egobia." The Web site warns that countless 419 e-mails come from bank managers, barristers, oil company executives, and government officials bearing the surname Egobia. While the Web site provides scores of examples of e-mails from people named Egobia and warns unsuspecting recipients to beware of such e-mails, it does not explain why so many e-mails come from officials supposedly named Egobia. Most likely, the folks who maintain the Scam-O-Rama Web site do not know that in Igbo, the language of one of Nigeria's three largest ethnic groups, *ego bia* means "money come." Despite the fun that Scam-O-Rama pokes at the "Lads from Lagos," in this case the lads appear to have had the last laugh. Knowing how creatively Nigerians use language in popular discourse, I have little doubt that the scam-letter writers use the name Egobia as both a kind of good luck charm—as in, let the money come—and a form of mockery of the potential dupes who do not realize that the truth of the scam is exposed in the name of the fictitious sender. (Recall that my friend AC's story about the scamming of the Texas oil executive contained a similar mocking name, Ibu Onye Biribe, the Igbo phrase for "you are a fool.")

While scam letters sometimes contain references whose meanings remain hidden from the recipients but are obvious to the senders, the structure and tone of typical e-mails are primarily designed to interest and ensnare the receiver. Most scam letters begin with appeals to confidentiality, secrecy, and trust. For example, an e-mail that one of my colleagues received on May 17, 2002, from Dr. Phillips Akande, who purports to be "the Secretary of the Federal Government of Nigeria Contract Award and Monitoring Committee (CAMC) of the Petroleum Trust Fund (PT)," begins: "First, I must solicit your strictest confidence in this transaction, this is by virtue of its nature as being utterly confidential and top secret." The references to secrecy and confidentiality are meant to reassure the recipient that the whole deal is clandestine and therefore safe. Establishing a relationship of trust is essential to hooking a dupe, and the letters employ a number of strategies, including appealing, ironically, to the honesty of the recipient. A letter from Mr. Agudo Ude, who purports to be a bank auditor, received February 19, 2004, starts with the appeal: "I want to ask you to quietly look for a reliable and honest person who will be capable and fit to provide either an existing bank account or to set up a new Bank a/c immediately to receive this money, even an empty a/c can serve to receive this money, as long as you will remain honest to me till the end for this important business trusting in you and believing in God that you will never let me down either now or in future."

Although it may strike Western readers as ironic that these appeals to honesty, trust, and religiosity are such prominent strategies in scams that are so blatantly premised on an original illegal act, in fact, actual practices of corruption in Nigeria depend heavily on trust relationships between the actors who conspire to funnel state resources into private hands. It is one of the paradoxes of corruption that it depends on the observance of a fairly strict ethical code among the collaborators. One reason corruption is so rampant and successful in Nigeria is that these ethical codes are well-known and usually faithfully adhered to, in part because they mimic a longer-standing moral economy tied to kinship and patronage, wherein loyalty and reciprocity have proven to be rational and successful cultural logics.

In my collection of 419 e-mails, a humorous example of such efforts to foreground ethics in the relationship between the scammer and the recipient came at the end of the opening appeal in a March 16, 2004, e-mail sent by Dr. Femi Adisa, who claims to be the chairperson of a Nigerian senate financial committee on foreign contracts verification and payments. After explaining that he needs a foreign partner, Dr. Adisa then writes: "Accept my apologies if this mail does not suit your personal or business ethics." Most of the scammers' appeals to ethics, trust, and confidentiality are, no doubt, some combination of a self-conscious strategy to hook victims and an implicit recognition that successful corruption always requires a high degree of trust between the actors. At times, the manners of everyday Nigerian society seep into the content of scam letters, perhaps unconsciously. A January 5, 2005, e-mail from a barrister Andrew Uban, who claims to need a foreign partner to transfer $38.5 million that allegedly belonged to a deceased U.S. consultant to the oil industry, closes with the ubiquitous Nigerian greeting: "My regards to you and your family."

Frequently, the effort to prove the trustworthiness of the sender is undertaken by flipping the focus to make the trustworthiness of the recipient the main issue. This is done by both the insistent appeals to the recipient to act secretly and honestly, and the explanation that the Chamber of Commerce or some other personal research has vouched that the recipient is someone who can be trusted. In perhaps the most elaborate example of this strategy that I have received, the sender describes how he was duped in a previous deal and appeals to the receiver not to let him down again. Mr. Donald Nnaji, claiming in a March 25, 2003, e-mail to be writing "on behalf of my colleagues at different Federal Government of Nigeria Parastatals," explains how some Moroccan partners absconded with part of the $35.5 million Mr. Nnaji and his partners are trying to transfer from funds left over from an overinvoiced contract:

> Precisely $5.0M (FIVE MILLION US DOLLARS ONLY) was transferred into a foreign account in MOROCCO (North Africa) but the provider of the account in Morocco is up to some mischief and has refused to comply with the earlier mutual agreement by insisting that the total amount be paid to his account before disbursement will take effect. . . . For some time now, this fellow has refused to contact us, and all efforts to reach him have failed so far. We cannot keep crying over this misfortune, but we have to forge ahead. . . . We are therefore seeking your assistance so that the remaining amount of US$30.5M can be speedily processed and fully remitted into your nominated bank account. . . . We cannot afford a slip in this transaction neither can we proceed with you without getting full guarantee from you that our shares will reach us safely after the money has reached your bank account! There must be a convincing way for you to assure us of this.

In an elaborate version of a common tactic, Mr. Nnaji shifts the burden to prove honesty and trustworthiness to the recipient, while also telling a story that reinforces that idea that the money is really there waiting to be transferred to a trustworthy partner.

Typically, the appeals for trust and confidentiality along with the explanations of where the sender learned the receiver's identity and e-mail address are followed by a brief description of the position of the writer, the amount of money involved (always millions of dollars), the scenario by which the money became available, the reason a foreign partner is required, and the proposed split if the recipient cooperates in providing a bank account in which to deposit the money. Most letters close with a request for personal information such as addresses, telephone numbers, and bank account numbers, or they provide phone numbers through which the recipient can contact the sender or, sometimes, the sender's lawyer, who will supposedly facilitate the transaction. The complications that require the remitting of advance fees typically only arise later, after the recipient has expressed interest.

The main genres of scam letters reveal Nigerians' perceptions of the primary mechanisms of corruption by which elites siphon state resources for personal enrichment. They also demonstrate popular awareness of the extent to which large-scale corruption in Nigeria is intertwined with and facilitated by Nigeria's position in the global economy as an oil-exporting nation, whereby Nigerian elites achieve power and wealth by exploiting unequal relationships with rich countries and multinational companies for their own benefit. A few examples of these principal genres show how scam letters are a form of critical commentary in which the connections between Nigerian corruption and global inequality are astutely expressed.

OVERINVOICED CONTRACTS

As indicated already, one of the most common Nigerian scam scenarios builds on the supposed availability of funds from an inflated or overin-voiced contract, typically involving the petroleum industry. The writer usually portrays themself as a government bureaucrat, a national petro-leum corporation executive, or a bank official who can gain access to the extra millions, but only with the aid of the recipient who will provide a much-needed foreign bank account. The e-mail below, received Septem-ber 20, 2002, with the subject heading "CONFIDENTIAL," is representative of this genre:

> From: Dr. Abubakar Usman
> Attn: Director/ CEO;
> Sir,
> I am Dr. Abubakar Usman, a top management staff in the Nigerian National Petroleum Corporation (NNPC). I came to know of you in my search for a reliable and reputable person to handle a very confidential transaction that in-volves the transfer of a huge sum of money to a foreign account. There were series of contracts executed by a consortium Multinationals in the oil industry in favour of NNPC.
>
> The original value of these contracts was deliberately over invoiced in the sum of THIRTY EIGHT MILLION SIX HUNDRED THOUSAND UNITED STATES DOLLARS (38.6M) which has now been approved and is now ready to be transferred since the Companies that actually executed these contracts have been paid and the projects officially commissioned. Consequently, my colleagues and I are willing to transfer the total amount to your account for subsequent disbursement, since we as civil servants are prohibited by the Code of Conduct Bureau (Civil Service Laws) from opening and/ or operating foreign accounts in our names. Needless to say, the trust reposed on you at this juncture is enormous. In return, we have agreed to offer you 30% of the transferred sum, while 10% shall be set aside for incidental expenses (internal and external) between the parties in the course of the transaction. You will be mandated to remit the balance 60% to other ac-counts in due course. You must however NOTE that this transaction is subject to the following terms and conditions:

Our conviction of your transparent honesty and diligence. That you would treat this transaction with utmost secrecy and confidentiality. That as a foreign partner, you will follow our instructions to the letter. Provide the account required, and competent to assist us on profitable investment areas in your Country in an advisory capacity. Furthermore, Modalities have been worked out at the highest levels of the Ministry of Finance and the Central Bank of Nigeria for the immediate transfer of the funds within 14 working days subject to your satisfaction of the above stated terms. Our assurance is that your role is risk free. To accord this transaction the legality it deserves and for mutual security of the fund, the whole approval procedures will be officially and legally processed with your name of any Company you may nominate as the Bonafide beneficiary. Once more, I want you to understand that having put in over 26 years in the service of my country, I am averse to having my image and career dented. This matter should therefore be treated with utmost secrecy and urgency.

Kindly expedite action as we are behind schedule to enable us include this transfer in the first quarter of this financial year. Please acknowledge the receipt of this message via Fax No: 234–1–7592604 ;Tel No: 234–1–7744044.
NOTE: PLEASE FURNISH ME WITH YOUR TEL/FAX$\frac{1}{2}$ SO THAT I COULD SEND ACROSS DETAILS OF THE TRANSFER AND OTHER RELEVANT DOCUMENTS FOR YOUR ENDORSEMENT TO ENABLE US TRANSFER THE FUNDS TO YOUR PROVIDED ACCOUNT. I AWAIT YOUR IMMEDIATE RESPONSE.
Yours Sincerely,
Dr. Abubakar Usman.

The fact that overinvoiced contracts are one of the most common scam narratives reflects a widespread perception in Nigeria that inflated and bogus contracts are one of the principal means by which government officials and their private-sector cronies loot the state (Bayart, Ellis, and Hibou 1999; Smith 2001b). Official corruption is so taken for granted by the Nigerian public that many popular debates about the ethics of corruption focus not on whether money was skimmed from a government project for private gain but on whether the contractor carried out the project at all, and if so, whether the work was completed at anything near a professional standard. Many Nigerians are so cynical about official corruption that their primary plea is that at least some of the money be used for the intended purposes. As countless friends and informants have said about government officials and their contractor collaborators, "Let them eat their share, but let them not eat everything!" The assurance in Dr. Usman's letter that the original contractors had been paid and that the project had been completed are meant to reassure the recipients that the money is not completely tainted. This concern may not even be apparent to a potential dupe, most of whom would be unaware of the nuances of moral assessments about degrees of corruption that are normal among

Nigerians, but its prominence in the text reflects the extent to which scam letters illuminate Nigerians' understandings and interpretations of corruption in their society.

Perhaps even more revealing than the nuances of Nigerian assessments regarding degrees of corruption is the fact that it is a government contract associated with the oil industry that is typically portrayed as the source of the millions. Nigerians are keenly aware that government contracts are the main mechanism by which elites divert national resources into personal wealth. The scam-letter writers' focus on oil industry contracts reflects widespread popular recognition that the biggest forms of national looting occur at the nexus of Nigeria's relationship to the world economy, particularly in the transactions between the government, the NNPC, and multinational oil companies. Another popular scam story highlights these international connections.

Dead Expatriates' Bank Accounts

In the second common scam scenario, millions of dollars are purportedly left unclaimed in a Nigerian bank because of the death of an expatriate account holder, who is usually said to have worked in the oil industry. In most cases, the account holder is reported to have died in a "ghastly" motor vehicle accident on one of Nigeria's highways. The letters almost always explain that extensive efforts have been made to locate the dead person's kin to no avail—indeed, the description of the car accident often includes the death of the expatriate's spouse and children to help buttress the claim that all efforts to locate heirs have been futile. Several letters I received included suggestions that if the money was not quickly transferred from its current limbo, unscrupulous elites would channel it to the military for nefarious purposes. The e-mail below, received on July 17, 2003, is fairly typical of the "dead expatriate" genre.

> Attn: sir,
> Permit me to introduce myself to you. My name is Johnson Elendu. I am one of the Senior Managers in the bank I work for (Union Bank, Nigeria PLC) and I work under the Director of Foreign Exchange Operations (International Remittance). I am contacting You presently because I need your urgent assistance in a business transaction that will be of immense benefit to both of us.
>
> I have the immediate need to transfer some money that has long been declared "UNCLAIMED" by the chairman and some members of the board of directors of our bank. The money is the closing balance of one of our best customers ever, Late Engr. CHAW, I was his personal account officer just before he died in the ADC plane crash of 1996 in Nigeria.

Engr. CHAW an American citizen was a contractor with the Federal Government of Nigeria, he supplied and installed equipment and his company Creekland Contractors completed some of the best construction contracts in the country. His closing balance in the Bank, Union Bank of Nigeria PLC (US$-40.Million) has been tagged Unclaimed because no relative of Engr. CHAW has come forward to make a statement of claim. We have no knowledge of a next of kin. At this point I trust you can picture what the situation is like. We have strong proof that the chairman and the board of directors will keep most of the money for themselves and donate the remainder to a discredited military trust here in Nigeria. This invariably is an attempt to infuse more money into the acquisition of military equipment (arms and ammunition) for use in an already prostrate Africa.

This of course, is senseless, hence my mission.

My colleagues and my self have made several attempts at locating persons that could be remotely related to Engr. CHAW and we have been doing this for about 4 years now. Right now I am almost alone in this enterprise and I have presently decided on moving the money to a foreign account. I am hereby soliciting your assistance and I will be very grateful if you will be willing to help in this regard.

We have access to most of what it will take to transfer the money. The only thing we do not have is a safe account. We will provide you with answers to all the security questions, which you will have to answer to move the process towards completion. We will also provide you answers to questions that only a person related to him will know. You may however not need to make any appearance; every thing will be concluded on phone and email between you and the bank [union bank nigeria pls, lagos] for your participation you will get 30%, 5% has been earmarked for the expenses that may be incurred on both ends. 65% shall be for my colleague and I.

I make this proposal in trust and in good faith, therefore, if you are interested and you agree to assist me then contact me immediately you receive this email, there is a lot more to talk about. If you are not interested, then, please, do get rid of this email and please forgive me if this message has upset you in any way. Thank you and best regards.

Mr. JOHNSON ELENDU

While this scam writer goes to great lengths to assure the recipient that Mr. Chaw's contract work in Nigeria was legitimate—his company "completed some of the best construction contracts in the country"—many other dead expatriate stories simply tie the deceased to the oil industry and presume that this connection is sufficient to explain why he would have tens of millions of dollars in a personal account. The scam writers thus represent the widely held Nigerian assumption that expatriates in Nigeria who work with the oil industry are getting fabulously rich. Awareness of the exclusive enclaves in which foreign oil company employees live in oil-producing centers like Port Harcourt and Warri, their large salaries, and the fact that big scandals involving foreign oil companies are sometimes exposed in the international and national media all feed public perceptions that expatriates associated with the Nigerian oil industry are making millions. The prevalence of the dead expatriate genre reflects a growing understanding among Nigeria's young population that corruption in Nigeria is intertwined with larger global systems of inequality. Some of the ambivalence ordinary Nigerians feel about the 419 scams is related to a perception that Nigeria in particular, and Africa in general, is often the victim of much larger mechanisms of resource redistribution in which Westerners are the primary winners and Africans are the primary losers; as the scam letter points out, Africa is "already prostrate."

A Deceased Dictator's Desperate Widow

A third common genre reflects scam-letter writers' knowledge that Nigeria's stolen billions are frequently expatriated to Western countries, highlighting popular awareness that Nigeria's history of military dictatorship was in many ways tolerated, and even facilitated, by rich countries whose primary interest was access to Nigeria's oil. In conjunction with popular discontent over the country's stolen billions, the name employed more often than any other in recent Nigerian e-mail scam scenarios is that of Mrs. Abacha, the widow of the late dictator. When General Abacha died suddenly in July 1998, it was widely reported in both the national and international media that he had looted several billion dollars during his five-year reign. Much of the money was believed to have been hidden away in foreign bank accounts. Since Nigeria's return to democracy in 1999, the civilian government has made efforts to recover some of the Abacha loot. Further, Abacha's son, Mohammed, was imprisoned for several years—accused of various crimes. Negotiations between the Abacha family and the government at one point reportedly included an agreement whereby the Abachas could keep one hundred million dollars in exchange for facilitating the return to the government of one billion dollars. After considerable media scrutiny, the deal fell through. As recently as late February 2005, the Nigerian government reached a final arrangement with Swiss banks to repatriate almost half a billion dollars of Abacha's money that Swiss authorities determined was criminally obtained. Forty million dollars was reportedly left out of the deal because it could not be conclusively proven that it was dirty money. Those accounts remain temporarily frozen.

The Abacha family has fought the Nigerian government's attempts to repatriate the late dictator's stolen millions, and the Nigerian media have carried extensive accounts of the whole process. While the predominant popular opinion seemed to favor the repatriation of as much Abacha loot as possible, there have also been media stories and some public discourse that portrays Abacha's widow as a victim of a vendetta by the current president, Olusegun Obasanjo, who was imprisoned by Abacha for two years for allegedly participating in a coup plot. Whatever public sympathy exists for Mrs. Abacha is related, in part, to the common refrain that plenty of other dictators have been allowed to keep their money. Ordinary citizens also express cynicism about what will happen to the Abacha loot if it is returned, the suspicion being that it will simply further enrich the current president and his cronies.

All of this plays into a common scam story in which Mrs. Abacha writes to appeal for help in transferring millions of dollars that have somehow escaped the hungry eyes of Nigeria's rapacious current rulers. The example below, received August 9, 2003, contains many of the characteristic features of the Mrs. Abacha genre.

Attention:

I am mrs. marriam Abacha, the wife to the late Head of State, of the federal Republic of Nigeria from 1993–1998—General Sani Abacha.

My late husband made a lot of money as the Head of state of Nigeria for 5 years. He has different accounts in many banks of the world. He has not left any stone unturned in accruing riches for his family. The present democratic government of Nigeria led by President (Gen. (Rtd)) Olusegun Obasanjo has not find favour with my family since their inception. This may be as a result of his hatred for my late husband who kept him in jail for over two years for a coup attempt, before the death of my husban. He was released immediately my husband died and he was later made the present President.

He has confiscated and frozen all my family account in Nigeria and some other American, Europe and Asian continents. It has been in both the local and international news. Presently my son mohammed Abacha has been languishing in different prison centers in Nigeria for a case against his father which he knows nothing about.

Now, my purpose of all these introduction and proposal is just seeking for your candid assistance in saving this sum of $30.8.000,000.00 [USD THIRTY.-EIGHT MILLION.DOLLARS] which my late husband had hidden from the Nigerian govt. during his regime. and which is presently somewhere in a financial and security company outside the entire Nigeria and West African region. This is a huge sum of money, I cannot trust much on most saboteur friends of my family in Nigeria who could not be trusted.

I got your contact through our trade mission. I deemed it necessary to contact you for this trustworthy transaction. All whom I needed is a sincere, honest, trustworthy and God-fearing individuals whom my mind will absolve to help me in this deal. If you have feelings about my situation, don't hesitate to stand for me.

If my proposal is sudden to you, all I need now is for you to stand as the Beneficiary of this money to claim it and save for me. There is no difficulty, I will send your name as the recipient as well as the beneficiary of the money. On your identification and confirmation from me, the fund will be handle to you. all i need is your confirmention of willingness and i will give you the full details. You will be compensated with 25% of the total fund for all your efforts in this transaction, provided this fund is save for me for your account in your country.

Please this is a very serious matter, it is a save my soul request from you and I will be delighted too much to receive a positive response from you in order to move into action. I will give you details on request from you.

THANKS YOUR FAITHFULLY MRS M ABACHA

Although the primary conscious strategy of the writer is to convince the recipient that the said millions are actually available for the taking, the Mrs. Abacha scam is instructive in what it reveals about ordinary Nigerians' assumptions regarding the workings of corruption in their society. In the Mrs. Abacha genre, scam writers assume that the recipients will be aware of the large amounts of money the late dictator allegedly looted as well as with the ongoing efforts of President Obasanjo's government to recover it. Most Nigerians also assume that no matter how much money the government recovers, Mrs. Abacha and her family will be able to keep millions that are somehow hidden from the inquisitors, or that they will be allowed to keep millions in exchange for large bribes to the authorities. These 419 scam letters frequently allude to instances of corruption and local current events that ordinary Nigerians take for granted, but that many Western recipients are unaware of. One variation of the Mrs. Abacha genre, an e-mail I received on October 15, 2004, explains the origin of the available money as "a result of a payback contract deal between my husband and a Russian firm in our country's multi-billion dollar Ajaokuta steel plant." However plausible or implausible such a scenario sounds to ordinary Western readers, millions of literate Nigerians know that over a period of more than twenty years, the Nigerian government has sunk over eight billion dollars into a steel plant that has never produced even one sheet of steel. The primary technical consultants for the project have, in fact, been Russian. To many Nigerians, including this particular scam writer, the Ajaokuta steel plant is a national symbol of official graft. Ordinary Nigerians recognize that corruption is most profitable when it involves an international dimension, and Nigerians are widely aware that their leaders depend on these international connections for their most lucrative looting of national resources.

Scams Letters, Corruption, and Global Inequality

The scam letters analyzed here are a tiny sample of a huge body of texts through which one segment of Nigeria's population produces cultural objects that convey popular conceptions of corruption. While my analysis has focused mainly on what these e-mails reveal about Nigerians' assumptions regarding corruption in their own society, they also illustrate Nigerians' awareness that corruption in Nigeria is intertwined with larger systems of inequality that link public and private economic spheres. It is no coincidence that the oil industry, expatriate contractors, and Swiss bank accounts are central figures in the scam stories. If one broadens the lens to include an analysis of the growing numbers of scam letters that focus on settings other than Nigeria, it is clear that the scam writers recognize that corruption is intertwined with the larger machinery for producing and maintaining global inequality. Scam stories that center on reconstruction contracts in Iraq, arms deals for Angola, refugee assistance in the Sudan, emergency aid in Indonesia, diamond deals in the Democratic Republic of Congo, or the pilfered millions of Charles Taylor, Mobutu Sese Seko, Gnassingbe Eyadema, and other dead or deposed African dictators demonstrate how attuned the scam writers are to the global ubiquity of corruption.

Nigerian scam letters are evidence that the young Nigerians who write and send these e-mails are aware of the importance of what Jean-François Bayart (2000) has called "a history of extraversion" in explaining patterns of inequality in African societies. Bayart argues that rather than seeing Africa's relative poverty as an indication of the continent's marginalization or exclusion from the world economy, we need to understand how profoundly Africa has been integrated in the global economy throughout history, in ways that deepen poverty and inequality. Bayart suggests that the structures of extraversion not only impoverish ordinary African peoples but also create the mechanisms by which African elites accumulate wealth and amass power. The complaint of my friend in the queue at the fuel station after the national strike protesting the rise in petrol prices, described in the introduction, typifies both the mechanisms of extraversion and ordinary Nigerians' awareness of them. My friend lamented that in a country that is a leading exporter of oil, petroleum products like gasoline, diesel, and kerosene must be imported because none of the country's refineries were working. He also expressed his belief that the country's elites intentionally preserved the nation's dependence on imported petroleum products so that they could profit from controlling the imports just as they profit from controlling the export of crude oil. His suspicion that former generals were building private refineries overseas expresses the extent to which Nigerians believe strategies of extraversion are at the heart of the nation's ills, providing cover for the most egregious forms of corruption. The most common genres of Nigerian scam letters also express, and indeed depend on, mechanisms of extraversion for their success.

While Nigerian 419 scam letters are an expression of awareness of these mechanisms of extraversion, the scams themselves are, of course, also an effort to participate in and benefit from these forms of corruption. But those who are actually getting rich from the hundreds of millions of dollars that are reportedly lost to Nigerian 419 scams are not the thousands of young people writing scam letters in the Internet cafés across Nigeria's cities and towns. These young people commonly reap little or nothing, and they participate with considerable ambivalence. On the one hand, they believe that those at the very top of the Nigerian political economy are corrupt to the core. Corruption frustrates the scam-letter writers, as it does most Nigerians. In an ideal world, almost all of these young people would prefer to do something different. In the abstract, Nigerians, including the scam writers I interviewed, know that 419 is inimical to their interests and those of their country. On the other hand, they are extremely cynical about the prospects for success without participating in the larger system of corruption, whether it is in scam-letter writing or some other arena of Nigerian society. Though the numbers of young people who write e-mail scam letters has multiplied with the advent of the Internet and the relative freedoms of democracy, scam writers still represent a tiny fraction of the population. Yet many other Nigerians participate in one way or another in the social reproduction of corruption, even as they simultaneously lament and condemn it. Nowadays, when Nigerians speak of 419 they frequently mean much more than the advance-fee fraud scams that fill Western e-mail in-boxes; 419 has become a metaphor for the pervasiveness of corruption in everyday life in Nigeria.

CHAPTER 2

From Favoritism to 419: Corruption in Everyday Life

IN JUNE 1995, the U.S. television news magazine *60 Minutes* did an exposé on Nigeria titled "Corruption, Inc." Among the most memorable moments in the piece is a segment where reporter Mike Wallace reveals that he has been able to procure a Nigerian passport with the payment of a small bribe. To further demonstrate the ease with which official documents can be created for the pursuit of 419, he arranges to have a letter produced on government stationery that asserts he is a deputy director in the Federal Ministry of Finance and has been authorized to award a contract of $1.3 billion "to supply earrings (left earrings only) to the Nigerian National Guard." To U.S. viewers, Wallace's Nigerian passport and preposterous scam letter appear as indisputable confirmation of rampant official corruption.

Few people in Nigeria ever saw the *60 Minutes* program. But several months after the original *60 Minutes* broadcast, and shortly after then head of state Abacha ordered the execution of government critic and activist Ken Saro-Wiwa and eight colleagues, which led to the widespread international characterization of Nigeria as a "pariah state," the Nigerian government aired and distributed its own television program, titled "Not in Our Character: Enough Is Enough in this Calculated Attempt to Smear Our Image as a People and Nation." I was in Nigeria from September 1995 to May 1997 conducting research, and I closely followed popular responses to Abacha's "Not in Our Character" campaign.

In 1995, and indeed both before and after these particular events, many Nigerians were quick to point out that corruption is a worldwide problem, almost every form of corruption that exists in Nigeria also exists in other settings, and much of the most detrimental corruption in Nigeria, particularly in the nation's lucrative oil industry, would not be possible without the collusion of foreign, mostly Western, partners. Educated Nigerians are well aware that their corrupt leaders' millions are deposited in Swiss bank accounts, illegally bunkered oil is purchased by Western merchants, and massive contracts related to the extraction and export of petroleum products frequently involve payoffs from multinational companies to their official Nigerian partners. Nevertheless, Abacha's "Not in Our Character" campaign was met mostly with intense cynicism on the part of ordinary

Nigerians. His propaganda was viewed as the height of hypocrisy because the Nigerian public was fully cognizant that Abacha and his cronies were looting the nation's wealth with unprecedented avarice and impunity.

The propaganda video and Abacha's larger campaign to deflect criticism by attempting to unite Nigerians through depicting foreign critics as anti-Nigerian, however, heightened what has been a perpetual preoccupation in Nigerian popular discourse: the question of why Nigeria and Nigerians are so corrupt. Not surprisingly, in some contexts Nigerians reject or at least resent the negative global stereotype of their country. For example, when Nigerians tell stories of their treatment at European and North American consulates, where visa interviewers interrogate them with questions and a tone that suggests each applicant is likely to be perpetrating fraud, they clearly resent the implicit insinuations of the interviewers. Similarly, when they tell stories of their treatment by customs and immigration officers on arriving in foreign airports, or they describe the special and difficult processes put in place for Nigerians who want to register for and take standardized educational tests such as the SAT or the GRE, Nigerians clearly take exception to the apparent assumption that no Nigerian can be trusted. Recently, a bright young Nigerian university graduate named Blessing, who has been helping me transcribe tape-recorded interviews, told me that she was angry at the arrangement I proposed regarding payment for work she would complete after my departure from Nigeria. She thought my proposal to pay most of the money after completion of the work smacked of distrust and she said, "Not all Nigerians are corrupt. This reputation is killing those of us who are honest." She convinced me to pay more of the money up front and completed all the work exactly as promised.

Despite widespread awareness in Nigeria that corruption is by no means a uniquely Nigerian phenomenon, and despite extensive resentment and frequent rejection of the stereotype that Nigerians as a people are corrupt, ordinary Nigerians regularly debate, argue, joke, and otherwise engage in a constant national discourse about the causes, culprits, and consequences of corruption. If one eavesdrops on Nigerian conversations, one will find corruption to be the most common and contentious topic. Discussions about corruption are rich in complexity, contradictions, and critical analysis. Discourse and debate about corruption are part of the stuff of everyday life in Nigeria. Even my brief recent exchange with Blessing over how to arrange her payment for transcription offered a small but telling insight. After I agreed to pay her more of the money in advance, I told her that there were two primary options to make the final payment: I could send the money by Western Union, or I could leave it with one of my friends, who would pay her on my instructions. She responded immediately, "Please, please, don't leave it with anyone, you can never . . ." As she realized what she was about to say, she gave me a look that said "touché," recognizing that she, too, often assumed the worst of her fellow Nigerians.

A good deal of the debate in Nigerian popular discourse about corruption focuses on who to blame, and in particular how much is the fault of leaders versus ordinary Nigerians. The dominant view is that Nigeria's corruption is principally a problem of leadership. In his classic book *The Trouble with Nigeria*, author Chinua Achebe (1983, 1) articulates the "bad leaders" argument: "The trouble with Nigeria is simply and squarely a failure of leadership. There is nothing basically wrong with the Nigerian character." Achebe adds that "if indeed there is any such a creature as 'an average Nigerian' he is likely to be found at a point in social space with limited opportunities for corruption as we generally understand the word. Corruption goes with power; and whatever the average man may have it is *not* power. Therefore to hold any useful discussion of corruption we must first locate it where it properly belongs—in the ranks of the powerful" (38).

Whether or not they have read his book, average Nigerians largely share Achebe's view that corruption is a problem that emanates from bad leadership. The vitriol that Nigerians express against their leaders in everyday conversation affirms how widely they blame their leaders for the country's predicament. Indeed, as an observer of Nigeria, it is hard not to sympathize with the view that Nigerian leaders bear much of the responsibility for the widespread corruption that stifles development, produces poverty, and reinforces inequality. But ordinary Nigerians, especially those whose life trajectories put them in contact with the state—whether through education, business, politics, or simply the seeking of social services—are also well aware of their own complicity in perpetuating corruption. The thousands of Nigerians I have listened to over fifteen years nearly all acknowledge that it is not just the country's leaders who are corrupt. Daily debates and conversations in marketplaces, offices, and bars, on buses, and in Nigeria's vibrant media excoriate not only the president and his cronies but corrupt Nigerians at all levels of society. In my experience, it is the exception rather than the rule to find a Nigerian who refuses to recognize their own culpability in reproducing Nigeria's notorious corruption. The same person who rails against General Abacha or President Obasanjo can, in a different moment, lament or laugh about their own involvement in corruption.

Corruption permeates nearly every facet of public life, and many facets of private life. The language and metaphors of corruption have even penetrated people's understandings of their intimate interpersonal relationships. To explain corruption in Nigeria, it is necessary to understand how many average Nigerians who condemn corruption also participate in its social reproduction. Further, it is important to be able to distinguish, where possible, between types of corruption that Nigerians undertake based on positive values associated with kinship, reciprocity, and loyalty, and those activities that Nigerians themselves label as 419. The ordinary Nigerians who participate in corruption often feel compelled to do so in the context of political and moral economies that seem to leave them little choice. Through examining the everyday workings of corruption in their most mundane forms—in bureaucracies, business, education, and health care, and even in intimate personal relationships—it becomes possible to see how Nigerians can be both critics and complicit participants in corruption, and in the many behaviors they associate with it.

OFFICIAL CORRUPTION: SETTLING OGA

When Nigerians seek a service from their government, they routinely expect that they will have to navigate corruption at all levels of the bureaucracy. Everything from obtaining birth and death certificates, to registering a company, to applying for a passport, to renewing a motor vehicle registration normally requires some sort of payment in addition to the official fee. Generally, the only way around paying extra money for routine government services is if one has a personal connection to someone with influence—a patron who will use their power to push on behalf of their client. But even then a relationship of reciprocity exists; the patron is helping with the implicit expectation that their act contributes to retaining and strengthening the loyalty of their client. Further, although a patron who helps a client navigate the bureaucracy may not expect payment, the client will nonetheless frequently offer a "dash" to say "thank you." Even in the simplest encounters with the state, the fuzzy boundaries between the forms of corruption identified by Giorgio Blundo and Jean-Pierre Olivier de Sardan (2001a) are apparent. The dynamics of patron-clientism can be quite complex, as the inequality inherent in patronage relationships often crosscuts other social bonds such as kinship, friendship, and ties of association that can be affective and relatively egalitarian (d'Azevedo 1962; Bledsoe 1980). Indeed, part of the complexity of official corruption in Nigeria is the way that the mechanisms of bureaucracy become personalized, not only in actual relationships between officeholders and their clients, but also in the language used to facilitate corruption, even in situations where the citizen and the bureaucrat are, in fact, complete strangers (Joseph 1987; Chabal and Daloz 1999; Blundo and Olivier de Sardan 2001b).

At the beginning of fieldwork in Nigeria in 2004, I bought a 1988 Nissan Bluebird to enable me to move more easily between two research sites separated by about forty miles. The process of registering the car and getting a new Nigerian driver's license illustrates some of the typical dynamics of routine official corruption. I bought the car in Owerri, the capital of Imo State. Frank, my friend and research assistant, had spent a whole day with me looking at cars and helped me decide which one to buy. He also agreed to accompany me the next morning to the licensing office to register the vehicle and apply for a driver's license. I told Frank that I wanted to get the registration and driver's license as quickly as possible, and that as long as the extra cost was reasonable by Nigerian standards, I was willing to pay whatever was necessary to grease the palms of the officials in charge. My past experience suggested that Nigerian bureaucrats tend to have one of two reactions to requests for services from foreigners. Either they are embarrassed or afraid to request bribes from an expatriate and therefore render the service more easily than to fellow Nigerians, or they see a foreigner as an opportunity to inflate the Nigerian prices and get even more money over and above the official and unofficial fees. As Frank and I parked at the licensing office in Owerri, I hoped for the former but expected the latter.

The office to register vehicles consisted of two rooms at the back of a large office block. In the first room were four desks, each piled with files. Behind each desk sat Nigerian civil servants. As we entered the room, a woman at the back desk was typing something on an old manual typewriter, and a man at the front desk was entering figures in a ledger. Two other people had their heads lying on their arms on top of their desks as if they were napping. After greeting everyone, I asked who we should see about registering a car. The man entering figures in his ledger perked up. "C. A. Okonkwo," he said, standing and holding out his hand to shake mine, "I am in charge of vehicle registration." I explained to Mr. Okonkwo that I had just purchased a car, and now wanted to register it and apply for a driver's license. "Of course," he said. Then Mr. Okonkwo's face grew somber. "Unfortunately," he continued, "there are no number plates. Imo State plates are finished." Frank immediately jumped in, knowing from experience that scarcity, whether real or faked, was a typical ploy for a bureaucrat to seek a bigger bribe. "Mr. Dan is our in-law," Frank announced. "He is just as much a Nigerian as you or me. You should treat him as a brother. We need the registration and plates as soon as possible." With these few words Frank had communicated to Mr. Okonkwo both that I was willing to "put something on top" of the official fees and that he should not try to take undue advantage of my being a foreigner. We were willing to pay the bribes but we would not be swindled.

When Frank announced that I was an in-law, the women who appeared to be napping on their desks sat up and we all engaged in a friendly discussion that included a brief story of how I met my wife, which village she is from, and whether I eat *akpo*, the local food most Igbos seem to assume will be least palatable to Westerners. I reinforced my desired "almost Nigerian" status not only by affirming that I did eat *akpo* but by switching my speech to the Igbo language. I gladly engaged in these minutes of friendly banter because I had long ago learned that the more personal I could make my relationships with Nigerian bureaucrats, the more likely they would treat me like a fellow Nigerian. I would still have "put something on top," but I would be less likely to be cheated by Nigerian standards.

Once everyone was satisfied that I really was an in-law, Mr. Okonkwo returned to the business at hand. "Imo State plates are finished," he said, "but I can get plates from Anambra State if you require urgent service." I told him I wanted urgent service so long as the price was fair. I informed him that I also needed the driver's license just as quickly. "Ah," Mr. Okonkwo sighed, "that might be a problem because the machine that produces the licenses is temporarily out of service." Frank and I exchanged smiles. "How much would it cost to put the machine back in service?" Frank asked. "Well, for five thousand naira our in-law can have his driver's license tomorrow," Mr. Okonkwo replied generously. Frank then said to Mr. Okonkwo, "See, *oga* [a common Nigerian word for "boss" or "big man"], just tell us the price for everything—the driver's license, the number plates, the insurance, and all the clearances so that Mr. Dan will not be hassled by the police. If we agree on the price, then you will do everything. You will be the one who settles all those people. We just want to collect everything tomorrow." Frank's reference to the clearances was a key part of the transaction. In addition to the actual vehicle registration certificate, Nigerian drivers are expected to carry several other official documents, including one that verifies that the police have determined the vehicle is not stolen. Without all the proper documents, one is likely to be delayed at police checkpoints with demands for money. Each of these documents has its own bureaucracy and officials who need to be "settled"—the Nigerian English verb for paying an expected dash, bribe, or kickback.

After doing some rough calculations, Mr. Okonkwo handed me a piece of paper with a large amount written down. Frank and I both shouted "heh!" expressing our assessment that the amount was too high. Over a period of a few minutes, Frank called me aside to discuss how much I would be willing to pay and then called Mr. Okonkwo aside to discuss how much he would be willing to take. Eventually, we agreed on a price. Mr. Okonkwo wanted all the money up front. I was reluctant because this left me with little leverage in case he failed to deliver as promised, but Frank convinced me I should go ahead. At least Mr. Okonkwo did not ask me to leave my car with him, I thought, stupidly imagining that the police might actually want to see the car to check whether or not it had been stolen. Mr. Okonkwo promised to have everything by the following afternoon.

When Frank and I showed up the next day, Mr. Okonkwo did not have the plates. He said that he had traveled to Anambra State only to find that their plates were also out of stock. But not to worry, he said, the Anambra officials assured him that in Ebonyi State plates were available, and if I gave him some additional money for transportation he would procure my plates by tomorrow. Frank suspected that he was simply trying to exploit me, and angrily told Mr. Okonkwo that we had a deal and that it was his responsibility to get the plates, whatever that involved. Mr. Okonkwo grumbled but seemed to accept the notion of a binding bargain, and he told us to come back the next day. Sure enough, the following day I had Ebonyi State plates and all the proper documents for my car. The only thing Mr. Okonkwo had not given me was my driver's license, for which five thousand naira had been included in the deal. "What about my driver's license?" I asked. Again Mr. Okonkwo frowned. "The machine is still not working," he said. "You can drive with your temporary receipt until the machine is fixed." I knew a temporary receipt would work because in the 1990s I had driven for nearly two years using just such a temporary license, and I was ready to resign myself to waiting again for the real one. But Frank was irate. He suspected that Mr. Okonkwo had simply pocketed the extra money for the urgent processing of the driver's license rather than settling whoever operated the machine. He demanded that Mr. Okonkwo accompany us to the office where drivers' licenses were issued.

Reluctantly, Mr. Okonkwo followed us to another office. After the usual greetings, I explained to the woman in charge that I had applied for a driver's license and that Mr. Okonkwo had promised it for the previous day. I pleaded with her to issue my license. She asked her secretary to bring my file, and then explained that the computer and printer that produce the plastic licenses required electricity, and the office had received no electricity for several days. Once there was electricity, she said, I would have my license. "What about the generator?" I asked. I had seen a small gasoline-powered electricity generator outside her office, obviously available precisely because the national power supply was so fickle. "No petrol," she said. At this moment Frank asked me to excuse them. Moments later, Frank emerged and said that I could come the next day to collect my license. When I asked what he had said to them in my absence, Frank reported that he told the woman that we had already paid enough money on top to get the license urgently, and that it was up to Mr. Okonkwo to settle her and assure that my license was issued immediately. She was apparently irritated with Okonkwo for "eating alone" and promised Frank that the license would be ready the next day. I have no idea how much Mr. Okonkwo had to pay to assuage the licensing officer.

The next day I came back to the office optimistic that I would finally get my driver's license. When I asked for Mr. Okonkwo, his colleagues said that he was "not on seat," but that the overall boss wanted to see me—a woman I had not yet met. I entered her office with a big smile and a warm greeting, hoping my friendliness would spare me from having to settle anyone else. Holding my plastic driver's license in her hand, she asked, "So Mr. Smith, you wanted to collect all your papers and your license without ever seeing me?" I tried to feign ignorance, pretending not to know that by seeing her she meant settling her—seeing being a well-known synonym for settling. I told her that I was happy to see her and that I had intended no offense. After all, I said, I would never want to avoid my in-laws, attempting to change the register of our conversation from that between a bureaucrat and a service seeker to one between two in-laws. Fortunately for me, it seemed to work, and as she handed me my license she said, "In future, you should see me, not just my staff." "Of course, madam," I said, as I departed happy to finally have my license. As difficult as it was to get my vehicle documentation, without the extra money I paid and without the aid of Frank, I might have waited weeks for these services, wasting valuable time with regular trips to the licensing office, only to be frustrated.

The help I received from Frank was out of friendship, but many Nigerians find navigating government bureaucracies frustrating and people frequently rely on the aid of intermediaries. Indeed, at almost every major bureaucracy that provides essential services, one finds a small army of intermediaries to expedite one's business. Nigerians sometimes derisively call these people "touts," the same name used to describe the urban urchins who populate lorry parks and bus stations trying to make a few cents shepherding people onto public transportation. Touts can be either employees of the bureaucracy or private entrepreneurs who have developed connections in the office that enable them to navigate the bureaucracy effectively. A good intermediary can save a service seeker time and money. But some intermediaries do not deliver what they promise, especially if their connections are not what they advertise or if they try to skirt settling their own patrons. Mr. Okonkwo's failure to settle the woman who issued the driver's license or to share any of my money with his own boss exemplifies this kind of problem. While intermediaries offer valuable services in the face of a corrupt bureaucracy, they are sometimes excessively venal and unscrupulous in their dealings with the public, and add yet another layer of interests invested in preserving practices of corruption.

It is important to point out that the story of my encounter with bureaucratic corruption is incomplete. I narrated it purely from the perspective of a citizen (or in this case, an alien) seeking government services. It is just as crucial to understand the perspective of the civil servants who sit behind those desks and expect to receive something on top. Typically, Nigerian civil servants are poorly paid, and salaries are often not remitted on time. At the time I applied for my license, civil servants in Imo State had not been paid for four months. People like Mr. Okonkwo sometimes rely on the money they make through corruption to feed their families. Furthermore, civil servants frequently have to provide services to people to whom they have affective or social obligations, such as kin or friends, without receiving anything on top. They might even be expected to provide services without collecting the official fees, since people in their networks may expect this help as a perceived benefit of having someone well placed in the bureaucracy. To refuse to help would risk being branded a bad person in a moral economy dominated by an ethics of reciprocal exchange. Thus, while civil servants collecting bribes to do their jobs are certainly using a public office for personal gain, they are often doing so in contexts of strong economic and moral pressures.

CHECKPOINT EXTORTION: CORRUPTION BY (THE POLICE) FORCE

My concern with obtaining all the correct paperwork for my car reflected fifteen years of driving experience in Nigeria and the awareness that the police are regularly looking for justifications to extort money from motorists. As a foreigner, I was less likely to experience outright threats of violence from the police than if I were Nigerian, but more likely to have my papers examined for any hint of an impropriety, looking for some justification to extract cash. In Nigeria, as in many societies (cf. Jeganathan 2004), perhaps the most notorious and popularly recognized symbol of everyday corruption is the roadside police checkpoint.

A legacy of military rule, Nigerian police and soldiers routinely set up roadblocks, where vehicles are stopped, drivers are besieged, and passengers are hassled. Many Nigerians are subjected to police and military checkpoints daily, and anyone who utilizes Nigeria's roads, whether in private cars or public transportation, encounters them frequently. Most people interpret these checkpoints as a means for police and soldiers to extract money from the public, symbolizing larger processes of control through which the powerful enrich themselves at the expense of the wider population. During the five years I lived in Nigeria under military rule, over a period spanning 1989–97, hardly a month passed without media reports or oral testimony from my friends and acquaintances about people who had been harassed, beaten, or shot in confrontations at checkpoints with the police or military. Stories about checkpoints, regardless of whether they were all true, became an important form of folklore that represented wider interpretations of military rule and the forms of everyday corruption it produced.

Interactions with the police at roadside checkpoints usually unfold according to a common script, with which nearly all Nigerians are familiar. After one is stopped by a barricade or a pointed weapon, police demands

Figure 4. Encountering roadside police checkpoints, at which armed officers extort tolls from drivers, is a daily experience for many Nigerians (photo by Rahul Kamath).

for money take several forms, including some in the euphemism of a polite request. Typical ways Nigerian police ask for money include: "Any weekend for us?" "We are loyal, sir," "Give us something for cigarettes," "Any 'pure water'?" "Any 'roger' today?" or simply "I salute you," followed by a look of expectation. When the Nigerian police or military say "roger me," alluding to how the word roger is used in radio communication—as in "roger, over and out"—all Nigerians know that in order for the encounter to end, the officer needs some money. The reference to "pure water," like the one to cigarettes, is meant to imply that the request is small—pure water being the popular name for the sachets of drinking water sold all over Nigeria for a few pennies.

The often friendly nature of the request for "something small" is belied by the guns and the behavior of the police when one fails to comply, or when the police are simply in a bad mood. In such cases, instead of a polite request, the driver of a private vehicle is, for example, likely to hear "clear well" or "park well," followed by a demand to see "your particulars." Official documents are examined to look for any omission or mistake, and if one is found the cost of continuing one's journey is inflated. Even when all is in order, a "hungry" police officer might demand to look under the hood, supposedly checking the engine and chassis numbers against what is written on the vehicle registration. The longer the delay, the more likely drivers will offer something just for the chance to get going.

As hinted in the earlier vignette in which my student asked about the half-concealed handoff between a minibus driver and the police, for commercial vehicles the routine is streamlined. It is expected that the driver or their apprentice/conductor will pay a small amount at every checkpoint, and this usually happens without delay or incident. Bus and taxi loads of passengers collectively condemn the police at virtually every checkpoint. But a driver who fails to pay will also be condemned by the passengers for delaying them. Despite the normally routine nature of these payments, several times a year the Nigerian press reports incidents where the police shoot and kill a driver or conductor over disputes escalating from transactions at checkpoints. The fact that corruption at police checkpoints occasionally ends in violence reinforces why ordinary citizens resent this form of corruption so deeply, even though the amounts of money are small. The money paid at police checkpoints amounts to what Blundo and Olivier de Sardan (2001a) describe as a toll or levy, in which no service is rendered. These tolls are seen as extortion, and people submit to police demands only because they are backed up by the threat of violence. Unlike many other forms of corruption, about which Nigerians are often ambivalent because they perceive positive as well as negative dimensions to particular transactions, checkpoint levies are widely viewed as forms of corruption with no redeeming features—except, of course, by the police who collect the money.

KLEPTOCRACY BY CONTRACT

Few events bring more excitement to a family and community than the news that one of its own has been appointed to an important government position. To have one's son or brother (terms used to describe a wide range of kin relationships) placed in a high public office is to expect access to the most notorious and lucrative form of Nigeria's infamous corruption: a contract. Contracts are the mechanism through which specific jobs—everything from refurbishing an oil refinery to building a road or supplying office stationery—are awarded. In Nigeria, by far the biggest source of contracts of all sorts is the government. Contracts are symbols for the whole system of patronage and corruption that dominates the Nigerian political and economic landscape, as coveted as they are reviled. The contract mentality is so prevalent in Nigeria it led one analyst to describe the government as a "contractocracy"—"a government of contractors, for contractors and by contractors" (Othman 1984, 452).

A contract is the most prominent symbol of corruption in Nigeria in part because of the critical significance of oil to the country's political economy. With the oil boom of the 1970s, Nigeria's economy became much less diversified, and the dependency of state and local governments on the federal government deepened. Investments in agriculture declined because the influx of petrodollars created an illusion of instant and seemingly unending prosperity. By 1980, more than 95 percent of Nigeria's export earnings came from oil, and that amount constituted 55 percent of the total government revenue (Watts 1992). Elites no longer depended on access to "surpluses generated by peasant producers but on oil rents redistributed through the state apparatus" (Watts 1992, 36). Central government control of and dependence on rents associated with the oil industry intensified the vertical hierarchy of patronage networks and the importance of government contracts as a source of wealth (Joseph 1987). Nigeria's dependence on oil revenues has only deepened in the early twenty-first century (Apter 2005).

The intensification of the reliance on oil revenues, with its concomitant concentration of government control over the national cake, contributed to the growing importance of social and political contacts as the basis for securing lucrative government contracts. Increasingly, success in business in Nigeria depended on cultivating partnerships with political patrons in positions to award state money. During its years in power, the military used the awarding of contracts to divide potential opposition by rewarding influential loyal civilians with huge deals. Since the transition to democracy, civilian politicians have used government awards to repay key supporters and cultivate additional clients. In most of these deals the Nigerian public is the loser, as politicians and their private-sector cronies loot the state in mutually beneficial bargains that unify government and business elites while perpetuating Nigeria's dramatic inequalities, a pattern of class formation that Jean-François Bayart (1993, 155–79) has described as "the reciprocal assimilation of elites."

One of the most striking things about corruption in the awarding of contracts in Nigeria is the fact that seemingly everyone knows exactly what is going on. Nigerians almost universally assume that virtually every state-awarded contract is corrupt. Talk about contracts and corruption inundates local discourse about Nigerian business and politics. Conversations routinely lurch between condemnation, on the one hand (as people lament a road repair contract that has been abandoned or concluded without noticeable improvements, wonder how a country so rich in natural resources can be so poor, or speculate about how a new political appointee will siphon government resources to their own people), and conspiratorial anticipation, on the other (as individuals survey their social networks for an "in" with a new big man, plan a "courtesy call" to a new official, or prepare a bid on a contract in hopes that family, community, or political connections will give them the inside track). People share a sense that corruption has perpetuated poverty in a land of wealth and that only the rich get richer. Yet few people see a realistic path out of the predicament.

Although Nigerians recognize and condemn, in the abstract, the system of patronage that dominates the allocation of government resources, in practice people feel locked in. One friend, a university professor who was appointed a state commissioner of agriculture, put it to me this way: "Even if I wanted to avoid the practice of awarding contracts on the basis of favoritism, I could not. My people would say that I am selfish and foolish. Who gets to such a position of power and then refuses to help his people? Only the worst kind of person." A man who enriches himself through emptying government coffers is, in his community, despised only if he fails to share enough of that wealth with his people—through direct gifts to individuals and community development projects, but also through more ceremonial distributions such as lavish weddings for his children, spectacular burials for his parents, and extravagant chieftancy installation ceremonies for himself. At such events his people enjoy his wealth—they "chop" (eat) his money.

The awarding of government contracts illustrates the ways in which local moralities intersect with state politics to create and reproduce a political economy grounded in patron-clientism, facilitating corruption. Examples of contracts that involve relatively small patrons and smaller clients support the argument that corruption is sustained precisely because people of all strata in Nigeria, except the very lowest, are invested in, and in some measure benefit from, the accumulation and distribution of public resources through informal private networks, even as corruption also has more general corrosive consequences. The cases below also highlight the importance of personal contacts, especially kin and affinal relationships, in negotiating a system in which patron-client ties become less dependable when social connections between ordinary citizens and the state are more impersonal.

Having a Powerful Patron

When I first met him in 1989, Chuka Okafor was a single young man of about thirty years. He lived in Owerri, the capital of Imo State. His late father was a relatively high-ranking policeman in another Igbo-speaking state. When I met him, Chuka had a low-paying job at the Imo State Sports Council. He played tennis at a local club, socialized there with many of the big men in Owerri, and used his impressive social skills to parlay his tennis playing into small contracts. Chuka was gregarious and funny, and quickly mastered the dynamics of club politics. Mostly because they liked him, many of the big men in his tennis club awarded him small contracts to supply stationery and buy minor equipment. Through these small enterprises he managed a comfortable if modest life.

Then, around 1994, a new military administrator was appointed for Imo State, a navy captain who hailed from Chuka's state, and specifically from Chuka's natal community. In a matter of months Chuka owned a car, had a phone, and dressed in the expensive linens that are elite Igbo men's favorites. The new administrator had welcomed Chuka into his inner circle, giving him a senior post in his security operation and signaling his self-appointed commissioners that Chuka was on the inside. Chuka benefited from much larger government contracts. People speculated that he passed much of his money back to the military administrator and that this was one of the reasons he was so favored. By 1997, Chuka had been elected president of one of the local tennis clubs. After the transition to democracy in 1999, he used his connections and newfound wealth to get elected to the national assembly. When Chuka comes back to Owerri nowadays, he is sought out by businesspeople looking for contracts.

A Little Contract Produces Bigger Rumors

In 1996, Emeka Okpara was about fifty-seven years old and a married father of six. He, his wife, Charity, and their children lived in Ubakala, about six miles from Umuahia. Emeka managed the family's small stall in the Apumiri market, where they sold a variety of everyday commodities and offered typing services. He also supplemented his small trade by acting as a sort of local medicine vendor, giving clients injections of B–12, penicillin, and chloroquine for common ailments such as "weak blood," gonorrhea, and malaria. Charity worked as a secretary in the Umuahia local government administration and took over at the family stall after work.

During my fieldwork from 1995 to 1997, Emeka managed to get a small contract from the Umuahia local government administration to build a fence at one of the primary schools in Ubakala. Emeka is not a builder and knows nothing of masonry, but such details are of little consequence in many government contracts.[1] Local gossip suggested that Charity had managed to persuade her boss to award Emeka the contract—the more salacious versions implying that Charity had a sexual relationship with her boss. With the proceeds from his contract, Emeka began the construction of a house and managed to pay the school fees for his daughter, who was the first in the family to attend a university. While some neighbors and kin admired and congratulated Charity and Emeka for managing to get their own small share of the national cake, the rumors about what Charity might have had to do to get the contract for her husband exemplify the moral ambivalence that accompanies the intense competition for contracts.

Compared with federal and state contracts, Emeka's primary school fence was insignificant. Nevertheless, it was a huge boost for him and his family. Further, just as Nigeria's leaders lack credibility with a public that simultaneously seeks their favor, so community responses to Emeka's success included both envy and disparaging gossip about his wife.

Unfulfilled Expectations

When I first met him in 1995, Levinus Okeh was in his late forties, married with five children. Levinus is popularly known as "World Biz"—short for World Business—among his friends, a praise name coined during his wealthier past. He hails from a local government area that was the home of a former civilian governor. World Biz married a woman from the former governor's extended family, and during the former governor's tenure, World Biz parlayed his affinal relationship into a series of lucrative contracts. For a number of years World Biz was a wealthy man.

Times were leaner during the military regime. His patron was long out of power. World Biz did not have a job but still managed to scratch out a living getting small contracts here and there. In 1996, World Biz campaigned hard for a particular candidate in his local chairmanship elections. He used to tell me—only half kidding—that he was the kingmaker behind the scenes. He also borrowed money from me and others, and assured us that when his candidate won he would "be in money, man." He expected lucrative contracts in return for his mobilization of followers.

His candidate won the election, but for months afterward World Biz complained that the man was ungrateful. He used to make frequent visits to the chairman's office in hopes of some sort of business deal. But the chairman kept putting him off—complaining about a lack of funds, debts to pay inherited from the last government, and increased state and federal scrutiny of local government spending. At first World Biz accepted the excuses and maintained hope. But eventually he concluded that the chairman had no intention of rewarding him. World Biz was bitter. The chairman was an ingrate, World Biz said, and he did not "know politics."

Within a few months the military again dissolved the local government councils. The chairman was out of office. Only weeks later, the former chairman died unexpectedly of a heart attack. World Biz said it was God's way of punishing him because he was not a good man.

World Biz's expectation that he would be rewarded was directly related to the fact that he "delivered his people" in the chairmanship election. Given World Biz's propensity to exaggerate on his own behalf, I have no way of knowing how instrumental he was in securing the chairman's election. Perhaps the late chairman saw things quite differently. Regardless, World Biz was calling on a widely shared value in Nigerian politics that one should be rewarded for delivering his people.

While there is no doubt that elites benefit disproportionately from the current structures of Nigeria's contractocracy, these structures are only sustainable because they are supported by a complex moral economy in which those at the top are forever fulfilling obligations and duties to their followers and clients (Joseph 1987, 7–8; Bayart 1993, 219; Olivier de Sardan 1999, 43). In the cases of Chuka and Emeka, social and political connections, mediated through kinship, directly determined the awarding of government contracts. World Biz's experience with his local government chairman illustrates that patrons and clients do not always agree on the extent of obligations. But World Biz's interpretation of the chairman's death demonstrates the strength of belief in the obligations implicit in a moral economy of patron-clientism. The fact that his affinal ties to the last civilian governor proved much more beneficial shows how much more secure one can be in ties created through marriage and kinship than in those produced through purely political alliances (Chabal and Daloz 1999, 27).

SUPPLEMENTARY ADMISSIONS AND MONETIZED GRADES

Over the past three decades, access to education in Nigeria has improved dramatically. Whereas in the 1960s a minority of children attended primary school and fewer attempted secondary school, by 2000 access to primary school education had long been available to the vast majority of the population. Secondary school attendance has climbed rapidly. Figures from the *Nigeria Demographic and Health Survey 2003* (National Population Commission 2004, 25) show that in southeastern Nigeria, approximately 67 percent of all women between fifteen and forty-nine years old had attended at least some secondary school; 27 percent had completed secondary education; and 12 percent had undertaken some level of post-secondary education. Among men in southeastern Nigeria between fifteen and fifty-nine years old the figures are similar, with 70 percent having attended at least some secondary school, 21 percent having completed a secondary education, and 17 percent having undertaken some level of postsecondary education. While the figures for southeastern Nigeria are slightly higher than the national averages, they represent a nationwide trend of increasing access to formal education.

Though university attendance is still limited, it is growing extremely fast. The number of government-supported tertiary institutions in Nigeria has grown from just a handful at independence in 1960 to more than thirty universities at the beginning of the new millennium, and more than one hundred government-supported tertiary institutions overall, if one counts teacher-training colleges and polytechnic institutions. In addition, several private universities have recently been established. Although millions of young Nigerians are currently in secondary school and several hundred thousand are at a university, students seeking admission still far outnumber the available places. The quality of secondary schools and universities also varies tremendously, creating fierce competition for the better institutions. In this environment of scarcity, corruption has become a major factor in the process of admissions. Once students are in school, furthermore, a combination of severe shortages of resources, poor teacher salaries, and a growing acceptance that even education must be bought has translated into extensive corruption in the educational system.

In contemporary Nigeria, aspirations for education are perhaps the most universally shared marker of modernity. In southeastern Nigeria, nearly every young person desires to complete secondary school, and most wish to attend a university. Parents and other elders widely support young people's ambitions for education. The pursuit of further schooling is not only an individual goal but also one of the most important motives in group life (Uchendu 1965). Families, kin groups, and communities mobilize resources and put strong pressure on their members to help educate others in the group. Parents make great sacrifices to pay school fees and assure that their children have resources for school. They frequently call on other kin to help. It is typical for older siblings to contribute to the education of their juniors. Family members contribute economically, and draw on whatever social capital they have to help kin get admission to a secondary school or university in a context where higher education is not available to all and admission often depends on patronage ties.

In 1996, my niece, Adanna, was admitted to a secondary school. In 2004 she entered a university. The story of Adanna's two admissions illustrates the role that patronage—and particularly what Blundo and Olivier de Sardan call "string pulling" (2001a)—plays in access to education in contemporary Nigeria. It provides some insight into the complexity of corruption, challenging simplistic moral judgments that associate it exclusively with individual greed.

My wife's brother, Christian, and his wife, Ulunma, live in Nigeria's huge commercial capital, Lagos. When I started my first fieldwork in 1995, Christian was struggling to make a small photocopying business profitable, while Ulunma had a steady but low-paying clerical job at a bank. They had been married more than twelve years and were about to have their fourth child.

Any child can attend a government-run primary school without paying tuition, but private primary schools are often better than the state-run ones. Many parents struggle, as did Christian and Ulunma, to put their kids in a private school so that they will be educated well enough to be competitive in the secondary school admissions process.

For secondary school, the national structure is quite different. The federal and state governments support relatively fewer secondary schools, and admission to them is highly coveted. Federal schools are the most selective and prestigious. Some state government secondary schools have good reputations, but there is much greater disparity than in the federal schools. Entrepreneurs also run private secondary schools, known as "commercial" schools, where anyone who can pay the fees can attend. But most Nigerians view these schools as second-rate and unlikely to lead to higher education.

In 1996, Christian and Ulunma's eldest daughter, Adanna, completed primary school at the age of nine, almost two years earlier than most students. She was a fine student, regularly finishing in the top five in her class of forty. Her parents had high aspirations that Adanna would be admitted to the Federal Government Girls College, Umuahia (FGGCU), a selective secondary school. They wanted the federal school in Umuahia because it is only a few miles from the family village of Ubakala, and if Adanna could attend school nearby her father's rural place of origin, relatives could more easily assist in looking out for her. Adanna scored well on her secondary school admissions test, but not well enough to gain automatic entrance.

Soon after the scores came out, it was clear that Adanna did not get admission. Christian asked me if I would talk to the principal at the FGGCU to see if Adanna could be admitted on her discretionary list. At secondary schools in Nigeria, some admissions slots are typically filled at the principal's discretion. In theory, these discretionary spots are meant for exceptional cases. In practice, they are doled out as part of a system of patronage whereby administrators help their friends, associates, and relatives—as well as powerful people who they cannot afford not to help.

Christian appeared to have no qualms about asking me to help Adanna get admission. He thought I might be able to assist because I had just recently conducted a study in Umuahia secondary schools as part of my research and therefore knew officials in the Ministry of Education. Additionally, I was teaching at Abia State University, and he thus believed I had status in the world of higher education. He also mentioned that I knew a lot of big men in Umuahia and that I would be well positioned to help. I did not know the principal personally, but Christian hoped my influence would be great enough anyway.

It is important to begin by understanding why Christian expected me to help. I was part of his social network, a potential ally and resource in seeking Adanna's admission. As his brother-in-law and Adanna's uncle, I was expected to help if I could. At the time I certainly felt that I had no choice but to try. Given what I knew about how the admissions process worked in Nigeria, and given my fondness for my niece and my desire to keep on good terms with my in-laws, I never hesitated to approach the principal. It seemed like the ethical thing to do, even though from another perspective one could argue that I was participating in corruption because I was going to ask that Adanna be admitted as a favor, when her scores did not merit it.

In any event, my effort failed. The principal told me that only those students with sufficient scores could be admitted, and no amount of cajoling on my part moved her. I believe my intervention failed precisely because I was not, in the eyes of the principal, part of a trusted social network. To her, I was an outsider with no roots in the community, no permanent identity, and no place in a web of social relations that she had a stake in perpetuating. Further, as a foreigner, I also represented a risk. To operate with me based on the informal rules of the game when I was potentially associated with formal rules of the game posed unknown consequences.

When I reported the results of my failed efforts to Christian and Ulunma they did not seem all that surprised. Christian said: "She was afraid because you are a foreigner. She just wanted to hide everything from you." Instead of the profound disappointment I had expected, Christian and Ulunma were upbeat. Since I had last seen them, Ulunma found out that her sister had a friend in the Federal Ministry of Education in Lagos. The woman in the federal ministry said that she would try to get Adanna admitted through the minister's influence. In the end, Christian and Ulunma had to pay the woman in the ministry five thousand naira (about sixty-five dollars, or more than a month of Ulunma's salary) for securing Adanna a place.

Christian and Ulunma's dependence on patronage and solidarity networks to facilitate Adanna's education did not cease in secondary school. In 2002, Adanna graduated from secondary school and began what in Nigeria is an extremely long process of preparing for and taking examinations aimed at securing admission to a university. Secondary school graduates aspiring to a university take the Joint Admissions and Matriculation Board (JAMB) exam, which all Nigerian universities require and which they use to determine admissions.

Over a period of almost two years, Adanna took the JAMB twice and several other standardized exams at least once. Unfortunately, she did not score well enough to get admission to her first-choice schools (under the Nigerian JAMB system, students are allowed to opt for only two schools). The only hope left for Adanna to gain admission in 2004 was to apply for something called "supplementary admission." Supplementary admission is meant to allow students with special circumstances to make their cases. In practice, the supplementary admissions mechanism is marked by patronage and corruption.

In Adanna's case, her parents decided that her best bet was to seek supplementary admission to Abia State University, even though technically she was not even eligible because she did not put it as one of her two choices. But they hoped that my connections would help, and in this case they did.

In addition to having taught at Abia State University in 1996 as a Fulbright Fellow, I had since maintained a continuous relationship with several faculty members with whom I collaborated on research. My best friend at the university had become a dean, and through him I also knew the vice chancellor, who is the university's chief executive officer. When I phoned my friend to explain Adanna's predicament, he said that I should instruct Christian and Adanna to come to the university with all her documents. I remember his precise words: "You are one of us. Even if I have to perform magic, your niece will get admission." Not only did my friend secure Adanna's admission but he also arranged it so that she would have university housing, a resource even scarcer than a place in the incoming class. Christian and Ulunma were ecstatic, and I was proud. I had proven myself to be a good in-law.

Reviewing Adanna's case does something more significant than demonstrate again how widely corruption permeates everyday life in Nigeria. It illustrates the complex relationship between corruption and a system of patron-clientism closely tied to a kinship-based reckoning of the importance of reciprocity. Helping one's people often supersedes obedience to the abstract rules of the state, especially in a context where people assume that others are breaking the official rules. The help I rendered my in-laws and that offered to me by my friend at the university highlight the degree to which so-called corruption can sometimes be undertaken for reasons that have strong moral justifications. To ordinary Nigerians, the good moral reasons to bend or break the official rules are bound up with obligations to family, kin, and community. Even with my Western sensibilities, as Adanna's uncle, I felt that helping her was the right thing to do. In some sense, what I did for Adanna and what my friend at the university did for me contributed to the social reproduction of corruption in Nigeria. Many instances of everyday corruption are of this sort: people doing what seems right, necessary, or imperative to fulfill their social obligations. Yet these same actions maintain a larger system of corruption that most people lament.

To recognize that a good deal of everyday corruption, including in the educational sector, makes sense, even moral sense, when one understands the position of the actors, is not to deny the often corrosive consequences of these actions. Nor should it obscure the occasionally dastardly aspects of some people's conduct, by standards Nigerians themselves uphold. Over the years I have collected countless stories of corruption in secondary schools and universities, many of them cases that everyone except the most immediate beneficiaries would condemn without reservation, frequently using the language of 419. Each year, the Nigerian media report thousands of cases of exam malpractice, where students sitting for the JAMB and other national exams have purportedly purchased the test questions in advance from unscrupulous officials. Sometimes tens of thousands of students have their results withheld, and are forced to pay again and retake their exams, delaying their possible admission by a year, because a much smaller percentage of the test takers were suspected of or caught cheating.

Each step of a Nigerian student's education is fraught with obstacles that are best understood in the context of the country's pervasive corruption. In addition to the connections and bribes often required for admissions, secondary students are frequently forced to pay fees and levies that are obvious efforts on the part of teachers and administrators to supplement their incomes. Further, students are often forced to perform labor for school officials—for example, working on their farms, bringing them firewood, or carrying their water. While some of these practices fit within an older tradition where young people routinely perform chores for their elders, many students and their parents resent this conscripted labor, but are afraid to protest because their children's school results could be affected if teachers are alienated. Stories of secondary school girls pressured or conned into sexual relationships with teachers in exchange for favorable treatment are also common. While I do not know how pervasive this is, even exaggerated stories are evidence of local communities' frustration with the exploitation of students in and outside the classroom. Once they have graduated, students face pressures to pay teachers and administrators to sign "clearance" forms, without which schools will not release official results, thereby suspending any future educational options. Adanna's younger sister graduated from secondary school in 2004, and I gave her several thousand naira to pay her clearance fees, without which she would have remained in educational limbo.

Corruption in the universities appears to be more extensive than in secondary schools, perhaps because the university is a much scarcer resource and university students are expected to have greater means than the larger population of secondary school students. While university students are rarely conscripted to perform menial labor for their lecturers, the purely monetary face of corruption is much larger. Nigerian universities are massively overpopulated and underfunded. Shortages of books, classrooms, and hostel accommodations are common. Expensive equipment like computers and vital infrastructure like laboratory space are minimal. Dormitory rooms meant for four students sleep sixteen.

Lecturers frequently teach courses without textbooks and write their own mimeographed "handouts" that they sell to students for a profit.

While some lecturers do their best to make these handouts useful teaching tools and sell them at or near cost, many others plagiarize from real text-books, sell their handouts at inflated prices, and require students to buy them under the threat that anyone who does not purchase the handouts will fail—a practice that students routinely brand as faculty 419. In recent years, students have told me (and many faculty have confirmed this) that those who cannot pass their courses, or do not care to try, have the option of "monetizing" their grades. Some lecturers will literally bargain with students over how much they must pay to pass a course or get a better grade. My sense is that only a small minority of lecturers are involved in monetizing grades, but stories of teachers selling handouts, pressuring female students for sex, or monetizing grades contribute to an atmosphere of corruption and lawlessness in Nigeria's universities (Bastian 2001; Gore and Pratten 2003; Oriji 2003).

In addition to the many aspects of corruption that are unique to campus life, Nigerian universities also share with other government bureaucracies many dynamics of institutional corruption. The Abia State University vice chancellor, who I came to know quite well since his installation in 2000, explained to me some of the kinds of opportunities for corruption common in university administration. He is known among his faculty and even in the student body as a scrupulously honest man, to the point where some people view him as a fool for benefiting so little from such an important post. The vice chancellor said that when he first began his job, he had a visit from a manager of the bank into which university salaries are deposited by the government each month—or at least in those months where the government pays salaries on time. The manager explained that the vice chancellor could make a lot of money by delaying the payment of salaries each month by two or three weeks. During the delay, the money could be placed in a short-term fixed deposit account and the vice chancellor could keep the interest—with a share, of course, for the bank manager. The bank manager said that the previous vice chancellor had done this regularly. The vice chancellor refused.

He also told me that some of the administrative officers he inherited from the previous vice chancellor had explained to him that the portion of the university budget known as the "security vote," for assuring security on campus, was not receipted. The vice chancellor could use it like a personal account. He further described the endless stream of contractors coming through his office looking for opportunities to build or supply something in arrangements where the contractor and the vice chancellor would share the overinvoiced portion of the deal. The vice chancellor clearly lamented the state of affairs in the university and had a reputation for trying to clean things up. But he did not claim to be a perfect person, and he admitted that he often succumbed to pressure to help the children of friends, colleagues, and kin get admission. Each time he visited his village of origin, he said, he prayed no one would know he was home, because the pressure was so intense.

Some pressures to be corrupt are irresistible, even for someone with the scruples of the vice chancellor. For example, Abia State's civilian governor, Orji Uzo Kalu, elected in 1999 and reelected in 2003, apparently never went to a university. Some rumors even suggested he faked his secondary school exit exams. During his first term, the governor wanted to complete his university education, including earning a PhD. Had the vice chancellor and his colleagues refused to admit the governor and eventually grant his PhD, they would have likely lost their jobs or imperiled the university's budget. The governor graduated with his PhD in record time, and ever since at every public event and in every mention of him on the state radio and television service, the governor is addressed as "His Excellency, Dr. Orji Uzo Kalu." Ordinary Nigerians believe his doctorate is 419, but at least as long as he retains the power of office, his title is recognized.

THE HYPOCRITICAL OATH: FAKE DRUGS, BOGUS DIAGNOSES, AND SLY CHARLATANS

Despite its oil wealth, relatively educated population, and remarkable human resource capacities, as well as an abundance of other natural resources, the health profile of Nigeria's 130 million people resembles that of its poorest African neighbors. Infant and under-five mortality rates are so high (98 out of 1,000 children die before their first birthday, and 198 out of 1,000 die before their fifth birthday) that many families plan their fertility against the possibility that at least one of their children will die (UNICEF 2004). Nigeria's maternal mortality ratio is among the highest in the world (with an estimated 800 maternal deaths for every 100,000 live births), making pregnancy a risky endeavor in a context where childbearing remains the single most important measure of personhood for a woman (UNICEF 2004; Fortes 1978; Smith 2001c, 2004b). Malaria is so common that even though it is a potentially fatal disease, most people see it as routine illness and typically treat it without the consultation of a doctor (Jimmy, Achelonu, and Orji 2000; Brieger et al. 2004). The HIV/AIDS epidemic currently infects an estimated 3.6 million Nigerians, and hundreds of thousands of people have already died (UNAIDS 2004). But by the end of 2004, only 10,000 adults were being treated in Nigeria's small pilot program to subsidize and provide antiretroviral medicine (Smith 2004c). Battling illness is one of the most painful realities of everyday life in Africa's giant.

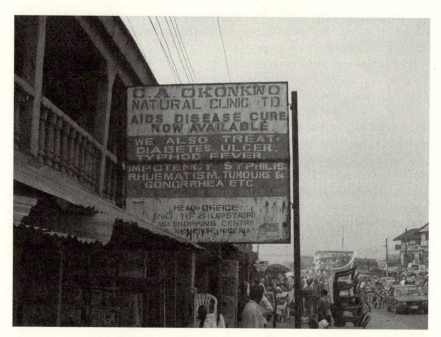

Figure 5. A range of quacks and charlatans exploit Nigerians' needs for health care, including advertising cures for AIDS (photo by author).

Contributing to this public health quagmire, corruption riddles the formal government health system. Further, the private and informal health sectors are meccas for quacks, charlatans, purported miracle workers, and other purveyors of 419 who exploit people's desperate desire to mend themselves and their loved ones. The Ministry of Health operates like every other Nigerian bureaucracy in the sense that it is run on principles of patronage, and a good deal of money and resources meant to serve the public end up in the pockets of bureaucrats and political appointees. As one of the arms of government that benefits most from international aid, there is much jockeying to control and benefit from donor dollars (Smith 2003).

It is important to acknowledge that even though the official health care system is plagued by the same problems of corruption as every arm of the government, there are many extremely dedicated and committed health professionals in Nigeria, in both the government and private sectors. Yet they fight an uphill battle, not only against parasites and poverty, but against the fraudulent practices of people looking to exploit ordinary Nigerians' ill health. Good people in the Nigerian government fight hard to try to stem a burgeoning trade in fake drugs, imported in huge quantities from places like India and China, and now apparently also produced in Nigeria. Even when Nigerians go to reputable doctors and pharmacies, they cannot always be sure that the medicines they are prescribed are real, because frequently even the doctors and pharmacists fall victim to fake drug fraud.

Nigerians often seek health advice and therapy from a range of nonbiomedical healers, drawing on a long history of traditional medicine (Buckley 1985; Wall 1988). As in the government health sector, the traditional sector includes many honest and dedicated practitioners. But there are also plenty of fraudulent "native healers" who exploit the plight of the poor and the sick. Modern scientific medicine and traditional healing are equally apt to be manipulated by the small army of quacks and charlatans who patrol Nigeria looking for opportunities to sell miracle cures. During my fieldwork in 2004, my wife, Ada, who is a registered nurse, encountered one of these charlatans in action.

Ada came to Nigeria at the end of August for a three-week visit designed to break in half our six-month separation for my fieldwork. For her it was, of course, a homecoming, and three weeks was hardly enough time to both greet and say good-bye to all her many friends and relatives. Several days into her visit she went to see her sister's mother-in-law, who lives in Ekenobizi, a village about six miles from my in-laws' community, Ubakala. Ada's sister's mother-in-law, Nwanyi Sunday, is probably in her early eighties. She had a mild stroke a few years ago and is no longer capable of carrying out all the routine tasks of village life. But she lives alone, except for a young girl who helps her with household chores in exchange for food, lodging, and the payment of her school fees. Despite the significance of the extended family system in southeastern Nigeria, Nwanyi Sunday's predicament is increasingly common. All her children have migrated away from the village for employment or in search of other economic opportunities. Although they visit regularly, remit money, and provide many other resources, none of them is willing to live in the village. While Nwanyi Sunday sometimes visits her children in their urban homes, she prefers to stay in the village. As with so many elderly, conversations with Nwanyi Sunday are dominated by her concerns about her failing health.

When Ada arrived at Nwanyi Sunday's compound, she found the front gate open and an old Mercedes Benz parked just inside. She wondered who else was visiting. When she entered the house, she found Nwanyi Sunday entranced by a young man in a suit with a stethoscope around his neck and a doctor's bag by his side. Ada greeted her in-law, who at first did not recognize her—it had been almost five years since they had seen each other. Nwanyi Sunday asked my wife to sit down, and the visitor continued his pitch. He explained to my wife that he had been sent by the

Federal Ministry of Health to provide home health care to the poor and the elderly. He was there to help. My wife sensed immediately that the man was a charlatan, if for no other reason than her cynicism about whether the federal government could possibly implement such an outreach program. But she was curious and played along, feigning interest in the man's skills. He proceeded to explain to the two women that he would check Nwanyi Sunday to see if her heart needed medicine. He then took an ordinary digital thermometer and touched it on Nwanyi Sunday's head and neck, and eventually between her breasts near her heart. As he did so a look of great concern crossed his face. He announced somberly, "I am afraid her heart is weak and it is very serious." My wife continued her act, "Oh my, what can we do?" The charlatan then smiled reassuringly, saying that he had medication that could treat Nwanyi Sunday's condition, and because of the federal government's new program he could make it available at a subsidized price. "Thank God," Ada said, looking at Nwanyi Sunday, "we are very blessed today."

Ada then asked if he wouldn't mind checking her. The charlatan gladly obliged, seeing another opportunity. Again he took his ordinary thermometer and ran it over parts of my wife's upper body. "Hmm," he said, "your heart is OK for now, but I am seeing some indication that you could also eventually develop a problem. But I have some medicine that can prevent it." "Oh, thank God," my wife exclaimed, "isn't it a miracle that I came here today." Seeing a blood pressure monitor beside the man's bag, she then asked, "What does that one do?" "Ah," the charlatan replied, "that measures the thickness of blood, a very important determinant of health." "Can you test me?" my wife asked, trying her best to seem enamored with the man and his technology. He proceeded to wrap the blood pressure monitor around my wife's forearm and squeezed the inflator. As the needle on the pressure gauge elevated, he again looked concerned. "Madam, your blood is very thin," he said as he pulled off the monitor without ever utilizing his stethoscope. "Do you have medicine for that?" Ada inquired. "Fortunately I do," he replied, "but it is from my own stock. The government does not provide it," thus preparing my wife for the medicine's exorbitant cost.

Ada then asked him to bring out all the medicines that she and Nwanyi Sunday would need and tell them how much they would cost, again reiterating her luck to have come by that day. Once the charlatan had brought out all his medicines, which were in unlabeled bottles and sachets, and he announced that the total cost would be "only" six thousand naira (about forty-five dollars), Ada decided to expose him. She cursed him, revealed that she was a nurse trained in the United States, and said that she knew he was a fake and a fraud. The man first tried to protest that as a nurse, she couldn't possibly know more than him, as he was a doctor. But that only made Ada angrier. Nwanyi Sunday didn't seem to understand initially what was happening, and begged my wife to calm down. But when Ada said, "It is 419," the old woman understood immediately. Once it was obvious that he had been exposed, the "doctor" packed his bag and headed to his car. As he departed, Ada told him that if he ever came back to Nwanyi Sunday again, or if she heard of him operating anywhere in the area, he would find himself confronted by the police.

Fake drugs, phony diagnoses, bogus treatment regimes, and charlatan service providers are, unfortunately, all too common in a country where frequent illness is the physical manifestation of poverty and inequality. Even the diagnoses and treatments people receive from seemingly reputable biomedical professionals are sometimes questionable. For example, doctors who diagnose malaria using blood tests also frequently diagnose a dual infection with typhoid. Over the past several years, dozens of people have told me they were diagnosed with malaria and typhoid. When I asked a friend who is the director of a Nigerian university teaching hospital about this common diagnosis, he said that the lab tests typically used in Nigeria to diagnose typhoid are extremely insensitive, producing many false positives. He suggested that a dual infection was much less common than reported, and that many doctors were deliberately adding the typhoid diagnoses, even without tests, because the medicines to treat malaria are cheap, while the antibiotics necessary to treat typhoid are expensive and profitable. Furthermore, the dual diagnosis enables doctors to convince patients they need to be admitted to the doctors' private hospitals, another crucial income generator. Most Nigerians would not easily be convinced to pay the high costs of in-patient care just to treat malaria, which is perceived as commonplace. How pervasively and deliberately Nigerian doctors resort to such tactics is impossible for me to say, but the fact that a top physician explained the typhoid epidemic this way is further evidence that ordinary Nigerians commonly encounter 419, even when they are just trying to heal their sick bodies.

Intimate Corruption: "He Played Me 419"

Deceits that Nigerians associate with corruption frequently occur even in the arena of intimate relationships between men and women. In Western societies, we tend to obscure or ignore the degree to which sexual and marriage relationships involve exchange, highlighting instead the importance of intimacy and an ideology of love; ideas of romance and expectations of emotional as well as sexual fidelity also infuse intimate relationships in Nigeria, perhaps more so now than ever before. Young Nigerians post messages on the Internet seeking their ideal partners; they send romantic text messages on the now-ubiquitous cell phones; and if they are Christians, they aspire to marry in the church to signify both modernity and monogamy. The expectation that romantic relationships and marriage can be an oasis of trust in a world of corruption is pervasive (Smith 2001c). But in reality, many intimate relationships end up as disappointments. Nigerians routinely interpret failures of fidelity, trust, and romance in the language of 419.

To hear Nigerians tell it, members of the opposite sex are biologically built for fraud. Women see men as cheap cheaters who will promise the world to persuade women to sleep with them or to win consent for marriage. But promises of material support and sexual monogamy are frequently followed up with phony cries of penury to avoid providing the promised resources and blatant lies to cover up infidelity. Men see women as mavens of materialism who use sexual and romantic guile to separate men from their money (Smith 2000, 2002; Cornwall 2002). Of course, when individuals are caught up in the heat of passion or the bliss of romance they do not often see their own relationships in these terms, but in analyzing the relationships of others or interpreting one's own failed relationships the attribution of fraud to the opposite sex is commonplace.

As in every society, sex in Nigeria is often a mode of exchange as well as an expression of intimacy. Stories of the relationship between sex and aspirations for money and power are the stuff of everyday rumor and gossip. Because Nigeria's political economy is in many ways patriarchal, it is not surprising that many stories about the way sex is transacted in the contexts of money and power involve men in the position of patrons putting pressure on women in the position of clients. Over the years, I have heard dozens of women tell stories of how men in positions of power expected sex in exchange for employment, promotions, business contracts, or even just the promise of no further harassment. Ifunanya's story is fairly typical.

After the return to civilian rule in 1999, Ifunanya, a recent graduate of the University of Ibadan, the oldest and most prestigious university in Nigeria, got a job working for a representative in the state assembly from her home area. She was able to get the job because her uncle was active in local politics and had helped the representative win his election. Ifunanya's job involved organizing youth-related development activities for the representative's constituency.

After several weeks on the job, Ifunanya's boss asked her to reserve a hotel room in town because, he said, he had an important guest arriving that evening. When she returned to the office and delivered the room receipt and the key to her boss, he smiled and asked her to meet him there after work. She knew immediately that there was no guest and that her boss wanted her to sleep with him. She told him that she already had plans after work, and invented the excuse that her mother was admitted in the hospital and she had to bring her food. The legislator was angry but relented. Yet he went on to say, "Ifunanya, you know that your position is a temporary post and that I will soon be making a decision about whether to make it permanent."

Ifunanya was the oldest child in her family with five junior siblings still in various stages of schooling. Her parents had sacrificed greatly to put her through a university, and Ifunanya faced strong expectations that she assist with the school fees of her juniors. Unemployment among recent graduates in Nigeria is rampant, and Ifunanya was very worried about losing her job. Under this threat, Ifunanya eventually agreed to meet her boss at the hotel. Several weeks later, after she had been asked to reserve the hotel room again for her boss to use with other women, her temporary position was terminated. Ifunanya was bitter and said of her boss, "He played me 419."

Men and women in Nigeria frequently use the expression "419" to describe the manipulations of the opposite sex. Men are more often in a position to pressure women for sex based on promises offered from positions of power. In addition, sexual mores make it much more acceptable for men to cheat than for women to do so. In the language of corruption, it is more likely that men will "play 419" on women than vice versa. But just as patrons complain about the demands of clients in a political-economic system where the patrons dominate, so men complain about the behavior of women in a sex-gender system where men dominate. As in patron-clientism, these complaints by the dominant party are both a way of protecting privilege and a reflection of the fact that even the less powerful can manipulate the symbols and structures of society for their benefit. Women sometimes acknowledge their own ability and conscious efforts to take advantage of men, using the phrase "no romance without finance" to express the common sentiment that a pragmatic woman is a fool to give herself for free.

Men believe that women consciously manipulate male sexual desires to extract material benefits. Men's everyday conversations about women regularly lament the manipulation of men for women's materialistic wants. Nigerian men talk of wives who consume their hard-earned paychecks, and resent that women always grumble for more money instead of showing gratitude. They speak about girlfriends who are "razor blades" that bleed them of their money (Smith 2002). Since the advent of mobile phone technology in Nigeria, men routinely complain that the first thing girls now request in a relationship is a cell phone. To many Nigerian men, women's proclamations of love are a cover for a more selfish agenda—the pursuit of wealth through feminine 419.

Women who reach positions of power are believed to have slept their way to the top. A friend who came from the same village as a recent female federal minister said that stories of her sexual stair-climbing were legion. Once she achieved a position of power, it was also rumored that she had an endless appetite for younger men. There is probably some truth to the idea that women in Nigerian politics face pressure to trade sex for the support of powerful patrons. But the stories about the minister are best interpreted as a commentary on the way that power is gendered in Nigeria, with allegations of sexual corruption used to maintain male superiority. Such stories reinforce the stereotype that women are not equipped to maneuver politically on male terms but can only get ahead by using sex. The stories of the minister's fondness for young men adds a further twist, depicting a powerful woman in what Nigerians normally see as a male sexual role—always wanting sex and using her position to get it.

The relationship between political and economic corruption and perceived corruption in sexual morality and behavior is nowhere more evident than in Nigeria's burgeoning video film industry. Churning out scores of videos every year that are seen by millions of Nigerians, the Nigerian film industry's staple plots intertwine political corruption, economic greed, and sexual intrigue. These films are filled with male and female characters who use sex to achieve selfish goals, and who promise love and fidelity to entrap partners they can use for their own selfish ends. Though Nigerian videos often depict heroes who battle against the tide of corruption in politics and try hard to maintain relationships of real love, the dominant message of these films is that intimate relationships are imperiled by deception and fraud, similar to everyday experience in the larger political economy.

As I was in the middle of writing this book, I received an e-mail from an American woman in Europe. Her story alerted me that Nigeria's international reputation for corruption had also penetrated intimate relationships between Nigerians and people of other nationalities. The woman was married to an Igbo man and was worried that he had lied about his past. Specifically, she suspected that he had another wife as well as children in Nigeria. She was looking for someone with expertise on Igbo culture to assist her in determining if this could be true. Excerpts from her two e-mails illustrate how her fears that her husband had lied to her intertwined with her broader conception that Nigeria and Nigerians are corrupt. Her first e-mail introduced her problem somewhat cryptically.

Dear Mr. Smith,

I am writing in hopes that you may have some insight into information that may help me. I understand that you have studied the Igbo culture. It is a challenge for me in my current situation to understand the culture or attempt to try. . . .
I am married to an Igbo man. However, I now believe that he may be also

married to someone in Nigeria. I believe that he has a registered marriage in Owerri, but I've found it difficult to locate the right agency or government office to assist me in getting a copy of this certificate. If it seems as if I am grasping at straws . . . I am. I understand that corruption is widespread in Nigeria but I am hoping that I can get to the truth.

I replied to her inquiry by explaining that there are many forms of legal marriage in Nigeria and that not all would be officially registered, and that in any case tracking down a license, if one existed, would be difficult without being in Nigeria. I also added, "Regarding your husband's marital status, I obviously cannot comment one way or another on your suspicions." Her reply made clearer the connections between her fears of her husband's possible deception and the prominence of corruption as the lens through which Nigeria is seen internationally.

Dan,

Thank you for your reply. I met my husband in England and in fact at a conference that was hosted by my church organization. He in fact presented himself to me as a reverend. He told me of his Anglican background and also told me of customs such as traditional marriages that continue to exist in Nigeria.

He explained that he had been a widower for eight years and that Muslims at a Christian crusade in the North had killed his wife and child. When I asked him about his wife's death certificate he told me that one did not exist and it is not customary to get a death certificate in Nigeria. After our marriage I by chance am reading one of his Bibles and flip to the front and there it is written a documented marriage to his wife the date and place of the marriage. The place is Owerri. The actual church or building was not documented. With this information I find it perplexing that the marriage is not documented. How would one legitimize the marriage? Are divorces also not documented?

I further suspect that he has not been forthright as we attempted to obtain a Visa to the U.S. for him and he was denied.

I've read portions of your studies and I wonder the motivations of people and what is deemed as ordinary or accepted in a culture. Is it accepted to have multiple wives in Imo State? Is it common to put forth all efforts to leave Nigeria even under falsehood? Is it a cliché what has happened in my life? Even though this is a personal matter I feel if I or others had a better understanding of Igbo culture, and not what is rumored of Nigerians, I would have been better prepared and may have heeded the advice of many.

Any insight is helpful.

In my next reply, which was the last correspondence between us, I tried to explain as best as I could about issues such as polygyny, marriage ceremonies, and the relative dearth of official documentation of events like marriage and death. Throughout my reply I tried to remain as neutral as I could. Near the end of my reply I wrote, "But none of that has any bearing on whether that has happened in your case. I am in no position to judge." I must be honest, though, and confess that my reaction to her e-mail was ambivalent. On the one hand, I worried that Nigerians' reputation for fraud had become so widely assumed that this poor woman wondered whether her husband might have invented the tragic death of his first wife and children at the hands of a mob in order to secure a marriage to her simply for the sake of obtaining residence in Europe. On the other hand, I suspected she might be right. A common joke circulating in Nigeria and on Nigerian Web sites gives some credence to her fears.[2]

> A Nigerian man living in Sweden decided to marry a Swedish lady in order to be legally certified via resident status . . . but the lady was not aware of this. She felt he really loved her. Anyway, seeing that Nigerian men had a bad rap in that particular part of Sweden, our chap decided to lie to the lady. He told her he was from Uganda.
>
> Upon marriage, the lady came home one day and informed our man that she had just met another Swedish lady who had married a Ugandan and they must all have dinner together.
>
> The Naija [Nigerian] man was somewhat perplexed, although not perceptibly, and wondered how he'd get out of this spot. He postponed and postponed until he could do so no more.
>
> Finally, the day came when they were to have dinner. The other Swede came in with her Ugandan husband and they all sat at the table. Our Naija chap was very quiet. "My own don spoil today" was all he could think.
>
> The two Swedish ladies, wanting their husbands to mingle, being from the same homeland, asked them to speak to each other. "Hey! It's not every day you meet people from home," they admonished.
>
> Our Naija man, being a man of great savvy, decided that he would just speak Yoruba, and the guy would probably assume he was from some part of Uganda where they spoke a different language. So looking across the table he said: "*Egbon Eko ni mi se? Ni bo lo ti ja wa?*" In Yoruba, this loosely translates to: "I'm a Lagos man. Where did you come from?"
>
> The fellow looked up at our friend. His eyes lit up as he said: "*Ah, bobo gan! Omo Eko ni mi se! Omo Eko gan gan!*" In Yoruba, this loosely translates to, "Hey buddy! I'm a Lagos child. A real Lagos child!"

Like so many Nigerian jokes about 419, this one is told and received in Nigerian conversation with a mixture of lament about the extent to which Nigerians have refined the arts of fraud and a certain degree of admiration for the skill it requires. While this joke had Yoruba characters, I have heard similar versions with Igbo protagonists. Nigerians recognize such stories as having to do with their national identity and they produce a familiar ambivalence.

CORRUPTION AND SOCIAL MORALITY

The examples of everyday corruption in this chapter suggest the complexity of the relationship between inequality, corruption, and social morality. Corruption is part of an explanation for the dramatic inequalities that characterize Nigerian society, and a strategy to survive in the face of these inequalities. Some forms of corruption, such as the types of string pulling that enabled my niece to enter a university, are widely considered morally justifiable, even laudable, in a society where everyone knows that favoritism is a major factor in gaining access to opportunities. My in-laws and friends rewarded me with obvious gratitude for using my connections to help my niece. I was made to feel that I had acted in the most morally upright manner under the circumstances. Further, many of the same people who expressed appreciation for my actions were able to see and articulate the destructive effects of favoritism on the educational system more generally. But understandably, in the struggle to survive and succeed in contemporary Nigeria, the immediate interests of assisting family, friends, and other allies usually trump a more abstract awareness of what might be in the best interests of the larger society.

Although cases of favoritism based on kinship and other close social ties sometimes elicit discussions about conflicts of interest, by and large such instances of corruption are socially accepted because they build on an established moral economy. Relatives helping their kin and patrons assisting their clients are long-standing strategies for navigating social life. Even forms of corruption such as the unwarranted payment for a public service (for example, obtaining a driver's license) are widely tolerated because they offer people a means to achieve their objectives in the face of an impersonal, unsympathetic, and often inefficient bureaucracy. A typical strategy in dealing with the state is to try to turn an anonymous encounter into a more personal relationship, so that the official with whom one is dealing is transformed into a provider of favors, and bribes are reconfigured as dashes. Actors on both sides of the exchange are frequently more comfortable operating in an idiom of accountability that humanizes the transaction between the citizen and the state.

But it is also true that bureaucratic rules provide opportunities for officials to exploit their positions. Instances of corruption where ordinary citizens are unable to transform their relationships into a more personal idiom provoke anger that is more intense than when favors are personalized. Cases of outright extortion, such as at police checkpoints, are seen as having no redeeming features whatsoever. With the growth in the size and scope of the Nigerian state, the relative anonymity created by internal migration and rapid urbanization, and the increase in the number of interactions that ordinary people must have with the state in order to achieve their everyday aspirations (for education, health care, jobs, business opportunities, and so on), the chance that encounters with the state will be more impersonal is escalating. Further, the squeeze placed on civil servants by insufficient and delayed salaries, rapid inflation, and the costs associated with achieving their own families' aspirations—all exacerbated by the continuing expectations to help kin, friends, and associates—create immense pressures to be corrupt.

Debates about the boundaries of acceptable corruption are common in popular discourse. In conversations that occur in marketplaces, at bus stops and bars, and in village community halls, national, regional, and local politicians are frequently judged by whether they are sharing the benefits of their offices with their people or eating alone. Years of military rule, where those who controlled the reins of power did so by the barrel of a gun, contribute to the sense that Nigerian elites have eschewed the traditional obligations of reciprocity long associated with a system of patronage in favor of more individualistic forms of accumulation and self-aggrandizement. Ordinary citizens see their leaders as having forsaken the obligations of sharing associated with patron-clientism in favor of personal enrichment and unabashed venality.

Nigerians recognize that many of the country's problems are due to a failure of leadership, and no segment of society is more condemned in popular criticism than the country's political and economic elite. But perhaps just as troubling to Nigerians is the sense that the amorality associated with military governance and high-level political corruption has diffused throughout society. Encounters with and stories about ordinary citizens who have adopted the ruses of 419 in order to survive in Nigeria's precarious economy are daily fare—whether it is medical charlatans, real estate swindlers, street hawkers who mix cheaper kerosene with more expensive gasoline, native healers who sell their magic in the service of crime, or lovers who deceive their partners for sex, money, or European visas. In the abstract, one might think it makes no sense to connect all of these phenomena under the rubric of corruption, but this is precisely what Nigerians do in the ways that they deploy the concept of 419. As the expansive meanings of 419 suggest, it is impossible to understand contemporary life in Nigeria without examining the intertwining of corruption and morality, and the relationship between Nigerians' disappointments with their postcolonial state and their sense that everyday life is increasingly amoral.

While Nigeria's mostly poor population has little opportunity to benefit substantially from corruption—indeed, it is important to remember that they are the principal victims—it would be a mistake to assume that ordinary citizens have little experience with corruption. As suggested above, the vast majority of Nigerians must interact in one way or another with the state, whether it is to put their children in school, seek health care, pass a police checkpoint on a public highway, vote in an election, or navigate some sort of bureaucratic office for a document necessary for civil or commercial life. As such, most Nigerians have firsthand experience with corruption, and all of the people I know, regardless of their social class, are aware that corruption is a prominent feature of national life. Because many poor people depend on the principle of reciprocity between elites and their clients to get access to basic resources, people of all social strata have a vested interest in certain forms of corruption.

While poor people continue to rely on networks of patronage to manage their relationship to the state, nowadays, as often as not, people are disappointed with their patrons. The confidence that social solidarities such as the obligations of kinship and community are effective in navigating the inequalities associated with an impersonal state is being eroded by experiences with patrons who neglect their clients and politicians who manipulate the facades of bureaucracy to enrich themselves. What is worse, the practice of 419 is widely believed to have infected every sector of social, economic, and political life.

Through this popular perception of social amorality ordinary Nigerians blame themselves, in part, for corruption. As an observer, one must be skeptical of an explanation that blames corruption on Nigerian culture and ordinary Nigerian citizens. But ironically, Nigerians themselves commonly participate in a social discourse that creates and perpetuates just this kind of thinking. Interpreting Nigerian self-blame is tricky. In one sense, it must be seen as an astute assessment, reflecting ordinary Nigerians' awareness of their own stake in corruption, even as they are also its main victims and loudest critics. In another sense, however, such self-blame must be interpreted as obscuring the structures of power and inequality that are at the root of continued suffering. Further, these discourses reflect a popular expectation that things could and should be different. Implicit in the intense collective concern with social morality is the awareness that some forms of corruption violate norms of kinship, community, and the reciprocal obligations of patrons and clients. Yet also implicit in this collective self-criticism are growing expectations about new forms of morality and accountability, associated with the ideals of democracy and development. Paradoxically, corruption and the discontents it fosters may be part of a process in which democracy and development are transformed from distant ideals into real expectations.

CHAPTER 3

Development Scams: Donors, Dollars, and NGO Entrepreneurs

ONE OF THE REIGNING jokes in contemporary Nigeria, told only partly facetiously, is that when students complete their education they have two options besides likely unemployment: founding a church or starting an NGO. Given Nigeria's weak economy and the dearth of decent job opportunities, the humor about churches and NGOs is a collective commentary on the difficulties of poverty. It is also an allusion to the entrepreneurial creativity of Nigerians who seek advantage and advancement in circumstances of great constraint. Obviously only a small fraction of Nigeria's population actually earns a living by establishing a church or starting an NGO. Yet the proliferation of churches and NGOs in Nigeria since the early 1990s has been striking and extraordinary, and has spawned an equally remarkable expansion and intensification of popular discourse about corruption in these domains.

I will return in chapter 7 to the phenomenon of new churches, particularly the dramatic increase in the popularity of Pentecostal and evangelical sects, which preach against corruption even as they open up new possibilities for its pursuit. In this chapter, I examine the world of corruption in Nigeria's development industry, particularly in the NGO sector. In Nigeria, as in many settings, development programs are a common cover for some of the most venal forms of corruption. An examination of NGOs offers a revealing window onto the dynamics of corruption for several reasons.

First, many development NGOs are international organizations, receiving much of their funding either directly or indirectly from the international donor community. An analysis of the corruption endemic in NGOs along with an exploration of the everyday practices and discourses deployed to facilitate and obscure corruption will expose the complicity of transnational institutions such as Western governments, multilateral agencies, and international development organizations.

Second, although in most academic literature NGOs are considered central institutions in civil society, and are frequently portrayed as bulwarks against state tyranny and venality, a realistic assessment of the machinery of corruption in Nigeria's NGO sector shows the inextricable intertwining with corruption in government. Understanding the dynamics of corruption in Nigeria requires unraveling the complexities of the state-society interconnections inherent in government-NGO partnerships in development. The intertwining of government and civil society in development reflects a broader blurring of state-society boundaries that is at once a realistic reflection of the social organization of Nigeria's political economy and a conscious strategy used by elites to facilitate corruption (Bayart 1993; Chabal and Daloz 1999).

Third, Nigerians running development NGOs appear to have refined corruption to an art form, and by studying the details of this art form one can better elucidate not only the embedded, systematic, and routine nature of corruption but also the complex ways in which so-called corrupt behavior can become morally justified and promoted by those involved (Smith 2003). Navigating and understanding the fine line between Nigerians' acceptance of and participation in corruption, on the one hand, and their frustration, anger, and imaginative responses to it, on the other hand, is one of the most important tasks of an ethnography of corruption. The production and circulation of rumors, stories, and other forms of imaginative discourse about corruption in NGOs aptly illustrate the creative collective interpretations and popular discontent about corruption in Nigeria.

Donors, International NGOS, and Corruption

International donors, Western development organizations, and expatriate aid workers are frequently complicit in facilitating corruption in Nigeria—a fact that is especially critical to demonstrate because Westerners working in Nigeria commonly and too easily attribute corruption solely to Nigerians. My first experience with NGOs and corruption in Nigeria came several years before I began thinking about corruption as an anthropologist. In 1989, following the completion of a master's degree in public health, I accepted a job with a U.S. NGO to serve as an adviser for a child survival project in Imo State in southeastern Nigeria. The project was funded by the United States Agency for International Development (USAID) and had begun in 1986. I was the third U.S. expatriate to serve in the project adviser position.

My job description called for me to provide technical assistance in the design, implementation, and monitoring and evaluation of child survival interventions such as the training of village health workers and traditional birth attendants as well as the delivery of basic primary health care services and education in areas such as immunization, the management of diarrheal disease, nutrition, and family planning. I was also responsible for documenting project accomplishments in the form of the many reports due to the NGO and USAID. In addition, I was a cosignatory on the project bank account and reviewed all expenditures before they could be approved.

The other cosignatory was the project manager, a Nigerian seconded from the Ministry of Health. She had been with the project from its inception in 1986. The nomenclature and much of the rhetoric in the project documents emphasized the superior role of the project manager in the overall program coordination. Nevertheless, certain aspects of the formal structure of the project and other de facto practices and implicit assumptions made it clear that as the NGO's U.S. representative on the project, I had equal and sometimes even superior authority to the Nigerian project manager. The structural aspects of our relationship merit further examination because they represent prevalent dynamics and assumptions in the relationship between the donors and recipients in the world of development. Most significant is the presumption on the donor/expatriate side that it is Nigerian actors who are corrupt or potentially corrupt and expatriate personnel who are the watchdogs able to prevent or minimize local corruption.

Donor Discourses about Nigerian Corruption

In my three years with the project, I spent considerable time worrying about and trying to prevent corruption. I cannot account fully for all the ways I had been predisposed to worry about corruption. Much of it is undoubtedly rooted in historical and cultural constructions that we in the West have created about non-Western societies in general and Africa in particular—constructions that I had internalized without really knowing it (Said 1978; Wolf 1982; Mudimbe 1988, 1992). These larger assumptions were reinforced by the kinds of stories that I heard about Nigeria from people in the development industry, both before I left the United States and once I arrived in Africa.

Preceding my departure from the United States, people warned me that Nigerians were notoriously corrupt. Some of the stories I was told focused on efforts at extortion by customs and immigration officials at the airport, and on the kind of intimidation one could expect at police and military checkpoints on Nigeria's roads, where the goal, I was warned, was to extract money from ignorant or fearful foreigners. More insidious were accounts that implied one must always be vigilant in dealing with Nigerian government officials and Nigerians working in development agencies. I was counseled that they frequently operated with a corrupt agenda.

My posting with the project in Imo State did not afford me many opportunities for interaction with other expatriates. I was based in the Imo State capital of Owerri, a small city that had few foreigners and no expatriate development community. But on the several trips a year I made to Lagos to meet with my supervisor as well as officials from USAID and other development agencies, I recall having numerous conversations with expatriates where the favorite topic was Nigerian corruption. Ironically, little is said about corruption in official development settings and program documents. It is part of a larger silence about the failures of the development enterprise (Ferguson 1990; Escobar 1995). Indeed, most development agency documents paint a remarkably rosy picture of their projects, and portray relationships between donors and recipients as equal and successful partnerships (Smith 2003). But in more informal settings, both the problems with development projects and the true perceptions that expatriates have of their partners are often revealed. At parties, and over drinks and dinner at the expensive restaurants in Ikoyi and on Victoria Island, the upscale areas in Lagos where the development and diplomatic communities entertained themselves in the early 1990s, expatriates told seemingly endless stories about Nigerian corruption.

These tales included cases where Nigerians working in internationally funded development organizations secretly hired relatives, steered agency contracts to friends, created ghost workers, submitted fake receipts, or just plain stole project money. For example, over dinner at Shalamar, an expensive Indian restaurant in Ikoyi, a U.S. official at USAID told a story of how a senior Nigerian staff member in his office hired her son in a midlevel position. The son managed to work at USAID for almost two years without any Americans finding out their actual relationship, in part because the mother and son had different surnames. In telling the story, the U.S. official emphasized that other Nigerians in the office had known about the situation and had colluded to hide what the American regarded as nepotism. The tenor of the story and the laughter it produced in the all-U.S. audience reinforced an "us" against "them" mentality that frequently surfaces in expatriate discourse about Nigerians.

During the time I worked for the NGO, one of the most trusted employees in the Lagos office was a bright young man named Emmanuel who came from the Igbo-speaking Southeast. The U.S. representative responsible for overseeing the NGO's operations delegated to Emmanuel various responsibilities that expatriate officials typically assign to their most trusted Nigerian employees. In all of his activities, Emmanuel had a reputation with the expatriate staff for being competent and honest. He was frequently authorized to do the organization's banking transactions, sometimes withdrawing the equivalent of several thousand dollars in cash to bring back to the office. One day, after Emmanuel was sent to the bank to withdraw approximately four thousand dollars, he simply disappeared with the money and was never seen again. The police were notified and the NGO placed wanted ads in the local newspapers, but Emmanuel was never caught.

Emmanuel's theft generated all kinds of talk both within the NGO and the larger development community in Lagos. Of course outright theft is not typically defined as corruption—at least not as Westerners usually apply the term in their society. But in the stories that circulated in Nigeria's expatriate community as news of Emmanuel's case spread, his act was depicted as yet another example of the deep and inherent corruption in Nigerian society. Even one's most trusted employee could not really be trusted. These stories reinforced a collective perception in the expatriate development community that it was Westerners who were honest and accountable while Nigerians were hopelessly corrupt.

I feel obliged to emphasize that not all expatriates were anti-Nigerian, and in many expatriate circles even the kinds of issues I am raising here, such as the misplaced presumptions of foreigners or the failures of development projects to benefit the neediest populations, were common topics of concern and conversation. But it is the way that even the most seemingly culturally sensitive expatriates could be sucked into prevalent assumptions about the dynamics of corruption that is most insidious and most revealing about the powerful ways in which prevailing patterns of inequality are reproduced and tightly intertwined with corruption.

Imagining Corruption Is Everywhere

The years with the NGO were a happy time for me. I established countless friendships that continue to the present. In addition, I met my wife in Owerri, and my relationship to Nigeria eventually became that of an in-law as well as an anthropologist. But in retrospect, as I have reflected on those years in light of my research on corruption, it has become clear that I was frequently a participant in processes that now appear much more troubling.

A few examples of the kinds of things that worried me when I worked as a project adviser suffice to illustrate the ways in which presumptions about Nigerians' corruption infused my thinking and actions. I report them because I have come to believe that my experience was not unique. Many expatriates who work for development organizations in Nigeria and other developing country contexts embark on their work full of good intentions, but often end up participating in discourses and practices that contribute to the maintenance of inequality and the reproduction of stereotypes about the corruption of Third World partners (Klitgaard 1990; Olivier de Sardan 2005).

Nigerian staff on the child survival project in Imo State consisted of four senior officers—including the project manager, an administrative officer, and two program officers—whose duties involved organizing training activities and supervising project-trained personnel, such as the village health workers and traditional birth attendants. In addition, the office included three or four clerical and support staff, two drivers, and three guards. Much of the actual work of the project was done in collaboration with personnel from the Imo State Ministry of Health and the local government health departments in the areas where the project was implemented.

As the expatriate project adviser, it was made clear to me by my supervisors that I had the primary responsibility for assuring that the project resources were utilized effectively and transparently. No one at the NGO office in Lagos or the Washington, DC, headquarters ever said explicitly that they feared my colleagues on the project were corrupt, but the message that one of my responsibilities was to be a watchdog was made apparent implicitly, both by the emphasis on my role in reviewing project expenditures and by stories I was told about instances of corruption that had been discovered on other projects. The first of three Lagos-based country representatives during my tenure told me angry stories about her most senior program officer on a large family planning project. She discovered he was selling medical equipment meant for free distribution. She also told me about another senior Nigerian program officer on a water and sanitation project; he was using the project's expensive well-drilling rig for personal enrichment, constructing wells for paying customers at the NGO's expense. While she never suggested that my Owerri colleagues were involved in such schemes, the message was plain to me that I needed to be vigilant.

I felt an obligation to make sure funds were not misappropriated, and it is important to point out that my worries were fueled not only by the implicit instructions from my supervisors and the stories that circulated in the expatriate community about Nigerian corruption but also by the prevalence of discourses about corruption among Nigerians. My Nigerian colleagues on the project sometimes discussed ways to discover or thwart the corrupt use of project resources by our Ministry of Health and local government partners. Further, my growing circle of friends in Owerri talked frequently about corruption, including not so veiled suggestions that my Nigerian counterparts on the project must be getting rich working on a "dollar" project. Stories about corruption were also rife in the Nigerian media. Indeed, my preoccupation with corruption seemed almost overdetermined.

The primary strategy of the project was to improve child survival by raising mothers' knowledge and promoting health protective behaviors through the training of village health workers, who would work directly with mothers in their communities. This strategy meant that our staff spent a lot of time in the intervention communities, organizing the training of village health workers and supervising their work. When our program officers would go to the intervention communities to train the village health workers, I wondered whether they always paid the trainees the full amount of the per diems allocated. When they came back late in the evening, I sometimes suspected they had used the project vehicles for personal purposes. I would occasionally later ask a village health worker how much she had been paid for the training, or ask a driver whether the team had come back directly from the field site.

The project had a number of vendors who provided us regular services—for example, the mechanics who repaired our cars, the printer who produced many of the materials used in the project training and monitoring activities, the technician who serviced our photocopiers, and the vendor who provided our office supplies. I sometimes suspected that these vendors had reciprocal relationships with the senior staff whereby each benefited from the relationship. On a couple of occasions, I checked prices on things on my own to try to make sure we were getting a fair deal. The reality was that my Nigerian colleagues could almost certainly negotiate better prices than I could, but I wondered whether they also got small kickbacks or favors from our biggest vendors.

In my last year on the project, one of my primary objectives was to try to assure that the skills for the tasks for which I had primary responsibility would be transferred to my Nigerian counterparts, as the plan was that the project would continue for another couple of years without an expatriate adviser. One of the main areas where I had done most of the work during my tenure as project adviser was in writing proposals for supplementary funding. In addition to our funds from USAID, for which I had written a renewal grant proposal, we also received funds for complementary projects from other donors. Although the Nigerian staff participated in the conceptualizing and planning for the new project proposals, the actual writing always seemed to fall to me. Alongside the myth that it is only Westerners who are honest and can keep a project from falling into corruption, control over the capacity to raise funds served as one of the few seemingly legitimate justifications for paying people like me to work on projects in places like Nigeria. When I started to work with our staff on grant writing, it was clear that the level of mystification about this process was deep and that I had contributed to it by taking almost sole control of the writing of previous proposals. The staff was as enthusiastic about their training in this area as anything we had done in my three years.

But again my presumptions and fears about corruption surfaced. My primary strategy for motivating the staff to take charge of the grant-writing process was to encourage each of them to submit proposals for funding for small projects through the U.S. ambassador's Self-Help Development Fund. The U.S. Embassy in Nigeria, as in many developing countries, maintains a fund of perhaps fifty to one hundred thousand dollars a year to finance small community development projects—projects in the range of one to four thousand dollars. Three of our staff worked hard on individual proposals, each designed to support a small project in the staff member's community of origin. I was extremely pleased with the quality of the proposals and felt that the skills transfer exercise had been one of my most successful efforts during my tenure on the project. All three proposals were submitted to the U.S. Embassy, and two of the projects were funded for approximately three thousand dollars each. Just as I was leaving Nigeria, those funds were released directly to my colleagues on behalf of the communities for whom they applied. I distinctly remember wondering how much of the money would be used for the proposed purposes, since there was no mechanism in place to monitor how the funds were utilized. I also remember feeling slightly embarrassed at thinking my colleagues might eat some of the money, but reassured myself that it would be naive to imagine they would not be tempted. I have no idea whether my colleagues misused any of the ambassador's Self-Help Fund money. More relevant is trying to understand my obsession with possible corruption and the contradictions it entailed.

Reorienting the Moral Compass

With hindsight and the aid of greater familiarity with social science literature about the dynamics of inequality, particularly in the arena of development, it is now much easier to see that I was not in fact a watchdog against corruption but a culpable and complicit actor in the whole enterprise of development-related corruption (Hancock 1989; de Waal 1997; Uvin 1998). During my years with the NGO I never stole any project money. I never took a kickback from a contractor, or awarded a job to a friend or a relative. I never submitted fake receipts to reimburse myself for expenses not incurred. By any conventional Western standard, I could not be reasonably accused of involvement in corruption. But if I examine my life as an expatriate working for a development project critically, it becomes clear that my vigilance regarding corruption among my Nigerian counterparts involved significant hypocrisy. My assumptions, privileges, and lifestyle were at least as morally problematic as anything I feared my Nigerian colleagues might have done with project resources.

It is not my intent to provide a confession. I relate these personal stories because I believe they represent common patterns of inequality and self-justifying perceptions of appropriate behavior on the part of many expatriate development workers. First and foremost, the hypocrisy of expatriates who criticize Nigerian corruption is evident in the inequality that characterizes the differences in economic position between expatriate staff and even the most senior local staff. For example, when I started as the NGO's expatriate project adviser in 1989, I was paid a salary of twenty-three thousand dollars per annum. Even in 1989 that was a modest salary by U.S. standards. Indeed, the NGO I worked for had a reputation in the development community for being stingy about salaries. But consider the following: the Nigerian project manager, who was supposed to be my counterpart—and whose job description gave her authority at least equal, if not superior, to mine—was paid less than four hundred dollars per month. In other words, she made less than a fifth of what I did, though by Nigerian standards her salary was quite good. The project's other personnel were paid much less, with the guards making as little as fifty dollars a month. I was also provided free housing by the project, and because my project-provided house was inside the NGO compound in Owerri, the office generator supplied my fully furnished house with electricity when there was no town power supply. The project's guards looked after my house at night, and the project's compound supervisor doubled as my steward, helping me with shopping and cooking, cleaning my house, and washing my laundry.

Of course, few Westerners would take a job in Nigeria for less than four hundred dollars a month, and it would be impossible for similar organizations to implement programs in places like Nigeria if local staff were paid salaries at U.S. levels. But what is rarely discussed are the cultural assumptions and mental blinders necessary to sustain a system of inequality wherein my time is worth at least five times as much as a more senior Nigerian colleague and more than twenty-five times as much as the night guard who has ten children to feed. Part of the context of understanding Western culpability, and in this case my own complicity, in sustaining Nigeria's notorious corruption is recognizing the peculiarity of a system that legitimizes my privilege, but is on the lookout for a local staff person who awards a contract to provide office stationery to an in-law to help a struggling business, or might terminate a driver who carries passengers for a fee in the office vehicle on his way back from an assignment in order to raise some extra cash for his children's school fees. These actions are viewed by Westerners as forms of corruption. Yet the larger system of inequality is taken for granted, at least by most of us who are its principal beneficiaries.

Certainly most Nigerians recognize, and many resent, the gross disparities between expatriate and local remuneration. But there is a degree of resignation as well. I never felt any open antagonism from my Nigerian colleagues that I was disproportionately compensated for my work, though it is worth noting that I knew their salaries and most of them did not know mine, at least not precisely. How much hidden resentment there was is difficult for me to judge. One might wonder whether awareness of these gross disparities served as a kind of justification for corruption. In other words, did Nigerians who garnered resources from development projects in ways that Westerners would describe as corrupt, see themselves as entitled to these resources as a kind of compensation for the overall inequities?

My experience and subsequent research suggest that this is much too simple a view. Nigerians often justify efforts to siphon off government money for personal benefit as trying to get their share of the national cake. International aid money is sometimes discussed in ways that imply it is seen as an "international cake," though I have never heard Nigerians use that phrase. To understand what drives the corruption condemned by Westerners, and indeed by many Nigerians, one certainly must recognize the profound inequalities that ordinary Nigerians face. In some cases, corrupt behavior is rationalized by its perpetrators as a legitimate response to inequality; in other cases, people see corruption as the only way to survive or get ahead in what they view as a broken system; and in still other cases, what might look like corruption from a Western point of view is undertaken as morally upright behavior from a Nigerian point of view. But despite the inequalities inherent in the development industry along with the moral questions raised by the gross disparities between expatriates and Nigerians, Nigerians are as ambivalent about corruption in development as they are about corruption in every other sector.

CIVIL SOCIETY AND THE STATE: PARTNERS IN CORRUPTION

The proliferation of local NGOs in Nigeria that gave rise to the popular joke about unemployed graduates' best career options is primarily a phenomenon of the last ten to fifteen years. Since the early 1990s, the number of local NGOs in Nigeria has grown exponentially. Three major causes combine to explain this upsurge. First, the global, Western-dominated international institutions that control development finance and aid—such as the International Monetary Fund (IMF), the World Bank, and the United Nations—moved over the last two decades toward a view that privileges civil society as a primary locus of social, political, and economic development. A major part of the justification for the emphasis on civil society, of which local NGOs are considered a key component, was the perception that governments in developing countries like Nigeria were bloated, inefficient, and in a word, corrupt.

Second, for much of its history since independence, and for the entire period from 1983 to 1999, Nigeria was ruled by military governments that came to power through coups. With Western tolerance of military governments waning, and the promotion of democracy in non-Western societies taking off in the wake of the dissolution of the former Soviet

Union and the end of the cold war, international support for Nigeria's military state diminished. In particular, the annulment of the 1993 election and the repressive actions of the military dictator General Abacha (1993–98) led to the suspension of much development aid to the Nigerian government and the transfer of some of that money to the NGO sector. Finally, the ability of Nigerians to see and interpret these changes in Western donor priorities as well as the entrepreneurial adaptability of Nigerians led to the dramatic multiplication of local NGOs.

By and large, in the early stages of the transition from colonial rule to independent nation-states, Western efforts to assist in the development of so-called Third World countries focused on aiding governments. The emphasis on governments was no doubt reinforced by the priorities of the cold war, when the Eastern and Western blocs jockeyed for strategic advantage in Africa, Asia, and Latin America. The perceived role of government in development was also part of a larger vision of how positive social change could be engineered—a view that dominated the development discourse for almost forty years after World War II (Escobar 1995). By the mid-1980s, however, the faith in governments had declined, and donor-driven policies such as structural adjustment programs (SAP) steered resources away from developing country governments toward the private sector and civil society. In Nigeria, the government of General Babangida (1985–93) navigated the donor community's call for structural adjustment with a dexterity that helped earn him his popular nicknames "Maradona" (after the Argentine soccer star known for his skill at dribbling through the opposition) and "the evil genius." Babangida, best known in Nigeria by his initials, IBB, managed simultaneously to placate Western governments and financial institutions, establish new mechanisms for the enrichment of the military elite and their civilian cronies, and sell the idea that he was acting in the national interest (Maier 2000). Yet the kinds of stories Nigerians told about IBB, SAP, and government-organized NGOs belie any notion that Nigerians were really hoodwinked.

Babangida managed to mollify Western governments and donors during most of his rule by appearing to accommodate the emerging international policy priorities, even as he put in place new mechanisms to loot the state. His successor, Abacha, failed to appease the international community and seemed to enjoy flouting Western pressure. When Abacha ordered the execution of human rights activist Ken Saro-Wiwa and his colleagues in November 1995, just hours after British Commonwealth leaders meeting in South Africa had called for clemency, it was clear that Abacha did not fear international pressure. In the wake of the execution, significant amounts of Western aid to Nigeria's government were suspended, and the channeling of some of that aid money to civil society contributed to the dramatic proliferation of local NGOs. Though the military government lost millions of foreign aid dollars because of sanctions, it is important to note that no sanctions were imposed on Nigeria's centralized oil industry, which generates billions of dollars annually for Nigeria's government and multinational oil companies. Abacha's main source of revenue was never threatened. Further, by the mid-1990s, Nigerian elites had already learned from IBB's model how to co-opt and redirect much of the money funneled to civil society.

"Better Life for Rich Women": The First Lady Syndrome and Other Military Ruses

In 1987, IBB's wife, Maryam, founded "Better Life for Rural Women," a quasi-governmental program run by the first lady. The Better Life Program (BLP) established a precedent and pattern for how Nigerian rulers at all levels of government along with their wives channeled resources to themselves in the name of development. It is a phenomenon that has been copied and repeated not only by Nigeria's subsequent rulers but by leaders throughout Africa (Mama 1995, 1998; Lucas 2000; Ibrahim 2004). Increasingly, venality became cloaked in the rhetoric and acronyms of development.

The BLP was billed as a vehicle for women's empowerment. Mrs. Babangida was the national chair. At the state level, the wives of the military administrators inaugurated state offices and programs and served as state chairs. Similarly, in each local government area, the lowest tier of formal government in Nigeria, the wives of the sole administrators launched and oversaw local branches. Thus, at each level of government, the wife of that level's most powerful person controlled the BLP. The program did carry out some activities designed to assist poor women, such as adult education programs, health promotion activities, and agricultural development and microcredit projects. But these activities were largely window-dressing to cover up the fact that the program was a boondoggle benefiting the elite. Large amounts of money were spent in launching BLP projects—events at which elite women enjoyed a moment of recognition associated with being a patron delivering benefits to the people.

Ordinary Nigerians are not easily fooled, and such schemes contributed to the popular cynicism about development programs. It quickly became clear that the only people who really benefited were the upper class. The Nigerian public coined new names for the program, such as "Better Life for Rich Women" and "Better Life for Ruling Women," reflecting popular awareness and discontent about the ways that ideals like gender equality, development, and democracy were used to further the privileges of the elite (Maier 2000; Ibrahim 2004). After the experience of the BLP and its descendants, it was easy for Nigerians to recognize the corruption inherent in the many local NGOs that have sprung up since the mid-1990s.

Mrs. Babangida's BLP was just one example of the way that ordinary Nigerians came to believe that her husband's government was cheating and even starving them. IBB created an alphabet soup of new institutions in the name of development ideals. Two of Babangida's most infamous creations were the Directorate of Food, Roads, and Rural Infrastructure (DIFRI) and the Directorate of Mass Mobilization for Social Justice, Self-Reliance, and Economic Reconstruction (MAMSER). Under the cover of these lofty names, IBB and his cronies were able to channel the nation's resources away from the government ministries that would normally control budgets for various development activities into institutions over which they had complete control. Babangida also created the Oil Minerals Producing Areas Development Commission (OMPADEC), which oversaw the allocation of 3 percent of oil revenues to oil-producing areas, primarily in the Niger Delta. OMPADEC was rife with corruption, and the mismanagement of these funds contributed to the frustration that would culminate in the escalating violence that has plagued the Niger Delta for over a decade (Akani 2002; Okonta and Douglas 2001). One of my friends, who once ran for governor of his state, knew the OMPADEC chairman in the mid-1990s and planned to finance his son's education in the United States with OMPADEC funds. My friend was neither poor nor from an oil-producing community, but the fact that OMPADEC funds could be available to him because of his connection to the chairman is illustrative of the corruption that riddled the organization.

Nigerians' experiences with corruption in government initiatives such as the BLP, DIFRI, MAMSER, and OMPADEC came at the same time that General Babangida instituted a homegrown SAP. Pressure to initiate the austerity measures of structural adjustment came from the IMF, the World Bank, and Nigeria's Western creditor nations. In one of his typical Maradona moves, Babangida publicly rejected international pressure for an IMF SAP, but instituted the homegrown program he called "SAP with a Nigerian face." This allowed IBB to appear to resist international pressure—something that appealed to both his military peers and the Nigerian public—but his indigenous program was close enough to an IMF-designed SAP that it kept his government in the good graces of the Western donor community. For ordinary Nigerians, the SAP with a Nigerian face was a cruel joke. Austerity measures aimed at a population reeling from economic hardship in a context where the military elite and their cronies were looting the national treasury seemed an injustice too harsh to bear.

But in their inimitable way, Nigerians articulated their suffering and hardship in widely circulating jokes that attested to the public awareness of the consequences of structural adjustment when implemented by a corrupt and despotic government. SAP was turned into a verb through which people expressed how their government and international powers were sapping their money, livelihoods, and very capacity to survive. In addition, people spoke of the adjustment in their diets forced by SAP. In the late 1980s and early 1990s, everyone in Nigeria knew what was meant when someone described his daily diet as "0-1-1," "1-0-1," "0-0-1," or some other permutation (Apter 2005, 250). Each numeral in the three referred to a meal: breakfast, lunch, and dinner. Someone on a 1-0-1 diet could afford to feed themselves and their family only breakfast and dinner, but no lunch. Someone with a 0-0-1 diet could afford just one meal a day. Only the wealthy could any longer eat "1-1-1," and people joked, but also genuinely worried, that the military government's SAP with a Nigerian face would soon bring a "0-0-0" diet. Although Babangida followed a long lineage of corrupt leaders, he raised the process of looting government money in the name of development to an art form, and ushered in an era in which government parastatals and NGOs would become primary vehicles for venality (Apter 1999).

IBB's successor, Abacha, who took control of the government just a few months after Babangida "handed over" in August 1993 to the short-lived transitional government of Ernest Shonekan, used many of the same mechanisms invented by the evil genius to loot the state. General Abacha and his wife, who is coincidentally also named Maryam, transformed Mrs. Babangida's BLP into the Family Support Program (FSP), shifting the emphasis from women to the entire family. While the rhetoric was designed to mark a change from the past and broaden the appeal, the structures through which the elite benefited at the expense of the public were the same. Each state military administrator's wife launched the program at the state level and assumed administrative control. A similar process unfolded in all the local government administrative areas. General Abacha further solidified his autocratic authority over the program with the FSP Trust Fund Decree of 1995, through which control over the trust fund was placed under the authority of the head of state.

The FSP trust fund was a small version of the larger Abacha strategy for looting the national treasury by siphoning funds away from the line ministries that were managed by civil servants into quasi-governmental organizations over which he and his cronies had complete control. Under the Abacha regime, the largest and most notorious of these schemes was the Petroleum Trust Fund (PTF), which Abacha created by decree in 1994. Although the rhetoric justifying the PTF spoke of utilizing the nation's oil revenues more directly to the benefit of the people (the presumption being that the normal bureaucracies were inefficient and corrupt), in reality the PTF gave Abacha and his closest allies direct control over hundreds of millions of dollars in oil money. He appointed a friend and former military ruler, General Muhammadu Buhari, to head the fund. During the Abacha years, everything from road construction to the building of schools to the purchase of essential drugs for government clinics was managed by the PTF. Signboards signifying PTF projects sprang up all over the Nigerian landscape, though eventually they came to be seen as icons of a corrupt government and a failed society where roads were not completed, health posts were without drugs, and schools lacked books and other basic supplies. Abacha and his military partners cemented the support of civilian collaborators by awarding them lucrative PTF contracts for projects that were frequently not finished or were executed below standard. As was well documented in both the Nigerian and international press, Abacha looted literally billions of dollars during his five-year reign. The irony that it was called a trust fund was not lost on ordinary Nigerians, who often quipped that the only thing they could trust about the trust fund is that they would see few, if any, of the benefits.

GONGOs and Other Schemes

The transition to a civilian government in 1999 did not diminish the symbiotic relationship between international donors and Nigeria's governmental and nongovernmental sectors in the social reproduction of corruption. If anything, the relationship was solidified. Donors could now more easily acknowledge and justify supporting programs that were partnerships between the state and civil society because the state now had the cloak of legitimacy conferred by democracy. By the time civilians returned to power, donor support for NGOs was undertaken not simply as an alternative to providing development assistance to a corrupt and despotic military government but as a means to promote and solidify democratic governance. The idea that institutions of civil society, such as local NGOs, were crucial to the deepening of democracy was something supported not only by donor nations and the development apparatus but by a significant body of literature in political science (Dicklitch 1998; Hudock 1999; Kleinberg and Clark 2000). A large proportion of the NGO sector in Nigeria, however, was created solely in response to the awareness that donor monies were available. As a result, donors faced great challenges in figuring out which NGOs were legitimate institutions of civil society that might really contribute to democratic and development ideals, and which were created simply to tap into the flow of international aid.

In Nigerian popular discourse, a humorous commentary emerged to describe and critique the proliferation of local NGOs. Many Nigerian observers were fully aware that new NGOs were created with the intent of benefiting their founders rather than the larger society. People invented and adopted all sorts of acronyms to depict the different kinds of NGOs that mushroomed over the past decade, as ever-entrepreneurial Nigerians realized that support for institutions of civil society was the latest fad in the donor-controlled development industry.[1]

When government elites in Nigeria recognized that significant donor dollars were flowing away from the state and into the NGO sector, they created NGOs of their own, relying on friends and allies outside government to serve as fronts. In local parlance these GONGOs, short for government-organized NGOs, included quasi-governmental entities like Mrs. Babangida's BLP and Mrs. Abacha's FSP. Similar efforts by wealthy persons in the private sector to "float" (a Nigerianism for founding or starting) NGOs were labeled BONGOs or IONGOs, short for bank-organized NGOs and individual-organized NGOs, respectively. NGOs where the proprietor lived in Lagos, but purported to be doing development work in poor rural areas were dubbed LABONGOs (Lagos-based NGOs). And NGOs that were complete scams, where an individual sent out proposals seeking funding, but had no office, no staff, and not even the appearance of ongoing activities were variously described as PONGOs (post office box NGOs), E-NGOs (e-mail NGOs), or TONGOs (telephone-operated NGOs), depending on the primary mode of communication.

During my fieldwork in Nigeria in 2004, I had the opportunity to observe firsthand several versions of GONGOs and other NGO inventions that must be understood, in part, as creative efforts to take advantage of the availability of funds for civil society. In the West, we would certainly call these efforts corruption, and many Nigerians saw it the same way. One powerful example is the first lady syndrome, which is still very much alive and well in Nigeria's current civilian administration. Both Stella Obasanjo, the president's recently deceased wife, and Titi Abubakar, the vice president's wife, established programs with lofty names and idealistic aims. Mrs. Obasanjo founded the Child Care Trust Programme. The trust is said to be an effort to empower special needs children who have suffered various forms of disabilities, abuse, discrimination, and neglect. Mrs. Abubakar's GONGO is called the Women Trafficking and Child Labour Eradication Foundation, and it is touted as a campaign against the destructive trade in Nigerian girls for sex work both within and outside the country. It was widely reported in the Nigerian press that each state governor gave Mrs. Obasanjo's NGO several million naira, presumably from government coffers. Whatever good these organizations may do, it is not surprising that ordinary Nigerians are skeptical and see these programs as a continuation of the corruption propagated by military rulers' wives in the name of needy women, children, and families.

As during military rule, under Nigeria's democratic dispensation the practices of first ladies at the federal level are reproduced at the state and local government levels. Perhaps in a nod to democracy, the wives of elected governors and local government chairmen now each have their own NGOs, rather than lower-tier versions of the president's wife's organization. I had the opportunity to observe one such NGO close-up, and the case highlights some of the intricacies of how these schemes work.

HER EXCELLENCY'S WIDOWS

I was invited to Abakaliki, the capital of Ebonyi State, by a close friend who teaches at one of the Nigerian universities. My friend, Onyi, had known the Ebonyi governor, Sam Egwu, for many years, and that relationship evolved when Egwu was elected the state's first civilian governor in 1999. Ebonyi State was created in 1996, during the most recent round of state creation in Nigeria. Onyi came from a prominent family in the state, so in addition to his personal relationship with the governor he also acted as a sort of political operative in his local government area. Onyi had his own political ambitions and he wanted to do everything possible to curry the governor's favor. To this end, Onyi wanted me to meet the governor's wife and possibly offer her assistance with her NGO efforts. He figured that based on my previous work with NGOs, I might be able to offer the governor's wife some advice about running her organization, called WidowCare, and maybe I could even be persuaded to help write some grant proposals for funding. At the very least, he reasoned that he would win favor with the governor's wife, and therefore with the governor, just for the effort of bringing a U.S. professor to help out. Our friendship is such that Onyi did not hide any of these things from me. I told him I would be happy to meet the governor's wife and hear about her NGO, but I also said that I could not make any promises about what assistance I might provide. I explained to him that my motive for agreeing, in addition to our friendship, was curiosity. For an anthropologist doing research, I reminded him, almost anything can be fieldwork.

When the governor's wife's personal secretary called to inform us that she was ready to see us, we drove immediately to the Government House. We passed through three different security gates staffed by armed police without any delay, hassle, or a search. Each time Onyi mentioned his name, the security personnel's demeanor went from menacing to welcoming, and we entered the governor's lodge, a compound that serves as both his official residence and a venue to host visitors after official business hours. My impression of the Government House in Abakaliki did nothing to alter my sense that Nigeria's civilian governors were doing quite well for themselves. The Nigerian press and popular discourse regularly suggest that the nation's governors are stealing many millions of dollars through one means or another. Egwu had a rather good reputation compared with others. He was praised for paying civil servants' salaries on time, investing in education, and building and repairing roads. Nigerians assume all of their political leaders are corrupt, but Egwu was considered less so than many of his counterparts in other states.

In the driveway in front of the main entrance stood a brand-new Mercedes-Benz sports car, which Onyi told me someone had given the governor for his recent fiftieth birthday. The lodge itself was a mansion by any standard, and the governor's wife's receiving parlor alone was the size of a small ballroom. The parlor was furnished with eight to ten comfortable sofas. CNN was playing on a large flat-screen television, and the walls were decorated with huge photographs and painted portraits of Mrs. Egwu, the governor, and their four children. Though she had not yet entered the room, it was clear where Her Excellency would sit (Onyi instructed me to call the governor's wife "Her Excellency"). At the far end of the room, one sofa looked more like a throne than a couch. Onyi assured me that everything in the governor's receiving parlor was even bigger and more expensive. There is a degree of ostentation in the way Nigerian elites display and enjoy their status that is quite different from the equally scripted false modesty that is expected of the rich and powerful in Western society. Even as Nigerians frequently resent the consequences of their leaders looting the state, they also expect that elites behave ostentatiously (Olivier de Sardan 1999). The expected conspicuous displays of wealth and power are part of the modern dynamic of patron-clientism—an aspect of what some have called Africa's big man syndrome (Price 1974; Bayart 1993, 60–87).

Her Excellency entered the parlor about ten minutes after our arrival; making visitors wait is another common Nigerian custom in performing power. After formal introductions, I expected we would chat for ten to fifteen minutes about WidowCare, and I would ask her for any brochures, reports, or other documentation about her projects. My plan had been to postpone any commitment to provide assistance with a request that I be able to study the materials first. To my surprise, Her Excellency informed us she was embarking on a tour of her projects and hoped that we would be able to accompany her. Onyi clearly wanted me to go along, so I assented and we all moved quickly to the driveway where a brand-new minibus waited along with an escort vehicle for the police who would accompany us. We were also joined by a cameraperson and a reporter from the state television station, which was going to run a story on Mrs. Egwu's good work for the local news. For the next three hours, we visited Mrs. Egwu's various charity and development projects.

Our first stop was a women's development center where Mrs. Egwu showed us several projects she had established and supported, mainly through WidowCare. One program provided legal assistance to widows who were having trouble securing access to family assets because of the patrilineal structure of inheritance in the region. Another project was providing widows with job training, including skills such as sewing, catering, and hairdressing. Also on the premises was a day care center meant for widows' children, though there was only one child present during our visit. The largest structure was a huge hall that the NGO built and rented out for conferences, wedding parties, and other events in order to raise money for its activities. When I asked the governor's wife who owned the center and the hall, Her Excellency said that it belonged to the NGO, and that the land was donated by the government (in other words, by her husband).

Before I could ask more questions, Mrs. Egwu described the part of her NGO's work about which she seemed most proud: the construction of housing for widows who have been largely dispossessed by their late husbands' families. She took us to visit the first of fourteen such houses that reportedly had been completed or were under construction. The house had been commissioned by Stella Obasanjo, and there was a plaque to that effect next to the front door. It was an awkward and surreal visit. Our entourage arrived at the little village compound unannounced. The lone adult in the compound—presumably a relative of the widow's late husband—informed us that the widow was not around. She had gone to the farm, he said. But he produced a key to the house and Her Excellency took us inside. The widow's house was modest and constructed from clay bricks, a material stronger than the mud walls characteristic of the houses of the very poor, but cheaper than the cement blocks used by those who can afford them.[2] The house consisted of two rooms as well as a small kitchen and a bathroom. In addition to the house itself, WidowCare had provided a bed and a couple of chairs for the parlor. What was most striking was that there was absolutely nothing else in the house—no clothes, no pots and pans, no mess. In short, it was clear that no one was living there. Before we left, Her Excellency showed us a small dilapidated thatch structure where she said the widow had lived before the project intervened.

As we drove away from this strange scene I asked Onyi whether he noticed that the house was uninhabited. He quickly hushed me and made it clear that we should not discuss it while we were still with Her Excellency and her entourage. Mrs. Egwu was obviously proud of the fact that these women were provided housing in their marital villages. Later, I explained to Onyi how ridiculous it seemed to me to build a house for a widow in the same compound where her in-laws had so mistreated her before the governor's wife and her NGO intervened. At the very least, I speculated, most women would be afraid to occupy such a superior house in the middle of an impoverished compound of antagonistic in-laws. It might be possible if a woman had adult children capable of supporting her position, but clearly these most desperate widows lacked such support, which is one reason they were so marginalized in the first place. Yet this seemed to escape notice. If anyone else saw the project as untenable, they certainly did not say so in front of Her Excellency. Throughout the day, everyone praised Her Excellency for her generosity and wisdom, perhaps especially my politically ambitious friend.

The ways that Mrs. Egwu financed her NGO projects reveal the mechanisms whereby GONGOs serve the interests of their creators. All of the land for Mrs. Egwu's projects was allocated to her by the state government; she would never have been able to gain access to these plots had her husband not been governor. In addition, some of the funding for both projects came directly from the state government. But besides the land, most of the money for these projects probably did not come directly from the government coffers. Mrs. Egwu was almost surely telling me the truth when she said that most of the money for her projects came from donations. Understanding who these donors were and what their motives are, however, is key to discerning the modalities of corruption in the nexus between state and civil society in Nigeria.

Throughout our journey, Mrs. Egwu happily informed me of various large donations that people had made to her projects. What she did not explain was why such people would give her money. I suspected, and Onyi confirmed that most of the donors were businesspeople who had been awarded or sought major state contracts, or they were political appointees who owed their own patronage positions to the governor, or they were aspiring politicians anxious to gain favor. What is more, fellow politicians, such as other governors, senators, and local government chairmen frequently make contributions to such projects in their own names, using government money. In Nigeria, it is a custom that the elite contribute handsomely to each other's public projects, including at events like launching ceremonies for a governor's wife's NGO. The tragedy for Nigeria's mostly poor masses is that almost all the money that politicians and their cronies give to each other comes from the same pot of state resources siphoned from the national treasury.

"RETURN TO SENDER": GOOD INTENTIONS, HONEST NGOS, AND THE CONSEQUENCES OF CORRUPTION

Although there are plenty of GONGOs, LABONGOs, and other suspect organizations, numerous NGOs in Nigeria are established by people with noble intentions, often in conscious opposition to the prevailing practices of corruption. Over the years, I have come to know many Nigerians working in the local nongovernmental sector who I would describe as committed, talented, and honest. But corruption affects even those dedicated to legitimate efforts.

In 2001, the World Bank loaned Nigeria approximately ninety million dollars to fight HIV/AIDS. The money was targeted to benefit eighteen states, including Imo State. The Imo State Action Committee on AIDS (SACA) used part of its several million dollar portion of the loan to support the work of NGOs working to combat HIV/AIDS. In 2004, the Imo SACA issued a request for proposals through which local NGOs could compete for grants of up to thirty thousand dollars to finance their activities. No more than a handful of NGOs in Imo State have been doing any serious work on HIV/AIDS in the past decade. But the SACA competition attracted seventy-nine applications, including many from organizations created purely in order to apply for the World Bank/SACA grants. The SACA grant-awarding process highlights how endemic corruption in the aid apparatus in Nigeria affects even those with the best of intentions.

Benjamin Mbakwem runs an NGO called Community Youth Development Initiatives (CYDI) in the Imo capital city, Owerri. Benjamin is perhaps the most knowledgeable person in the state about HIV/AIDS. I have met few people anywhere in the world who are more dedicated and altruistic. With a tiny budget, Benjamin initiated the state's first support group for people living with HIV/AIDS. Further, CYDI began working with the city's most difficult-to-reach populations, such as adolescents who have dropped out of school and adults working in the city's informal economy. CYDI also provides one of the few HIV/AIDS counseling and resource centers in the region. Any time Imo State Ministry of Health officials need serious advice about their HIV programs they consult Benjamin. Although he is well aware of the endemic corruption in government and is sometimes frustrated with the efforts of the Ministry of Health, he works closely with them because, he says, "HIV in Nigeria is a Nigerian problem. AIDS in Imo State is, in the end, not America's problem, not the World Bank's problem, and not the United Nations' problem. It is our problem and only we can fix it."

Benjamin conceived and wrote an outstanding proposal for the SACA grant competition, focusing on working with adult male traders and their young apprentices in some of the roughest sectors of Owerri's markets. If Benjamin's organization won a thirty thousand dollar grant, it would be the largest amount of money CYDI had ever had to work with. The Imo State AIDS coordinator, Dr. Nwamadu, who frequently consulted Benjamin for advice, indirectly assured Benjamin that funding CYDI would be one of SACA's highest priorities. The seventy-nine applications would be reviewed by a technical committee appointed by the Ministry of Health, but Dr. Nwamadu had little doubt Benjamin's proposal would rank at or near the very top. Benjamin joked that because of all the help he provided

Dr. Nwamadu, he would not even be expected to provide the typical return-to-sender portion from the grant. "Return to sender" is the phrase used to describe the fact that in most competitive bids or proposal competitions, the winners are expected to give 10 to 15 percent of the money back to the government official(s) in charge of awarding it.

In the weeks leading up to the proposal deadline in October, Benjamin was deluged with requests from other local NGOs wanting help with their proposals. Even though they would be his competitors, Benjamin offered help to all that he believed were legitimate efforts. He was also bombarded with appeals from people who wanted to start NGOs in order to compete for the money. In those cases, he simply referred them to the SACA office where the proposal application was available. The proposal's guidelines stated that to be eligible for the World Bank money, competing NGOs had to have been registered with the appropriate federal or state bureaucracy for at least three years. Benjamin told me that a colleague informed him that all the newly formed NGOs were getting backdated registration certificates from an official in one of the state ministries who seized an opportunity to address the new demand.

Benjamin also provided help on two proposals where he felt he had no choice but to assist if he wanted his own project funded. Dr. Nwamadu came to Benjamin requesting help with a proposal for his own NGO, and also pleaded that Benjamin assist him with a proposal on behalf of the Imo State governor's wife, Mrs. Chika Udenwa. The Imo first lady wanted to use the thirty thousand dollars to support AIDS orphans—a seemingly noble gesture, except that actually identifying such orphans conclusively has proved notoriously difficult in Nigeria, where intense stigma means that few families will openly admit that one of their own has died from AIDS. The governor's wife asked Dr. Nwamadu to write her proposal. He passed the task to Benjamin. Benjamin said Dr. Nwamadu begged for his help, saying, "I don't want to lose my job." Who could blame him? Dr. Nwamadu was doing very well for himself as the state's AIDS coordinator. Benjamin helped craft these GONGO proposals and ensured that, at the very least, they met the criteria of the proposal guidelines, but he was skeptical about the efficacy and sustainability of the governor's wife's plan to aid orphans.

The proposals were reviewed in November 2004 by a technical committee appointed by Dr. Nwamadu—a group made up mostly of academics from the local universities. After a week at a resort hotel and with consultant payments of approximately a hundred dollars a day (a sizable sum in Nigeria, even for the relatively well-off), the technical committee presented its ranking. The first lady's project ranked first and was praised by the technical committee's chairman in a press release. Dr. Nwamadu's GONGO was also among the ten NGOs slated for funding. Benjamin's

CYDI proposal did not rank in the top ten. It fell in the second ten, and by the original SACA criteria it would not be funded. Benjamin was crestfallen and told me that he had not even heard of some of the NGOs that were going to get the money.

Dr. Nwamadu himself was shocked and embarrassed that CYDI was not ranked in the fundable category. He had just assumed Benjamin's proposal would rank at or near the top, and he had not really monitored the review process. In the end, he initiated a course of action to get the second tier of high-ranking proposals funded, and CYDI eventually received a portion of the World Bank money. But so did fifteen other NGOs, and some of them appear not to be the least bit credible or capable (and perhaps have no intention) of carrying out effective HIV/AIDS-related projects. Benjamin's experience illustrates a common pattern in Nigeria, where aid dollars flow in ways that further corruption as much as (or more than) they promote their ostensible development objectives.

PARTNERS IN CORRUPTION

Elite control of the relationship between Nigeria and international development donors contributes to the fabric of corruption and the maintenance of inequality in the country. Increasingly, as wealthy Western countries have adopted neoliberal strategies for development, emphasizing civil society and privatization over government-controlled social welfare programs, greater amounts of donor resources have been channeled to NGOs. Nigerian elites have responded by creating a plethora of NGOs designed to tap and control these resources. Politicians and other elites manipulate the promises of development, claiming to assist the most desperate and marginal in Nigeria's large impoverished population, even as they funnel a disproportionate share of development aid into their own pockets.

Western donors and their expatriate development agents in Nigeria frequently view themselves as watchdogs against corruption, but are often complicit in the perpetuation of the gross inequalities that are the backdrop of corruption. Stories about NGO project drivers who carry private passengers for small personal profit, administrative officers who try to steer petty contracts to their friends, or program officers who attempt to get their own kin included in a training program reinforce the stereotypes of corruption in Nigeria. But these stories are told too easily and gleefully by expatriates who reward themselves so handsomely for "aiding" Nigeria. The reality is that while local elites are often stealing huge sums of money and expatriates are living lifestyles they could not afford even in their wealthy homelands, many ordinary Nigerians feel compelled to participate in what Westerners view as corruption simply in order to survive. The stories about Nigerian corruption that are so pervasive in expatriate discourse serve to mask the degree to which many development programs depend on collaboration between donors and local elites. The ideals promoted in development rhetoric are often belied by the realities of how development projects become vehicles for corruption and mechanisms for the reproduction of inequality. Yet even as development projects frequently fail to deliver their promised benefits, they contribute to the transformation of expectations, such that people like my friend Benjamin believe that Nigeria could and should be different.

CHAPTER 4

"Fair Play Even among Robbers": Democracy, Politics, and Corruption

SINCE INDEPENDENCE IN 1960, the military has ruled Nigeria for approximately thirty of the forty-five years of its postcolonial history. Beginning with the first successful coup in 1966, a primary justification for every putsch has been the venality of the previous government. Each new regime promises to clean up corruption, and seemingly inevitably, each administration eventually loses its legitimacy because of its own venality. Almost every successful coup in Nigeria has been initially welcomed by much of the public, as people hoped that the new government would exhibit greater sympathy for and ensure better accountability to the masses. Even as Nigerians came to disdain military rule after more than a decade of unprecedented looting of the state by the Babangida and Abacha regimes, a certain nostalgia for military government still surfaces in the twenty-first century, perhaps especially as people have become disenchanted by the obvious corruption of the current civilian administration, which has failed to deliver the expected dividends of democracy.

It is probably not coincidental that the two military regimes Nigerians remember most fondly are those that were among the shortest lived. General Murtala Muhammad's reign lasted just a few months. He was assassinated in 1976, and to this day he is the most beloved and revered of Nigeria's past military rulers. Seemingly millions of Nigerians believe that had Muhammad lived, he would have put Nigeria's house in order. The international airport in Lagos is named for him, and he is the only former military leader to have his face on Nigeria's currency. His statements along with some historical and biographical accounts suggest that Muhammad was more of a maverick than other generals who have ruled the country, but given how entrenched corruption is in Nigeria, it seems likely that his shining legacy is mostly due to the fact that he was murdered before he could govern long enough to ruin his reputation (Panter-Brick 1978; Kirk-Greene and Rimmer 1981; Forrest 1993; 58–62).

The other military government that evokes considerable nostalgia is the Buhari regime that ruled for less than twenty months from 1983 to 1985. On December 31, 1983, Muhammadu Buhari led a coup to overthrow the four-year-old civilian administration of Shehu Shagari, a government racked by widespread corruption and gross mismanagement (Joseph

1987). Nigerians enthusiastically embraced the Buhari coup and initially supported his famed "War against Indiscipline." Buhari and his deputy, General Tunde Idiagbon, launched the War against Indiscipline with the familiar promise of rooting out corruption, but extended the fight to include a campaign against all kinds of petty forms of indiscipline, such as coming late to work, failing to queue for public transportation, and urinating in public places (Agbaje and Adisa 1988; Forrest 1993, 93–104; Osaghae 1998, 163–87). Eventually, Nigerians came to realize that even as the War against Indiscipline cracked down on ordinary people's behavior, it did little to change the culture of corruption at the highest levels. Although Nigerians generally welcomed the loosening of military repression brought by Babangida's bloodless coup of August 27, 1985, in the decades since the War against Indiscipline ordinary people often speak nostalgically of the Buhari regime—part of a common discourse in which Nigerians view their society as deeply corrupt and themselves as disorderly people in need of iron-handed leadership. At times, it seems almost a national fantasy that only the military can provide the strong leadership necessary to curtail corruption.

Nonetheless, by the time the military finally oversaw the most recent transition to a civilian government in 1999, popular sentiment had long swayed in favor of a new democratic dispensation. Relying on a combination of his military background and democratic credentials, Obasanjo swept to victory in the 1999 polls.[1] Although many accounts suggested widespread irregularities in the election, the popular consensus in Nigeria seemed to be that Obasanjo was legitimately elected, and that even without rigging he would have easily defeated his main opponent. Obasanjo's first term began with many promises, most prominently cleaning up corruption as well as improving the country's failing electricity supply and other basic services. In his inaugural address he assured the nation that before the year 2000, they would see a difference. But by the end of the year, and in the five years since, most Nigerians perceived that the nation's economy was worse, the country's basic services had further eroded, corruption remained endemic, and the leaders were not accountable.

Nigerians' experiences with democracy suggest that the trappings of political parties, elections, and the bureaucratic institutions created to manage the process are just as susceptible to manipulation as other features of the postcolonial state. Elites have managed to hijack democracy in the same ways that they have benefited from military rule, the facades of bureaucratic officialdom, and the institutions of development. But in the discourses of complaint that have emerged in the wake of the transition to civilian rule, in the public airing of political scandals, and even in the failed and seemingly futile efforts of opponents of electoral corruption, public expectations for greater transparency and accountability are

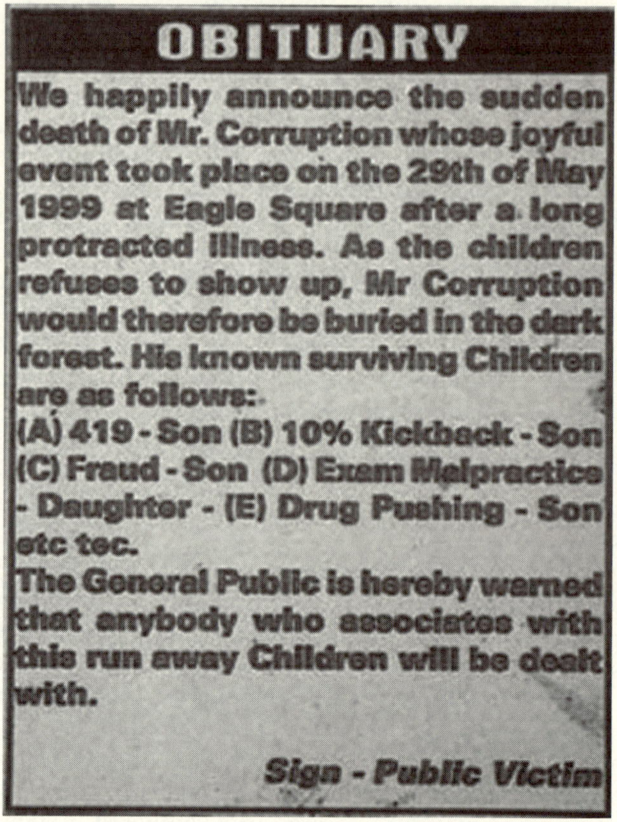

OBITUARY

We happily announce the sudden death of Mr. Corruption whose joyful event took place on the 29th of May 1999 at Eagle Square after a long protracted illness. As the children refuses to show up, Mr Corruption would therefore be buried in the dark forest. His known surviving Children are as follows:-
(A) 419 - Son (B) 10% Kickback - Son (C) Fraud - Son (D) Exam Malpractice - Daughter - (E) Drug Pushing - Son etc tec.
The General Public is hereby warned that anybody who associates with this run away Children will be dealt with.

Sign - Public Victim

Figure 6. This obituary of "Mr. Corruption," from a popular poster, "War against Corruption," reflected many Nigerians' hopes that the transition to democracy in 1999 would curtail the rampant corruption prevalent under military rule (photo by author).

fueled. Although ordinary Nigerians tell stories and lay complaints against their government that can sound cynical and resigned, it would be a mistake to underestimate the degree to which these discontents are generating aspirations for change.

"WORSE THAN ABACHA!"

Obasanjo's first four years were marked by a litany of initiatives that promised much and delivered little to the nation's mostly poor masses. People expected a great deal when the military finally handed over the reins of power. Though some Nigerians were cynical from the beginning as to whether the civilians could do any better, generally speaking there were unrealistically high hopes for what a new democratic government could accomplish in four years. Obasanjo was probably destined to disappoint, no matter what he did. But by the time I saw a June 2003 front-page newspaper headline emblazoned over Obasanjo's face that read "Worse Than Abacha!" the paper was simply following public opinion rather than leading it. Obasanjo failure to deliver the expected dividends of democracy in his first four years culminated in the widespread public perception that his reelection in 2003 was rigged, and that corruption in the new civilian government was as bad as or worse than under the military.

Early in his first term, Obasanjo kindled expectations by setting up the Human Rights Violations Investigation Commission, modeled loosely after South Africa's Truth and Reconciliation Commission, to investigate human rights abuses from the beginning of military rule in 1966 to its end in 1999. The commission, known in Nigeria as the Oputa panel after the former Supreme Court justice who headed it, held two years of hearings that occasionally gripped the nation's attention. Though President Obasanjo himself testified, the failure of the government to compel testimony from three former military heads of state (Buhari, Babangida, and Abubakar), as well as the fact that the government has refused to release the report submitted in May 2002, led most Nigerians to conclude that the leaders most responsible for past injustices were immune from any process of accountability, much less criminal prosecution. Although President Obasanjo was initially praised for creating the Oputa panel, in the end its failures were added to the litany of disappointments Nigerians have experienced with their fledgling democracy.

The promised improvement in electricity and other basic services also failed to materialize. Most people experienced only a worsening of the country's anemic power supply, reinforcing the humorous popular view that the acronym for the National Electric Power Authority, NEPA, should actually stand for "Never Expect Power Anytime" or "Never Ever Power Always." Sales of small Chinese-made electricity generators boomed. Many small businesses such as barbershops, bars, and restaurants relied on these small generators, known widely by the most common brand name, Tiger, to keep their trades afloat. One astute friend noted that the world has two kinds of "tiger economies," the Asian type that produced these generators and the Nigerian type that relied on them because nothing in the country worked as it should. As with many of the country's problems, most Nigerians chalked up NEPA's failures to corruption.

To implement his espoused crusade against corruption, President Oba-sanjo created two new government entities, the Economic and Financial Crimes Commission and the Independent Corrupt Practices and Other Related Offences Commission, each mandated to pursue various forms of corruption in Nigeria. These commissions' investigations have led to a number of highly publicized criminal indictments of politicians and gov-ernment officials. But few have resulted in convictions. In addition, in some of the most highly publicized cases, media accounts and popular discourse suggested that those targeted by the commissions were being prosecuted primarily because of some kind of political falling out with the presidency, rather than for their crimes. Nigerians commonly believe that almost every prominent politician is guilty of prosecutable offenses, but assume that the state apparatus is only turned against those who have committed some other offense that has antagonized the president or his powerful allies.

Through his first four years in office, President Obasanjo lost the confi-dence of the people not only because of his failure to deliver on his prom-ises but because he himself was perceived to be highly corrupt. Countless stories circulated in everyday Nigerian discourse about the multiple ways that President Obasanjo, his family, and his cronies were getting rich at the expense of the people. The most common stories focused, naturally, on the lucrative oil industry. As indicated in the introduction, for more than a decade Nigeria's four domestic oil refineries have been regularly out of service. As a result, Africa's largest petroleum producer imports most of its refined petroleum products for domestic consumption, such as gasoline, diesel, and kerosene. Many, if not most, Nigerians believe that the failure to maintain the country's oil refineries, despite contracts awarded worth hundreds of millions of dollars, is a deliberate act by the president in order to assure that he and his friends reap the benefits not only from Nigeria's lucrative exports but by controlling the import and marketing of refined products. In the minds of average Nigerians, their leaders are exploiting them doubly, by stealing much of the export oil revenue and then making ordinary people pay the high costs of imported fuel. Stories about how Obasanjo benefits from the petroleum industry are legion, including that his son owns one of Nigeria's biggest oil firms, and that his old military pals have built refineries abroad to profit from Nigeria's domestic fuel needs. It is difficult to verify stories about corrup-tion at the highest levels of the government, but the popular currency of these narratives is undeniable.

In addition to the widespread belief that Obasanjo and other politicians are ruthlessly corrupt, the president has done himself no favors with vari-ous public statements that seem to downplay or even mock the suffering of ordinary Nigerians. My brothers-in-law in Lagos reported to me one instance where Obasanjo purportedly declared that the population in Lagos was not as poor as was proclaimed because even though people lived in cramped quarters, many had basic amenities like televisions, radios, and refrigerators. Whatever the distribution of consumer commodities in Lagos, my in-laws and many other Nigerians viewed the statement as callous, given the absence or poor quality of public services in the city and the luxury in which Obasanjo lives at Aso Rock, the presidential villa in the capital, Abuja. Public perceptions of Obasanjo's apparent insensitivity to popular suffering were further exacerbated by the large role Obasanjo chose to play on the world stage. His frequent trips abroad led to newspaper editorials, television and radio talk-show banter, and widespread public and private discussions focusing on the perception that President Obasanjo spent too much time and too much of Nigeria's money on his international image, even as the Nigerian masses faced increasing hardship. All this meant that when Obasanjo ran for reelection in 2003, much of the Nigerian electorate was disillusioned with his rule. Among ordinary Nigerians, his landslide victory and his party's dominance in federal, state, and local elections were widely believed to be rigged.

Conscience Party or Fool's Quest?

When the phone rang at 5:00 a.m. one March 2003 morning in our Providence, Rhode Island, home waking me from sleep, I knew the call would be from Nigeria. The six-hour time difference between Nigeria and the East Coast of the United States has long produced sleep-depriving phone calls from family and friends in Africa. I was prepared for the sad news that someone was sick or dead, or for a request to help with school fees, or even just to hear "Happy New Year" from a friend I had not spoken to in 2003. I was correct in assuming that the call came from Nigeria, but I could not have guessed the purpose.

On the line was my wife's brother, Christian, who along with his wife and four children live, as I mentioned earlier, in Lagos, Nigeria's commercial megacity. After the usual greetings and inquiries about family members, Christian informed me that he was calling with an urgent request. Instead of the usual story about overdue rent, hospital bills, or school fees, however, Christian explained to me that his younger brother, Moses, had decided to run for the federal house of assembly. Moses, also a resident of Lagos, had already traveled home to the semirural community of Ubakala, the family place of origin in Abia State in southeastern Nigeria, where he planned to contest the election under the banner of the National Conscience Party.

Politics in Nigeria is very much rooted in ethnic, regional, and community ties (Joseph 1987). Successful politicians almost inevitably depend on strong support in their places of origin. It was natural that if Moses wanted to run for political office, he would do it at "home" in Ubakala because as a member of the Igbo ethnic group, no matter how long he lived in the Yoruba-dominated southwestern city of Lagos, he was a migrant, and therefore a "stranger" (Skinner 1963; Shack and Skinner 1979). But politics in Nigeria is also very much about money (Reno 1993). A successful run for public office, especially a national office, costs a great deal of money. National politics in Nigeria is generally the province of the rich. I knew that Moses was poor. With a diploma from a vocational college in civil engineering and a more recent master's degree in business administration from Lagos State University, Moses eked out a living by getting occasional contracts to supervise other people's construction projects. Much to the consternation of my mother-in-law, Moses remained a bachelor even though he had reached his mid-forties, and he explained his postponement of marriage by saying that he did not have the economic resources necessary to start a family. In addition to being relatively poor, Moses was soft-spoken, almost shy. I could not imagine him as a successful politician, even supposing he had the money to campaign.

Further, the party under whose banner Moses would run, the National Conscience Party, was a fringe one at best. It carried somewhat greater name recognition than some of the other small parties because its founder and presidential candidate was the maverick lawyer Gani Fawehinmi, who became famous in Nigeria for frequently standing up to military governments, and speaking out forcefully for human rights and against injustice and corruption. Indeed, Gani, as he is widely known in Nigeria, probably had more credibility on these issues than any presidential candidate. But he was given no chance to win the presidential election, in part because people viewed him as too radical to be president, but mainly because Nigerians knew too well that the political process depended on power, patronage, and corruption, and in that realm many candidates were far more accomplished than Gani.

Moses apparently had a friend in Lagos who was closely tied to Gani's campaign. Without resources, the Conscience Party had difficulty creating a national base, and though Gani's presidential run attracted some press coverage, in many political zones and wards the party could not find candidates to run for office. Moses's friend convinced him to run for the federal house of assembly, the lower house of Nigeria's bicameral federal legislature. Moses set out for Ubakala with almost no material support from the party, little or no money of his own, and absolutely no previous experience in politics.

Needless to say, I was skeptical about the viability of Moses's run for office and assumed that any money I sent would be a waste. On the other hand, I later joked with my wife, if Moses won, he would become rich and the whole family would be transformed. My assumption about Nigerian politics was the same as what I learned from Nigerians: anyone elected to national office would use that position to benefit themselves, their families, and their communities of origin. Though Christian also had serious doubts about the viability of his brother's run, I could almost hear him salivating at the prospect of having Moses in a position of power. I decided to send Moses three hundred dollars by Western Union, calculating that it was enough to show affinal solidarity without putting too large a stake on such a high-risk bet. As I filled out the Western Union form, I wondered what happened to the thousand dollars I had left Moses during my previous visit to Nigeria in summer 2002—money I gave him with the explicit instructions that it was meant to help him pay for the costs of getting married. If it was used for the campaign my mother-in-law would be even more dismayed than me. I have not had the nerve to ask, but Moses remains a bachelor.

Beginning in March, Moses campaigned for several weeks, and when the election was finally held on April 12, 2003, he garnered less than one hundred votes, compared to the several thousand commanded by the winning candidate from the People's Democratic Party (PDP), the party of both incumbent President Obasanjo and Abia State's incumbent governor, Orji Uzo Kalu, who also comfortably won reelection. During the campaign, Moses met leaders in many of the communities in the three local government areas that made up his constituency. Local government areas are the lowest tier of formal government in Nigeria. Below the local government level are so-called local autonomous communities—villages or clusters of villages that are historically and politically tied together. In the Igbo-speaking Southeast, each local autonomous community is headed by a traditional ruler, known in Igbo as an *Eze*.[2] The support of the Eze and other influential people in any community is the key to securing local political support, as many people follow the recommendations of their leaders in deciding who to vote for, particularly when leaders are able to share some of the money that is typically given to them by politicians to mobilize supporters.

Moses used much of his limited campaign funds simply to bring the offerings necessary to seek audience with Ezes and the other local chiefs and influential people. Traditionally in Igbo culture one cannot seek an audience with an Eze, or with any important person, without presenting some kind of gift or offering, what Igbos frequently call *kola*, in order to show respect and goodwill (Uchendu 1965). Most typically the kola offered by a visitor takes the form of a bottle of wine, brandy, or hard liquor, or what Nigerians call "hot drink." Moses bought a lot of hot drinks for his campaign. But he could not compete with candidates from the wealthier parties who had much bigger bankrolls. These candidates not only presented the required kola, they gave community leaders large amounts of money to distribute among people they could recruit to vote as they instructed. Of course local leaders and common folk take full advantage of this system, collecting as much money as they can from as many candidates as possible, but those with the biggest bankrolls generally win. If the richest candidates are from parties or factions out of favor with the ruling powers, however, there is always the option of rigging or annulling the election. I will describe one such case below.

On my visit to Nigeria later that summer I asked Moses about the campaign. He mostly laughed it off, but told some revealing stories about how the local leaders he met with listened to his campaign appeal and responded with comments like, "We have heard you, my son, but is this all you have for us?" or "You have tried, my son, but next time you must try harder." I do not think Moses ever really believed he could win, yet he also never realized just how much elections in places like Ubakala were driven by processes of patronage in which the candidate's message was inconsequential in comparison with the power of the purse.

Another of my in-laws, Uzoma, who is based permanently in Ubakala, became active in local party politics in the 1999 election. He was an officer in the one of the major party's local hierarchy. Though his party did not win the local government chairmanship, the governorship, or the presidency, it was the main opposition party and had significant resources. Uzoma's position in the party's local organization was technically voluntary and therefore unpaid. But during the 1999 election season Uzoma began building a house. When the campaign ended, the construction stopped. During the 2003 election season Uzoma was the ward chairman of his party, again a losing party, but the largest of the losers. When I arrived in Ubakala after the election in 2003, his house was almost finished, but again construction had ceased. Everyone said, only half joking, that if Uzoma had cast his lot with the PDP (the winning party), his house would surely have been finished by now. "Do not worry," Uzoma's cousin said, "he is bound to complete his house during the next election in 2007." Uzoma was playing Nigerian politics correctly. Many of my in-laws and other friends viewed Moses's run for national office as foolish. How could a poor person ever be elected in Nigeria? Why cast one's lot with a fringe party that could not even provide any money? Maybe it was a silly effort, but the derision people in Ubakala expressed about Moses's attempt, voiced even by the very poor who ought to be the natural constituency for the Conscience Party, illustrates just how deeply embedded are the obstacles to a more truly democratic process in Nigeria.

"Fixing" Elections

The elections for the national assembly on April 12, 2003, were followed a week later by the election of state governors and the president. Obasanjo won a landslide victory with almost 62 percent of the vote, while his main rival, Buhari, received only 32 percent. Reports by observer groups and the international media suggested that voting irregularities and outright rigging were widespread.[3] Western nations expressed concern about the conduct of the election but generally accepted Obasanjo's victory.

The United States in particular was predisposed to favor and recognize Obasanjo's reelection. First, with the ongoing war in Iraq, uninterrupted access for the United States to Nigeria's oil had become even more crucial. The Obasanjo administration had demonstrated its commitment to keep the oil flowing, even at the cost of massive human rights violations in the oil-producing Niger Delta. Second, Obasanjo's main challenger, Buhari, is a Muslim, while Obasanjo himself is a born-again Christian. Given the controversy over the institution of Islamic sharia law in some northern states, and the general sympathy in mostly Muslim northern Nigeria for the Arab and Islamic resentment of Western domination, the Bush administration perceived President Obasanjo as a more reliable ally in its war against terrorism. Third, Nigeria had never had a successful transition from one civilian administration to another—not even an incumbent handing over power to themselves. Obasanjo continuing in office appeared to be the most stable prospect for Nigeria's struggling democracy. Finally, Obasanjo had shown a willingness to take the lead in trying to create "African solutions to African problems," a strategy much favored by a U.S. administration that was originally elected on a noninternationalist platform, but that had seen itself stretched thin by the interventionist policies in Iraq and Afghanistan. The official position was that the U.S. government recognized President Obasanjo's reelection and supported Nigeria's progress in establishing a stable democracy.

When I visited Nigeria less than two months after the 2003 elections, people were still abuzz about the massive and flagrant rigging that took place. Common stories included ballot boxes being stuffed or stolen, supporters of the ruling party being allowed and encouraged to vote multiple times, thugs hired to intimidate the opposition, and returning officers reporting results completely different from the actual vote count. In most parts of the country, the ruling People's Democratic Party seemed to be the primary beneficiary. Both the president and most of the incumbent PDP governors won landslide victories. Election fraud, though, is certainly not the sole province of the incumbents. Opposition candidates also know the unofficial rules of a Nigerian election and any candidate with a realistic hope of winning is engaged in the same practices as the incumbent.

Although the number of votes a candidate receives does not necessarily determine victory in Nigerian elections, the degree to which a particular candidate or party can mobilize followers and resources, sometimes including violence, is in fact some measure of a candidate's strength. Because ordinary Nigerians generally have access to their leaders only through the structures of patron-clientism, and because they have learned to have little faith that their leaders will actually represent their interests while in office, they will often vote for the candidate who looks like the best patron—that is, the person who gives them the most money or might be able to deliver the most government resources, even if the mechanism of delivery is corruption rather than transparent public policies and programs. Ironically, many candidates who win through rigging would probably win in a fair election. But given that everyone assumes the electoral process is corrupt, few are willing to take the chance that they might win without rigging.

Considering how widely Nigerians assume that elections are fixed, it is hard to sort out fact from rumor. But official 2003 election results in some states reported turnouts larger than the number of eligible voters, clearly suggesting something suspicious. International watchdog groups documented numerous cases of irregularities and outright rigging (National Democratic Institute 2003). Even if some of the stories that circulated in postelection Nigeria were myths or exaggerations, they represent a widespread belief on the part of Nigerians that their leaders are not elected but selected, and that even with the transition to a civilian administration they are still ruled rather than represented.

The most detailed description I recorded about the way rigging and corruption work in a Nigerian election came from a friend who was heavily involved in the local government council vote in his place of origin. Election of the country's 774 local government councils and their chairmen was originally scheduled to take place in 2002, but the poll was eventually postponed until March 27, 2004. Much is at stake in local government elections because under Nigeria's federal system, the central government makes a huge statutory allocation of funds to each local government administration each month. Everything from teacher salaries to funds for health services to money for capital projects and an allocation for state security is dispersed to the local governments. Local government administration in Nigeria has been notoriously corrupt. Besides federal ministerial posts and governorships—and of course the presidency—becoming a local government chairman is viewed as one of the best ways to get rich in political office. Many people have told me that being a local government chairman is more lucrative than being a senator or a member of the house of assembly in the national legislature. The people who run local governments not only amass great personal wealth but also control a huge patronage purse that trickles closer to the lowest levels of Nigerian society than any other government monies. Therefore, competition and factional fighting in local government elections can be even fiercer and more violent than in state and national elections.

One of my best friends in Nigeria, Kalu Onuoha, arrived in Providence three days after the 2004 local government elections to attend a conference in Boston. When we were arranging his itinerary, Kalu wanted to be sure that he would be in Nigeria through March 27. Kalu is a businessperson, but like many Nigerians who are successful in their chosen fields, he remains active in the politics of his place of origin. Though he had built a house in his village, Kalu had not actually lived there permanently since he was a child. Yet that in no way reduced his sense of having a stake in the local government election. If anything, being a successful out-migrant heightened his stake because having influence in the election was one way of assuring his continued relevance at home (Geschiere and Gugler 1998; Gugler 2002).

On his first night in Providence, Kalu recounted a harrowing story of the previous weekend's election in his local government area. The local government was bitterly divided between two candidates, and tensions escalated in the days leading up to the election. The candidate from the party of the state's governor was Kalu's person; the other candidate had the support of the state's senator, who belonged to the main rival party. Reportedly, the rival candidate also had the secret support of the state's deputy governor. The deputy governor was supposedly worried that the incumbent governor, who would reach his two-term limit in 2007, would not support the deputy's own gubernatorial candidacy. By secretly supporting the opposition, the deputy was building an alternative coalition of support for himself—or at least so Kalu explained to me.

On the ground, the contest involved much more than a campaign for votes. Each faction assumed the other would resort to all possible means of rigging, and each planned not to be outdone by the other. Each candidate's group used some of its funds to import large numbers of political thugs from towns and cities as far away as Lagos. The importation of "area boys," the common term Nigerians use to describe unemployed young men who are easily tempted into crime and violence, contributed to an atmosphere of anxiety. Kalu said that several of these area boys were stationed at his house and the homes of other prominent supporters of his candidate for protection in case the opposition sent their own thugs to try to intimidate them.

In addition to the support of a senator and the purported secret backing of the deputy governor, Kalu and his allies were also concerned that the rival candidate had the support of the richest man in the local government, a reputed 419 kingpin nicknamed "Big Boy." Big Boy apparently made his fortune engineering the scams for which Nigeria is notorious. Kalu said that he and his allies had spies in the other camp, and that they were given regular reports about the discussions and planning that took place at meetings in Big Boy's compound—though he looked a bit puzzled when I asked how he could be sure his faction's spies were not double agents. Although my double agent query left Kalu perplexed, he and his group did assume that the opposition had their own spies, and they expected that the discussions at any large meeting would leak to the other side. They relied on much smaller meetings for the really important strategizing.

On the night before the election, each group held supposedly secret meetings that were in fact premised on the knowledge that the other side would know what happened; they were designed as one final attempt to intimidate the opposition. The strongest and richest supporters of each candidate contributed money at these meetings. Kalu himself contributed over a hundred thousand naira (close to one thousand dollars), which he had been given by one of the governor's aides on instruction from the governor. Other people gave similar amounts—some their own money, and some also distributed indirectly by the governor. At Big Boy's compound the same process unfolded, and when the meetings ended well after midnight and reports from the spies circulated, Kalu and his group were satisfied that they had outspent the opposition.

I did not understand how all this money contributed in the wee hours before the election could make a difference to the outcome, so I asked Kalu. He replied that the money would be used to buy ammunition, and that the amount contributed would be a signal to the other side how well its opponents were armed. At the time I was told this story I had worked in Nigeria for fifteen years. I had been in the country during countless outbreaks of deadly violence. I knew that guns were so common that armed robbery was a national fear. Further, I had directly observed the aftermath of multiple incidents where the military government (and more recently the civilian administration) used force to quell various kinds of civil disturbances. But I was nonetheless shocked at the extent to which control over the means of violence was so openly a part of the tactics in a local government election.

The next day, during the election, there were several incidents of gunfire and several people were wounded, but according to Kalu no one was killed. He said he had narrowly escaped being shot himself when he approached a roadblock set up by the opposition's area boys. Kalu saw the roadblock just in time, and turned and sped in the other direction as shots were fired at his car. Apparently the opposition's area boys knew his vehicle. Each faction set up roadblocks to try to thwart the other group's stealing of ballot boxes. After the voters had gone to the polls, the real contest was to see who could actually control the ballot boxes.

Kalu said that his group dominated that process and they were confident of victory. But they made one huge mistake. The official who actually recorded the election results when the votes were counted had been bought off by the other faction. When they realized that they did not control the documents that were used to report the official election results, they searched frantically for the official, but he was not to be found. In the end, the results submitted to the electoral commission showed that Kalu's candidate had lost.

But that was not the end of it. Because the governor had supported the losing candidate and because the election was so obviously marred by fraud, the governor used his powers to annul the election. Another election would have to be held. When Kalu arrived in Providence on March 30, the governor had not yet acted. Kalu made several phone calls to the governor's office and was anxious about the situation throughout his conference. When he learned just before he left to go back to Nigeria that the governor had annulled the election he was greatly relieved.

Later in the year I visited Kalu in his village home. He was busy lining up support for his candidate in the new election that would take place in November. Several people who had supported the opposition had come to Kalu asking for forgiveness and wishing to demonstrate their allegiance to Kalu and his patron, the governor. They wanted to cast their lots with the likely winner. In a situation where the entire electoral process is corrupt, but where those who control the government can much more easily use the official rules against their opponents, the advantage to those in power is immense. Incumbents control the preponderance of resources to make them more effective cheaters, and if that does not work they can annul an election and prosecute their opponents for cheating. In the November rerun Kalu's candidate—the governor's candidate—won handily.

THE GODFATHER AND THE GOVERNOR: THE ANAMBRA CRISIS

As indicated, the 2003 elections were, by and large, an overwhelming victory for incumbents. Ironically, the single incident of election corruption that has become the most powerful symbol in popular consciousness of the venality of contemporary Nigerian politics occurred in a state where the ruling PDP chose another candidate to head its ticket, dropping the incumbent governor altogether. The electoral crisis that unfolded in Anambra State included almost incomprehensible intrigue and drama, capturing the popular imagination. The Anambra crisis exposes the extent of corruption in Nigerian politics, illustrates the public fascination with

corruption, reinforces the conclusion that corruption is the primary discourse of national complaint, and serves as a potent example of why Nigerians are so cynical about democracy so soon after the transition from
military rule.

On July 10, 2003, a little over a month after Dr. Chris Ngige was sworn
in as the new governor of Anambra State under the banner of President
Obasanjo's ruling PDP, police attempted to arrest Ngige and literally remove him from office. The justification for the attempted arrest was that
Ngige had purportedly resigned the governorship several days earlier and
therefore was illegally holding onto the reins of power. Though Ngige was
temporarily detained by police and security officers, his arrest and removal
from office failed in part, as the newspapers reported, because Ngige managed to make a call on his cell phone to the country's vice president, Atiku
Abubakar, who contacted the inspector general of police for the federa-
tion, who in turn issued an order ending the police action against Ngige.
But the failed arrest set in motion a series of revelations and subsequent
events that would shake the still-fragile foundations of Nigeria's nascent
democracy and cement the public's perception that its leaders were corrupt to the core.[4]

In the days after the story of the attempted removal of a sitting governor
broke, Nigerians learned that Ngige had indeed signed his own resignation letter, but that the letter was signed prior to his taking office, as part of
an agreement with his political godfather, Chris Uba, who had bankrolled
Ngige's run for office. The undated, signed letter of resignation was Uba's
insurance that Ngige would be beholden to him once he assumed office.
In fact, not only had Ngige signed a letter of resignation before taking
office, Uba and his allies had filmed the signing and extracted an additional verbal oath of Ngige's loyalty on videotape. It was later further revealed, or at least widely reported, that Uba had sent Ngige to one of the
most feared traditional shrines in Anambra State to make Ngige swear his
loyalty in a blood oath.[5] Believers in the shrine expect that violating a
sworn oath results in catastrophe and probably death.

The political godfather, Uba, had gone to great lengths to assure that
he would control the levers of power in Anambra State from backstage.
He had bankrolled the governor's election, but he had also installed a
loyal deputy governor and speaker of the Anambra State house of assembly,
who by some accounts, was one of his senior sisters. Even as the arrest of
Ngige failed, the state house of assembly set in motion the swearing in
of the deputy governor, Okey Ude, to replace Ngige. Shortly after the
aborted arrest and Ngige's denial that he had resigned the governorship,
Uba's supporters tried to initiate impeachment proceedings against the
governor. This effort failed only because by this time the story had become
a national scandal and the PDP hierarchy purportedly put pressure on its

members in the Anambra house of assembly not to allow the impeachment to succeed. Eventually, Uba's self-selected speaker of the house of assembly resigned, and following a brief internal police investigation, the assistant inspector of police who had led the attempted arrest of Ngige was retired from service. But no action was taken against Uba and the full scope of the Anambra crisis was only just beginning to unfold.

President Obasanjo had been at an African summit in Mozambique when the police tried to arrest Ngige. On his return, he ordered an internal police investigation that resulted in the retiring of the assistant inspector. With regard to the struggle for power in Anambra State between the governor and the godfather, early on Obasanjo issued a now-infamous statement that the crisis was a "family affair" within the PDP, and suggested that the dispute should be resolved by the party rather than the federal government. The irony of the president's wording became clear as Nigerians learned that Uba was Obasanjo's in-law. Uba's senior brother, Andy Uba, was both a special adviser to the president and married to the first lady's sister. In the minds of ordinary Nigerians, every action taken (or not taken) by the federal government in the Anambra crisis had to be interpreted in light of Obasanjo's affinal ties to Chris Uba. Indeed, once their relationship came to light, the media reported, and popular discourse embellished, a huge range of stories, many of them almost certainly false, about the dealings between the president and Chris Uba. While the unfolding crisis led to a massive production of rumors, the aspects of the Anambra saga that can be established as fact are themselves so disturbing that they leave little wonder why most Nigerians are convinced that their entire electoral and political system is hopelessly corrupt.

Initially, Ngige denied that he had ever signed a letter of resignation. But when the videotape came to light, his strategy for survival and hope for legitimacy switched to portraying himself as a populist governor who resisted his political patron's efforts to control the state government. It was widely reported that Uba demanded three billion naira (approximately twenty-two million dollars) from Ngige for installing him as governor. He planned to collect this money through controlling major government contracts issued by the governor and by placing his own people in Ngige's cabinet of commissioners who would control the budgets of the line ministries. Indeed, Uba reportedly demanded that he choose or approve all of the governor's key political appointments to assure his control of the state coffers.

In the eighteen months after the crisis erupted, Governor Ngige proved adept at generating popular support in Anambra State. The administration of Ngige's predecessor, Chinwoke Mbadinuju, had a reputation for being one of the most venal on record. At the end of the Mbadinuju administration, all public schools had been closed for almost an entire year because teachers were not paid their salaries, and the entire civil service was owed seven months of salary arrears. Most people assumed that the former governor and his cronies simply ate the money. The reputation of Ngige's predecessor meant that just paying salaries on time made Ngige popular. Ngige also issued construction contracts to repair some of Anambra State's notoriously poor roads. Further, his efforts to resist what was increasingly perceived as a conspiracy at the highest levels of the federal government to remove him from office added to his populist reputation. Though some people continued to question the legitimacy of a governor who ran for and took office based on a corrupt bargain with his political godfather, the fact that Ngige reneged on the agreement and was now the apparent target of the larger political machine was enough to make him something of a folk hero. In my conversations with Anambra indigenes and other citizens across southeastern Nigeria, it was clear that Ngige was increasingly admired even as new revelations suggested that his entire election was a fraud.

Ngige's populist stature was enhanced by the fact that he operated as governor for almost a full year without any government-provided security services. Both the police and the state security services in Nigeria are federal institutions, ultimately under the authority of the president. The withdrawal of Ngige's security detail came as the result of a lawsuit filed by one of Chris Uba's supporters in the high court in Enugu, a neighboring state to Anambra. The plaintiff had been suspended from the Anambra State house of assembly in the wake of the initial crisis. He sued, claiming that Ngige had resigned the governorship, and asserted that the events that led to his own suspension were based on the false premise that Ngige was actually still governor. The court sided with the plaintiff, and declared that Ngige's resignation was legal and that the inspector general of police and the federal minister of justice should forcefully remove Ngige from office. Ngige quickly went to court himself and won a counterorder restraining the police from executing the Enugu's judge's order. But meanwhile, as appeals wound their way through Nigeria's courts, federal police and security service protection for Governor Ngige was suspended pending the judicial system's final ruling. Few Nigerians believed that the withdrawal of a governor's security detail could be undertaken and sustained without the direct consent of President Obasanjo. Ngige continued on as governor, using a private security detail, made up partly of the remnants of a vigilante group, the Bakassi Boys, who had been popular several years earlier for their violent efforts to control crime in the state's major cities. All kinds of unsubstantiated rumors circulated in southeastern Nigeria, including that the president himself had helped to plot the Enugu court case. Even if these rumors are false, few people disputed the fact that the president could have ordered the restoration of Ngige's security detail had he so desired. To the Nigerian public, and particularly the Igbo-speaking people of southeastern Nigeria who have seen themselves as losers in Nigeria's federal system for four decades, a governor operating without a federal security detail represented their own fortitude in the face of continuous marginalization.

As part of the president's effort to portray the Anambra crisis as a family affair and resolve it within the structure of the ruling PDP, a peacemaking effort was led by senate president Adolphous Wabara (a politician whose own dubious election was the subject of massive media attention, and who eventually resigned the senate presidency over his alleged involvement in a bribery scandal) and Governor Chika Udenwa in the Imo State capital of Owerri. Ngige and Uba were brought together to negotiate a truce and a peace accord. To the consternation of many Nigerians, this so-called Owerri accord stipulated that Uba would be given a say over a certain number of Ngige's political appointments, a quasi-official recognition that the beleaguered governor did, in fact, owe a debt to his political godfather. The Owerri agreement broke down, and tensions between Uba and Ngige as well as their respective supporters remained high. To Nigerians observing the whole surreal affair, it was further evidence that Uba had support at the highest levels of government. How else could a political godfather who admittedly engineered a governor's election and then tried to remove him from office be allowed to "negotiate" with the governor under the observation of the federal senate president and another governor?

The Enugu court ruling that led to the removal of Ngige's security detail occurred early in January 2004, almost six months after the initial "godfather's coup," as it was dubbed in the Nigerian media. Over the first nine months of 2004, Ngige held on to power, building his populist image, but also occasionally partaking in various mediation efforts arranged by prominent politicians. The case frequently dominated the front pages of Nigeria's newspapers and magazines, capturing the popular imagination like no other political story in President Obasanjo's second administration. But over time the scandal grabbed less attention than in the first six months after it broke. Then, on November 10, 2004, massive violence erupted in Anambra State and the intensity of the crisis reached an even higher pitch.

That day hundreds of young men attacked major symbols of the state government in Awka, the state capital, and Onitsha, the commercial capital.[6] The mob, portrayed by Uba's supporters as protesters and by Ngige's supporters as thugs, burned, bombed, and looted the Government House, the governor's lodge, the state judiciary building, the state house of assembly, the state radio service, and other public buildings. The violence continued for three days before the police and the military finally cracked down. Indeed, video footage of the destruction on the first day, run on national news broadcasts, showed the police standing by idly as the mayhem unfolded. Once again, the Anambra crisis was on the front pages and in the forefront of popular consciousness. Media accounts and popular speculation assumed that the uprising was sponsored by Chris Uba in an attempt to make Anambra State ungovernable, a desperate attempt to accomplish what he had so far failed to do: have Ngige removed from office. His strategy, it was widely assumed, was that by making Anambra ungovernable, he would create a justification for the president to declare a state of emergency, thereby removing the governor and installing the president's handpicked acting administrator. A precedent had been set earlier in the year when President Obasanjo, with the support of the federal house of assembly and the senate, declared a state of emergency in Plateau State after an eruption of communal violence between Christians and Muslim communities that killed hundreds.[7]

The November 2004 mayhem in Awka and Onitsha brought increasing attention to the president's role in the Anambra crisis. Igbo leaders in the Southeast spoke out more forcefully about the crisis, asserting that it was not only a blight to Nigeria's democratic aspirations but also that the president's failure to resolve the crisis represented overt discrimination against the Igbos. The more critical voices suggested that Obasanjo not only failed to prevent the November 10 violence but that he had encouraged it, plotting with his in-law to take back control of the state from the now-popular Governor Ngige. It is impossible to know Obasanjo's role, if any, in the November 10 events, but he and his government came under a barrage of criticism more intense than any it had faced since the initial godfather's coup in July 2003. If there were ever plans to declare a state of emergency, they were scrapped in the wake of the public reaction to the violence. Indeed, within days of the incident, Obasanjo restored Ngige's security detail, and promised that the violent events would be investigated and those responsible would be prosecuted.

THE LETTERS: "FAIR PLAY EVEN AMONG ROBBERS"

Most ordinary Nigerians who viewed the video footage of the riots on television or heard the stories about it assumed that the destruction of state government property by a mob of thugs occurred because the police who looked on had been ordered not to intervene. The inspector general of police claimed shortly after the mayhem that the police did not have the personnel on the ground to confront the large and violent mob, but the popular consensus was that he was covering up after the fact. Even to high-ranking members of President Obasanjo's ruling PDP, the Anambra crisis and the appearance that the president condoned the actions of his in-law, Chris Uba, had become a huge political liability. These concerns led the national chairman of the PDP, Chief Audu Ogbeh, to write a letter to President Obasanjo criticizing his handling of the crisis and calling on him to put the affairs of Anambra State in order. Ogbeh dated his letter December 6, 2004. It was widely published in the Nigerian media. Six days later President Obasanjo sent a lengthy reply, also widely published in the media, which is almost certainly the most extraordinary public document regarding political corruption since the transition to civilian rule in 1999.[8]

President Obasanjo's reply to Chief Ogbeh's letter is such an unusual and revealing document that I have included a copy of it, as well as Ogbeh's initial letter, in the appendix. The letter is worth reading in its entirety for what it divulges about the dynamics of political corruption in Nigeria, particularly as seen through the eyes of President Obasanjo, Nigeria's most powerful person. While one cannot be sure that Obasanjo wrote every word himself, unedited by his aides, it certainly reads that way. Indeed, one suspects that if any of the president's talented political advisers had been given the chance, they would have counseled Obasanjo not to send or publish the letter. One can only imagine how the president's top advisers must have cringed when they eventually saw the letter and realized that it would be read throughout Nigeria and beyond.

Ogbeh's initial letter, less than two pages long, expresses his concern that the Anambra crisis along with the failure of the president to handle it effectively had deepened public anger and disappointment with the head of state, his government, and the PDP. Ominously, Ogbeh compares the present crisis with the situation in 1983 when the last civilian administration was overthrown by a military coup. The letter concludes with a call for the president to act decisively, and "bring any, and all criminal, even treasonable, activity to a halt." Ogbeh's reference to treason echoed widespread popular dismay that the federal government appeared to stand by passively while a political godfather whose aim was to loot a state treasury acted deliberately to destabilize and end the administration of a sitting governor. Ogbeh's letter did not explicitly accuse Obasanjo of condoning Uba's actions, but the reference to a previous coup must certainly have been viewed by Obasanjo as threatening and inflammatory.

The president's extensive reply opens with language that suggests Obasanjo viewed Ogbeh's letter as a betrayal. The focus on Ogbeh's person foreshadows the extent to which the letter uses idioms of kinship—such as failures of reciprocity, respect, and loyalty—to interpret and explain the Anambra crisis. The letter begins, "I am amused and not surprised by your letter of December 6, 2004 because after playing hide and seek games over a period of time, you have finally, at least in writing, decided to unmask and show your true colour." The letter attempts, in Obasanjo's words, to "go over systematically and, in some detail, through the whole episode of the Anambra saga." Obasanjo begins by recounting the process of withdrawing support for the previous incumbent PDP governor in the state, Mbadinuju, who had been an "unmitigated failure." Obasanjo mentions Mbadinuju's "failure to pay salaries in some cases for over 7 months which led to school children not being able to take the WASCE [a standardized school-leaving exam]." Regarding Mbadinuju, Obasanjo writes, "You rightly, I believe, requested that I should work with you to give him a soft landing and we agreed to make him an ambassador after the election and we even agreed on which mission abroad." While such soft landings are common for disgraced ex-politicians in Nigeria, the fact that Obasanjo would describe the process in such a matter-of-fact manner in a letter he knew would be widely read by the Nigerian public shows that either he had no sense that such a course of action could itself be perceived as abetting corruption or he felt he enjoyed absolute impunity. I suspect it was a combination of the two, as well as the fact that the intense rage he felt toward Ogbeh (an emotion that pervades the letter), prevented him from reading his own words objectively.

Obasanjo then includes a telling anecdote about his dealings with Ngige after he learned Ngige had emerged from the primaries as the candidate of the PDP—a process over which Obasanjo claims he exercised no influence. He writes that "after enquiries about the situation in Anambra and about Ngige himself, I made a point to him that he should go and reconcile himself with his father with whom he was not on talking terms as I believed it was an abomination for an African son to be in a state of enmity with his father to the point of absolute non-communication. I advised Ngige to reconcile with his father and the rest of his family and he reported to me that he did." Given that Obasanjo, and Nigerian leaders in general, tend to use the idiom of fatherhood to describe their position vis-à-vis their clients and the public more generally, Obasanjo's reference to Ngige's poor relationship with his father as an "abomination" presages the president's interpretation of Ngige's behavior as governor. If Ngige could fail to communicate with and respect his own father, Obasanjo's anecdote suggests, is it any wonder that he would behave so poorly in his relationship with his political godfather? Again the idiom of kinship, and particularly the failure of key actors to behave like good kin, is deployed to explain the underpinnings of the Anambra crisis.

Obasanjo then writes: "The election took place and Ngige was declared the winner." In describing the initial weeks of Ngige's administration in Anambra State, prior to the godfather's coup on July 10, 2003, Obasanjo acknowledges that Chris Uba came to him early on, "to report that things appeared to be going wrong between him [Uba] and the governor." Obasanjo reports that he asked an elder politician in Anambra State to try to mediate. Obasanjo does not explain why Uba had direct access to the president, or why Uba and Ngige had any relationship at all, much less why this should be an issue that Uba could bring to the president of the country. Perhaps needless to say, many Nigerians interpreted these passages in Obasanjo's letter as confirmation of Chris Uba's close relationship with the president and as an indication that Obasanjo knew from the beginning that Uba was Ngige's political godfather, with all that it implied.

After explaining that he was in Mozambique when Ngige's supposed resignation was revealed, Obasanjo repeats his well-known phrase that the Anambra crisis "required urgent party action to resolve it as a family affair." Obasanjo then proceeds to recount how he distanced himself from the crisis and its protagonists, asking "both Ngige and Chris Uba never to come to my office or my residence." The president proceeds to blame Chief Ogbeh for failing to resolve an intra-PDP problem, and suggests that he, Obasanjo, only waded into the problem again because Ogbeh "had shirked your responsibility as party chairman." Obasanjo then describes a private meeting he reluctantly had with Uba and Ngige. At that meeting, Obasanjo writes, "I got the real shock of my life when Chris Uba looked Ngige straight in the face and said, 'You know you did not win the election,' and Ngige answered, 'Yes, I know I did not win.' Chris Uba went further to say to Ngige, 'You don't know in detail how it was done.' I was horrified and told both of them to leave my residence." While Obasanjo's intent in revealing this private conversation seems to be to show that Ngige is not the legitimately elected governor of Anambra State, his alleged horror was seen as completely disingenuous by most Nigerians. The fact that the president simply dismissed the men from his residence, but did not initiate a federal investigation, suggested to Nigerians that Obasanjo was not as shocked as he claimed. Further, media accounts and popular discourse following the publication of the letter focused on the fact that if Ngige's election in Anambra State was rigged, then the president's victory in the state (and by implication, in others states) was surely also rigged. None of this was particularly surprising to the already cynical Nigerian public, but the fact that the president would risk his own credibility so openly in order to discredit Ngige was seen as further evidence of the president's personal stake in the Anambra crisis.

After explaining why he continues to deal with Ngige as governor constitutionally, despite his moral misgivings, Obasanjo's letter then launches into its most revealing passage. Obasanjo writes:

> I told Chris Uba and Ngige that their case was like the case of two armed robbers
> that conspired to loot a house and after bringing out the loot, one decided to

do the other in and the issue of fair play even among robbers became a factor. The two robbers must be condemned for robbery in the first instance and the greedy one must be specially pointed out for condemnation to do justice among the robbers. To me, the determination of the greedy one is also a problem, maybe they are both equally greedy. Justice, fairness and equity are always the basis of peace and harmony in any human organization or relationship. Anambra issue is essentially a human organizational and human relationship issue.

Nigerians who read Obasanjo's analogy could not but think "robbers, indeed!" Most revealing in Obasanjo's analogy is that he is primarily concerned not with the fact of robbery itself but with the conduct of the robbers in their own relationship.

This little story stands as a metonym for the whole way in which political corruption unfolds in Nigeria. The fact that politicians will enrich themselves through their offices is taken for granted. Understanding who is "in" and who is "out," or who gets the weapons of the state used against them and who is able to act with impunity, requires an assessment of precisely the kinds of personal relationships Obasanjo alludes to. In a sense, he is completely correct that the Anambra crisis is essentially "a human relationship issue." From Obasanjo's perspective, and in the logic of Nigerian politics, Ngige behaved badly to his godfather, failing to deliver on the promises implicit in their relationship—a behavior foreshadowed by his problems with his own father.

Nigerians at every level of the political hierarchy understand the importance of these kinds of personal relationships. Values such as respect and loyalty are widely cherished. The expectation that patron-client relationships will be characterized by mutual reciprocity is rooted in the fundamental structures of kinship that serve as a template for the moral economy that frames political dynamics in Nigeria (Joseph 1987; Oliver de Sardan 1999). Indeed, although most Nigerians lamented the consequences of rigged elections, godfathers, and massive corruption, they also participated in discussions and debates that revealed the extent to which they shared Obasanjo's concerns about the conduct of "the robbers" in their relationship with each other. I heard many arguments about whether it was Uba or Ngige who was at fault for the Anambra crisis. Though in some moments almost everyone could acknowledge the corrosive and defective nature of the whole political system, it was not unusual to hear some people saying that Ngige should have "settled" his godfather in order to avoid the crisis, while others contended that Uba had sought too much control, even for a godfather. Nigerians discussed the Anambra crisis within a taken-for-granted perspective on politics in Nigeria—a perspective that recognizes both the moral and amoral dimensions of corruption.

"Share the Money"

In the 2003 elections, Obasanjo's PDP consolidated its grip on power in Nigeria, controlling larger majorities in the federal senate and house of assembly, and taking twenty-eight of thirty-six governorships. The joke among my in-laws—that Uzoma would have finished his house in 2003 had he been affiliated with the winning PDP instead of the second-place party—symbolized local knowledge that with political office come the spoils. The practice of using public office for private gain was by no means an invention of the post-1999 civilian administration. Nigeria's military governments were notorious for their corruption, and the roots of corruption precede independence. Historians and other analysts have documented the role that colonialism played in setting up political structures across Africa that would breed inequality and corruption (Afigbo 1972; Mamdani 1996; Mbembe 2001). While ordinary Nigerians do not often look to these antecedents to explain the present situation, after the transition to democracy comparisons with military rule were common.

The difference in how Nigerians perceive military and democratic corruption is illustrated by two common phrases I heard in southeastern Nigeria—one during my dissertation fieldwork from 1995 to 1997 under the Abacha regime, and the other while doing research in 2004. During Abacha's rule, one of the military administrators in Abia State, where I was living, was a navy captain named Temi Ejoor. Ejoor quickly earned the nickname "Where my own?" among locals because of his reported penchant for asking this question with regard to any proposed state government project. He was only interested, people said, in collecting his own share. If you could assure him that he would get his own large cut of the money involved, he would likely approve the project. During Ejoor's administration, people in the town of Umuahia, the capital of Abia State, commonly asked each other "Where my own?" both in situations when they actually hoped to be given a share of something, and as a joke that there was nothing for them—because the military had taken it all.

In June 2004, five years into Nigeria's new democratic government, I remember entering a bar in Umuahia to join some friends for a drink and hearing them laugh as one person shouted "PDP" and the others responded in unison "Share the money!" Among my friends in the bar was Oke Nwafor, who was involved in politics in his local government area. He had just returned from a PDP meeting in Abuja, the nation's capital. Chanting "PDP: Share the money!" was meant both to put pressure on Oke to buy the beer and to acknowledge that as a PDP stalwart he was receiving a disproportionate share of the national cake. After that evening I heard the chant many other times and I asked numerous friends what they thought it meant. Almost everyone said that it meant that those in power were the ones who got to share the money. Nonetheless, the way it was deployed by my friends in the bar to pressure Oke to buy the beer highlighted the fact that the onus to share was more powerful in the new democratic dispensation than during the military rule, when Ejoor could ask without concern for anyone else, "Where my own?" Political corruption is no less prevalent under the new civilian administration—indeed, many Nigerians argue that it is worse—but under democracy, people's sense is that they have more leverage to demand part of the spoils.

The cases described here are just a few examples of the ways in which political corruption functions in Nigeria. Recognizing the dominance of discourses of complaint about corruption in the popular imagination is perhaps just as important as understanding the mechanisms for perpetrating corruption. No other issue generates more debate and discussion. By the time I last left Nigeria in December 2004, some people were again questioning whether the military should come back, rejuvenating the long-standing fantasy that only an ironfisted leader can clean up corruption. One evening at the tennis club in Umuahia, several men were arguing over how many political elites a revolutionary leader would have to kill in order to root out corruption. After concluding that shooting down a plane full of ministers or sinking a ship with thousands of the country's most powerful people onboard would not be enough, Goddy Nwogu said, "Let's face it, we would all have to die, because we all know that any Nigerian who gets to a position of power would do the same thing." There was laughter but also grudging acceptance that he might be right.

In part, this collective self-criticism must be interpreted as a product of history and a factor in the perpetuation of the very problems Nigerians so deeply lament. To understand why Nigerians are so cynical about their capacity to overcome political corruption, one must account for the legacies of the past: colonialism, years of military misrule, and the long-term complicity of Western governments, development donors, and multinational oil companies. But one must also recognize that in a political economy dominated by patron-clientism, most people perceive that their present needs can only be met if they participate in the system. Many organizations, journalists, and politicians routinely campaign against corruption, but everyday experience suggests that most aspirations, certainly most political aspirations, are only achieved by successfully navigating the Nigerian factor. Nevertheless, as accustomed as Nigerians are to corruption, there is a widespread sense among ordinary citizens that things have gotten out of control, and that politics represents the worst of it.

Discontent seems to be greatest when the structures of a modern state allow elites to keep a disproportionate share for themselves, making a mockery of the reciprocity expected in traditional patron-client relationships. The anger and frustration expressed about corruption in contemporary popular discourse suggests that the current situation is not sustainable indefinitely. People are disillusioned with the very system that they are obliged to participate in and reproduce. It is easy to hear the stories of Nigeria's seemingly intractable corruption and conclude that the future looks grim. But Nigerians' remarkable capacity for self-criticism is, I think, hopeful. The invention of politically critical phrases like "democratic selection" and "civil rule"; the uncanny ability to speak humorously and insightfully about their troubles, such as in references to the "real" meaning of NEPA and the unique Nigerian tiger economy; and the self-critical diagnosis that in order to root out corruption in Nigeria, everyone would have to be killed: all of these examples suggest that Nigerians have a tremendous capacity not only to endure and understand their predicament but perhaps to change it. The popular chant "PDP: Share the money!" represents both the problems with the present system and the potential for a better future—as ordinary Nigerians feel more entitled and empowered to demand their share of wealth and power, drawing not only on an idiom of accountability tied to patron-clientism but also on expectations for democracy.

CHAPTER 5

Rumors, Riots, and Diabolical Rituals

NIGERIANS' DISCONTENTS ABOUT corruption are intertwined with growing expectations for democracy and development, and with the experience
of inequality that characterizes contemporary social transformations. While
these discontents take many forms, they are nowhere more poignantly expressed than in people's ambivalence about money (Barber 1982, 1995;
Watts 1994). On the one hand, ordinary folks see themselves as necessarily
engaged in the pursuit of money and readily admit the lengths they will
go—the lengths they have to go—to try to get more money. On the other
hand, people see the single-minded pursuit of money as patently amoral, a
perversion of long-established values in which notions of wealth were much
more closely tied to social relationships (Guyer 1993, 1995; Smith 2004b).
The socially constructive principle of building wealth in people is perceived
as having been transformed into a socially destructive pursuit of wealth
measured only in money. When Nigerians talk about 419 as a new form of
corruption they typically associate it with an absence of or decline in morality. But the extent of discontent about corruption in Nigeria illustrates the
continuing power of moralities that privilege people and the obligations of
social relationships above the naked pursuit of riches.

Nigerians' moral distress about the prevalence of corruption is expressed
in everyday conversation, but it also frequently takes other forms. Many
important trends and prominent events in contemporary Nigeria, including
some that look bizarre to unfamiliar observers, can be better understood
when seen as expressions of popular discontent about corruption. Nigerians
interpret, criticize, and challenge corruption through a host of varying beliefs and behaviors. In this and the following two chapters, I show how
events and movements as diverse as riots over accusations of occult rituals,
the rise of urban vigilantism, the resurgence of ethnic nationalism, and the
burgeoning popularity of Pentecostal Christianity are all better understood
in the context of popular discontents about corruption.

THE OTOKOTO SAGA

Rumors of child kidnappings had been circulating in Owerri, the capital
of Imo State in southeastern Nigeria, for more than a year. One Saturday

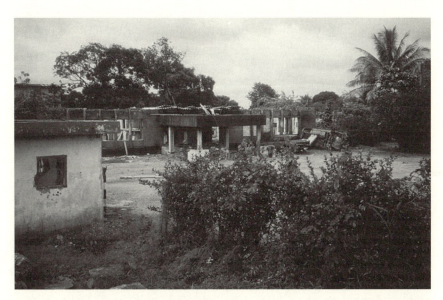

Figure 7. The Otokoto Hotel in Owerri was one of many premises believed to belong to 419 men that were razed in riots in September 1996 (photo by author).

night in September 1996, a local television station broadcast pictures of a man holding the freshly severed head of a child. The video was accompanied by an announcement that the man with the head had been arrested the previous day. The police did not know the identity of the child and were asking for the public's assistance. Early Sunday morning, the alleged perpetrator died mysteriously in jail. On Monday, news of the man's death in police custody began to circulate in Owerri. Tuesday morning, a police team moved to the premises of Otokoto Hotel, a popular lodge in town where the alleged murderer had been employed. That morning, police unearthed the headless body of a boy from the hotel grounds. A large gathering grew as the police worked. When the police team left the scene with the boy's body, having first arrested the hotel owner and all of the hotel's staff, the crowd became an angry mob. The irate throng burned all of the buildings and vehicles in the Otokoto Hotel premises. They then moved across the street to burn an upscale supermarket catering to Owerri's elite. From there, the crowd grew still larger and moved across the city burning many of Owerri's most select stores and hotels. The crowd also burned the palace of one of the traditional chiefs of Owerri as well as the houses of other wealthy people.

The rioting and burning continued into Wednesday, sparked by the alleged discovery the next morning of a roasted human corpse at the residence of Damaco, one of Owerri's young millionaires. In addition, word spread of the purported finding of human skulls and human-meat pepper soup at the Overcomers Christian Mission, the Pentecostal church where Damaco worshipped, implying a practice of ritual cannibalism.[1] More than twenty-five buildings and dozens of vehicles were torched before the riots subsided. The cessation of violence was due in part to a strict curfew imposed on the town by Nigeria's military government.

The rioters did not target places and people randomly. In the retrospective accounts that I collected through interviews with participants, the explosion of press coverage that followed (Bastian 2003), and the government report that was produced five months later describing the findings of an official judicial inquiry into the events (Imo State Government 1997), the "Otokoto saga" was portrayed as a cleansing of connected evils. The Owerri riots were widely viewed as a popular uprising against intertwined social problems. The rioters and much of the public believed that many of the town's young elite had achieved their "fast wealth" through occult rituals that included child kidnapping, ritual murder, and cannibalism.[2] Collective anger was vented not only at the nouveaux riches suspected of ritual murder but also at the police, politicians, and religious leaders who were believed to have encouraged, protected, legitimized, and consorted with these alleged evildoers.

Rioters explained that the properties targeted in the Owerri uprising were owned by 419 men. The town had developed a reputation over several years for being a hub of 419 activities and a haven for the main actors. In addition to being suspected of garnering their riches by conning foreigners and wealthy Nigerians in highly elaborate scams (Apter 1999; Hibou 1999), Owerri's 419 men were also suspected by both law enforcement officials and the Nigerian public of participating in the highly lucrative international drug trade (Bayart 1999). Whatever anger or ambivalence ordinary Nigerians felt about the typical 419 activities, accusing the young elite of kidnapping, cannibalism, and ritual murder implied much greater evils.

In the wake of the Owerri riots, stories of kidnapping and ritual murder in the pursuit of fast wealth circulated widely in the press and popular discourse. Why did 419 men specifically feature in popular accounts of ritual murder? What did the accusations against them mean? Why did the Owerri riots generate so many rumors and stories of similar evils in other places throughout Nigeria? I argue that the Owerri riots and the stories of ritual murder that proliferated in their aftermath are related expressions of Nigerians' constructions and understandings of the changing nature of inequality in the maintenance of political power in contemporary Nigeria, and are partly expressions of anger and discontent about the consequences of corruption. Strikingly, popular rumors and stories circulating in the wake of the Owerri crisis demonstrate not only public discontent over corruption and inequality but a collective recognition of the role that common people play in supporting corruption and bringing about the very changes in the structure of inequality they find so troubling.

PATRON-CLIENTISM, CORRUPTION, AND MILITARY RULE

Corruption in Nigeria was exacerbated by years of military rule, during which those who controlled the official means of violence plundered the nation's resources. The Nigerian public's conclusion that the kidnapping and beheading of a young child served to advance the achievement of fast wealth must be interpreted in the larger context of violence wielded by despotic leaders in order to maintain power and accumulate fantastic riches. At the time of the Owerri riots, General Abacha ruled Nigeria in what has been widely acknowledged by both international observers and the Nigerian people as the country's most brutal regime. But the Owerri riots were not simply an expression of popular anger over violent oppression by the military. Stories of ritual murder and fast wealth reveal the ambivalence about corruption created in the entanglements of class and kinship, the tensions between military rule and patron-clientism, and the conflicts between individual desires and social obligations.

The many stories about the events in Owerri suggest that Nigerians both welcome and reject the emergence of social structures no longer securely rooted in systems of reciprocity associated with kinship and patron-clientism. The burdens and obligations of kinship and patron-clientism often frustrate Nigerians, both rich and poor. The poor suspect that their wealthy patrons are not sharing enough of their riches, and the prosperous feel obliged to assist their networks of clients, even as they complain that the demands are too much. Nonetheless, as ambivalent as Nigerians are about the disparities in their patronage-dominated society, the Owerri riots and the discourse produced in their aftermath suggest that new forms of corruption, where the beneficiaries are less bound by the moral obligations of kinship and patron-clientism (forms of corruption often described specifically as 419), are even more troubling to them.

On the surface, Owerri residents condemned fast wealth as prosperity allegedly accumulated through unworthy means. But to the rioters, and indeed to a broad range of Owerri residents and other Nigerians I interviewed in the wake of the riots, perhaps the greater evil than the speed and means by which this wealth was accumulated was that it was not shared. The beneficiaries of fast wealth flouted the customary obligations of the haves to the have-nots—much as the military flouted the traditional obligations of national leaders. 419 men, like military rulers, accumulated and displayed their wealth in ways that exacerbated their differences with common people rather than reinscribing social ties by sharing their wealth through the customary networks of patronage.

The Owerri riots and the popular interpretations, rumors, and related stories that proliferated afterward serve as a window onto the Nigerian public consciousness about corruption and class, and wealth and politics. These events and the public response they generated illustrate how the traditional institutions of kinship and patron-clientism are being threatened by new patterns and structures of inequality. Attacks on swanky stores and hotels, posh cars, and the residences of some of Owerri's wealthiest people can be read as a kind of class warfare, targeting the most obvious symbols of corruption and inequality. Owerri's angry rioters were acting against changes in the structure of inequality—changes that include the breakdown of the obligations of the rich to share with and assist the poor. Child kidnappings and ritual killings stand for the violence and polarization that increasingly undergird the structure of inequality in contemporary Nigeria. These stories also highlight the intimate connections between popular condemnation of the unequal accumulation of great wealth and widely shared fantasies about being rich. Nigerians recognize and condemn the new structures of power that facilitate corruption and create new forms of inequality, but they also implicate themselves as sharing the motives and producing the very social changes they find so disturbing.

WITCHCRAFT ACCUSATIONS: A CRITIQUE OF CORRUPTION?

A growing anthropological literature has explored the way in which emerging and exacerbated inequalities in sub-Saharan Africa are played out in discourses about the occult (Comaroff and Comaroff 1999a; Geschiere 1997; White 1997). Much of this literature focuses on understanding what Peter Geschiere (1997) has called the "modernity of witchcraft." The anthropology of witchcraft in contemporary Africa emphasizes that occult happenings and the popular dialogues they engender "are not archaic or exotic phenomenon, somehow isolated or disjointed from historical processes of global political and economic transformation. Rather, these are moral discourses alive to the basic coordinates of experience, highly sensitive to contradictions in economy and society" (Auslander 1993, 168). Anthropologists have long interpreted witchcraft as being about moralities related to production and reproduction (Ardener 1970). Witchcraft accusations have been described as responding to and addressing the social, moral, and emotional consequences of selfishness, greed, and excessive accumulation in societies organized around obligations of reciprocal exchange. Archetypal witches consume their kin to satisfy avaricious desires to prosper at the expense of others. The failures of production (for example, on the farm or in business and trade) and reproduction (say, infertility) of some people, and the dramatic successes of others, are explained and acted on through accusations of witchcraft.

Much of the literature on the proliferation of witchcraft in modern Africa has focused on the dramatic nature of contemporary inequality (Bayart 1993), and the fact that capitalist penetration and postcolonial politics have produced wealth along with disparity by means that are largely beyond the view and control of most people. Witchcraft accusations distill "complex material and social processes into comprehensible human motives" (Comaroff and Comaroff 1999a, 286). Rather than being projected directly onto the "mysterious mechanisms of the market" (Comaroff and Comaroff 1999a, 284) or the power of the postcolonial state, discontent is often refracted back onto those symbols of the traditional social structure that people perceive as inhibiting their own participation in the dramatic appropriation of wealth and power by a privileged few. But one of the most intriguing features of the Owerri events is the way in which accusations focused precisely on those young men who succeeded outside the structures of kin-based patron-clientism. The alleged 419 men had flouted the expectations of reciprocal obligation and flaunted their ill-gained wealth.

Jean Comaroff and John Comaroff (1999a) and others (Fisiy and Geschiere 1991; Geschiere 1997) have argued that the proliferation of witchcraft in postcolonial Africa is directly related to the penetration of neoliberal capitalism as well as the articulation of the local and the global. The essential condition that gives rise to "occult economies" (Comaroff and Comaroff 1999a) is inequality. To ordinary Nigerians, the main mechanism that explains inequality is corruption, both in its practical political and economic manifestations and its moral dimensions. But popular sentiments about corruption and inequality are marked simultaneously by resentment and attraction. In other words, people resent the gross disparities of wealth created by corruption in contemporary Nigeria, yet they also wish that they could be the beneficiaries of great wealth themselves (Barber 1982, 448–49; Meyer 1995, 249).

Few of the popular stories that circulated in Owerri after the riots referred to the millionaires specifically as witches. Nonetheless, stories of child kidnappings, ritual killings, trades in body parts, and other magic practices form part of a dynamic cultural complex for which "witchcraft" serves as a crude but widely recognized label. It is important to understanding why stories of the occult—of witchcraft—are so prominent in Nigerians' interpretations of corruption and inequality in contemporary society. The events in Owerri along with the rumors and stories that surrounded them make sense only in their particular social, political, and historical contexts. Many facets of the Otokoto saga link it to other accounts of the modernity of witchcraft in Africa, but the differences raise crucial issues, particularly with regard to popular participation in and ambivalence about corruption and the role of ordinary citizens in transformations in the structure of inequality.

The major difference between the Otokoto case and many other instances of modern witchcraft accusations is with regard to the targets of antiwitchcraft violence. Unlike many documented episodes of witch finding in Africa—in which elderly, female, or marginal people are often the targets of accusations and anger—the rioters in Owerri attacked the property of the elite, especially the young elite, popularly known as 419 men. The rioters were themselves primarily young men, mostly of lower socioeconomic status. The fact that the rioters and their targets were all mostly young suggests that the intersection of age and class is complicated for Nigerians. These complications arise from young Nigerians' contradictory feelings about generational inequality, where privileges accrued traditionally according to seniority, reinforcing a generational dimension to the structures of patron-clientism. While youth have often bristled and rebelled against these age-based hierarchies, the targeting of the young elite in the Owerri riots suggests that the rioters were acting against wealth accumulation no longer regulated by obligations of reciprocity rooted in a kinship-based patron-clientism. Rather than targeting people who symbolized the constraints of traditional hierarchies, the rioters and the subsequent accusations focused on those who had escaped and abandoned the traditional obligations of patron-clientism.

419 AND FAST WEALTH

The practice of 419 has always held a precarious place in relation to Nigeria's system of patron-clientism. On the one hand, 419 men are admired for their ability to circumvent the system and get rich without having to negotiate the obligations of kinship and patron-clientism. The tremendous burdens and obligations to family and community are such that people who can escape them are often envied. On the other hand, 419 men are often despised precisely because they fail to fulfill many of the duties that are expected of big men.

Stories such as the one I described in the introduction about the scam perpetrated on the Texas oil executive are common topics of popular discourse in Nigeria. Whether they are true or apocryphal, they reveal much about the ambivalent place of 419 in Nigerian society. Those who fall for

419 schemes are often depicted as so greedy that they are easy dupes and so selfish that they do not care how the fantastic profits they are promised might be obtained. The 419 men are sometimes portrayed as skillful entrepreneurs who can outcon the wealthy and the powerful. Also, they are envied and admired for their wealth. They are able to wield many of the symbols of success in Nigerian society that most people can only dream of—the newest Mercedes cars, modern houses, and fancy linen clothes.

But it was clear, even prior to the Owerri riots, that 419 men were also engendering anger and resentment. In ordinary people's accounts of the appearance of 419 men at weddings, funerals, and other social events, awestruck descriptions of the huge amounts of money they "sprayed" mixed with criticisms of their outlandish self-aggrandizement.[3] People said that these 419 men were "buying" honorary traditional titles, acquiring special vehicle license plates from the government that told the police and military that they were untouchables, and having the streets they lived on renamed after themselves. Their wealth and the privileges it bought created jealousy and resentment as well as admiration.

THE RIOTS

When Owerri exploded, I was a little more than a year into a field research project in Ubakala, about an hour's drive from the Imo State capital. As mentioned earlier, I had worked in Owerri for three years on a public health program. I knew the small city in the heart of Igbo-speaking Nigeria quite well, and during my years there I enjoyed its relatively calm and peaceful atmosphere. As a civil-service town that had become a state capital with the creation of Imo State in 1976, Owerri was a quiet place compared to the bustling Igbo commercial cities of Onitsha and Aba. When I lived there from 1989 to 1992, I heard occasional stories of carjackings and armed robbery, but Owerri residents I knew at the time told me they were grateful that their town was not afflicted with the same degree of violent crime that characterized places like Lagos, Benin City, and Onitsha.

When I returned to Nigeria in 1995, Owerri was more crowded, traffic was worse, and people talked a lot more about violent crime. In addition, I was told that a wave of child kidnapping plagued the city. Armed robbers entered homes and sometimes took children, later asking for ransom. In a handful of well-known cases, the children had yet to be recovered. The people I knew suspected that the police were as likely to be involved in crime as trying to prevent it.

I happened to be in Owerri on the Saturday night that Innocent Ekeanyanwu, the alleged murderer, was shown on local television with the child's head. The next morning, at a local tennis club, talk of the beheading and the television broadcast dominated conversation. Club members were shocked and outraged by the broadcast—both by the fact that this man was caught with a child's head and that the police decided to show it on television. Imagine the reaction of the child's parents if they saw the horrible image, my friends worried. Much of the talk centered on the decline of Nigerian society and the depths of evil to which people had become willing to descend in order to prosper. What, I asked, would the man have wanted the head for? For some kind of *juju* (a popular term for various forms of traditional medicine and black magic), my friends said. Probably to get rich or overcome some kind of political rival, they speculated. The association of child kidnappings with ritual murder and of ritual murder with black magic to obtain wealth and power is widespread in Nigeria and throughout much of Africa (Geschiere 1997; Meyer 1998; White 1997), and has a long history (Middleton and Winter 1963; Shaw 1997). But that Sunday morning, in their casual analysis, none of my friends drew explicit connections between the beheading and Owerri's 419 men. And certainly no one implicated Eze Onu Egwunwoke, whose house was razed by the mob. He was an honorary trustee of the tennis club. The elite status of my tennis partners prevented them from anticipating the popular uprising that was brewing.

Indeed, part of the morning's discussion was about the club's preparations to host "Larry," one of Owerri's wealthiest and most widely known nouveaux riches. My friends hoped that a party in his honor would encourage Larry to give the club a generous donation. Two days later that would all change. Larry was one of the 419 men targeted by the Owerri mob. His businesses, cars, and fancy modern house were torched. Larry disappeared from Owerri, no doubt in fear for his life. As a result of the riots, he went from being a highly sought-after guest to being a suspected ritual murderer accused of using child kidnapping and cannibalism to magically manufacture his outrageous prosperity.

I returned to my village field site that Sunday evening and related the shocking television broadcast to my wife and friends at home. Wednesday night, the local evening television news (in nearby Abia State, where Ubakala is located) broadcast scenes of devastation in Owerri. The riots had been underway for two days and were attracting regional press coverage. The television report showed burned buildings and cars. The segment included a video clip of a crowd carrying to the state military administrator's office the burned human corpse that was allegedly found in Damaco's residence. The video also showed a large pot of pepper soup found cooking at the Overcomers Christian Mission church compound. The television reporter said the pepper soup supposedly contained human meat. The picture of a headless body that had been deposited by police in the federal hospital mortuary was described as "one of more than a dozen bodies" that had been unearthed at Otokoto Hotel.[4] The rioters were said to be targeting the property of people suspected of masterminding a spree of child kidnapping and ritual murder in the pursuit of fast wealth.

An Evil Conspiracy

One of the most remarkable aspects of popular and media reactions to the riots was the intense focus on Ekeanyanwu's death in police custody. Although the beheaded eleven-year-old boy became the primary symbol for the evils committed in the pursuit of illegitimate wealth, it is at least arguable that it was the death of the alleged killer in police custody, rather than the young child's beheading, that actually triggered the rioting.[5] The public almost uniformly assumed that Ekeanyanwu was killed to cover up the involvement of important people in the spree of kidnapping and ritual murder purportedly plaguing Owerri. The following accounts from Nigerian newspapers reflect the public mood and the widespread interpretation of Ekeanyanwu's death:

> On Sunday last week, as the normally sedate Owerri city began to hear whiffs of what started as rumour, news came that Ekeanyanwu had suddenly died in the police cell where he was held. The mysterious death . . . heightened the drama and the possibility of highbrow involvement in the whole thing. The cynical public began to seethe and also began to accuse the police of complicity in a grand cover-up design. (Nwakanma and Onwuemedo 1996, 20)

> The incident [Ekeanyanwu's death] was nowhere near mystery to most residents. Their conclusion was that the suspect was eliminated to close the tracks of the other head hunters. (Akor 1996, A23)

> It is suspected that Ekeanyanwu was killed by his sponsors who must have colluded with officialdom to bury any evidence that might lead to the arrest of the perpetrators of the heinous act of ritual murders in Owerri. (Obibi 1996, 11)

Public anger focused on three groups in addition to the 419 men: the police, the administration of former military governor Navy Captain James Aneke, and traditional rulers, especially Eze Onu Egwunwoke, the Owerri chief who was also the chairman of the state council of traditional rulers. Each of these actors was targeted for their perceived complicity with the 419 men—cooperating in their corrupt endeavors, protecting them, and conferring them with social legitimacy. These people, along with the 419 men, became symbols of corruption and inequality. Nevertheless, anger was channeled and ultimately focused on a few individuals and material symbols, rather than on the nature and structure of these institutions themselves. The emphasis on individuals and symbols meant that the riots ultimately had little effect on the larger structures that facilitate corruption and solidify inequality.

An Accused Military Ruler

The Owerri riots occurred barely a month after Navy Captain Aneke handed over the position of Imo State military administrator to his successor. Aneke had been reassigned by Nigeria's ruling generals after thirty months on the job in Owerri. In popular discourse and press accounts in the aftermath of the riots, explanations for the mob's anger at Aneke's administration focused on a number of public complaints about his tenure in office: failing to pay civil servants' salaries, consorting with 419 men, and enriching himself and his cronies.[6] According to the people I knew, the most salient reason for the public's anger at Aneke was his sale of large electricity generators at the Amaraku power station shortly before he left office. The power station had been purchased and commissioned by the state's only civilian administration from 1979 to 1983, and it symbolized the state's ambitions and efforts to develop the region. Prior to the Owerri riots, stories circulated that Aneke sold the generators to a Lebanese company for 114 million naira, reported the sale for only 30 million naira, paid the smaller amount into the government coffers, and pocketed the difference.

After the Owerri riots, the official judicial commission of inquiry set up by the government to investigate "the remote and immediate causes of the Owerri disturbances" (Imo State Government 1997, 4) focused a great deal of attention on the Aneke administration. The probing of former military rulers by their successors is usually taboo in Nigeria's military culture; thus, in promoting the investigation the military revealed its substantial anxiety over the Owerri riots. In allowing accusations against Aneke to receive official sanction, the military was offering up a scapegoat. By laying blame for the Owerri riots on the Aneke administration, the military was able to deflect attention from the more general discontent with military rule.

Making 419 Men Chiefs

Nearly all of the people I interviewed said that traditional ruler Egwunwoke's palace was razed by the mob because he was conferring honorary chieftancy titles on 419 men. In southeastern Nigeria, as in other parts of the country, it has become commonplace for people who acquire significant wealth to try to translate their economic success into social prestige. The connection between wealth and the taking of chieftancy titles is not a uniquely modern phenomenon, but many Nigerians believe that the honor of chieftancy has been demeaned because titles are awarded to the highest bidders rather than through assessments of people's contributions to community and society. Ordinary Nigerians derisively refer to these modern chiefs as "naira chiefs," a reference to the fact that titles are bought rather than deserved. Even more troubling to ordinary citizens is the notion that much of the money used to purchase chieftancy titles is believed to be the product of corruption. In common cynical discourse, the more elaborate a man's title-taking ceremony or the more titles a man accumulates, the more money he is believed to have stolen. Thus, 419 men taking chieftancy titles in lavish ceremonies and accumulating a host of praise names affiliated with their titles became a prominent symbol of popular discontent over corruption. Egwunwoke was thought to have profited handsomely from the money of 419 men paid him to crown them. The angry crowd that set off from Otokoto Hotel did not spare his palace.

One newspaper account of his escape as the crowd torched his palace took apparent pleasure in relating details that emphasized the disgracing of this traditional ruler who many believed had demeaned the institution of chieftancy: "It is reported that Eze Onu-Egwunwoke had escaped from the irate crowd through the bush path, from where he took *okada* [motorcycle taxis] to the State House" (Nwakanma and Onwuemedo 1996, 20). The report that Egwunwoke fled by "bush path" lowers him to the standard of the poorest farmer because only village people going places where there are no roads traverse bush paths. The fact that he then took okada to the state house implies the same thing, but with an urban twist. Most people in Owerri rely on okada for public transportation— the common person being too poor to own a car or take automobile taxis.[7] Egwunwoke was known for his fleet of fancy cars, so the insinuation that he was reduced to fleeing by bush path and hiring okada reverberated powerfully in the public consciousness.

Newspapers and magazines featured numerous stories about Egwunwoke in the weeks and months following the Owerri riots. Some of them said that he was living as a refugee in government quarters, afraid to be seen in public among his own constituency (Anyaehie 1997, 7). Several accounts implied that the government was protecting him (Hart 1996, 3)—a charge that is not surprising given that the Eze had a reputation for strongly supporting the military government. Within a few months of the riots, Egwunwoke lost his position as the chairman of the state council of chiefs and was rarely seen in public up until the time of his death in 2000. At the tennis club where he was an honorary trustee, and where he used to be feted lavishly when he came to play, he was never seen again.

The Police: Partners in Crime

Egwunwoke came to represent traditional rulers' complicity in the events leading to the Owerri riots. Aneke served the same role for the military government. Similarly, former Imo State police commissioner David Abure was denounced for the police role in protecting and collaborating with 419 men. Like Aneke, Abure had left office before the Owerri riots, retiring from government service and returning to his home state. But popular rumors, newspaper stories, and testimony at the judicial commission of inquiry implicated him in the underlying causes of the riots. Abure was accused of consorting with known 419 men, providing them police protection for their nefarious activities, and failing to investigate reported cases of kidnapping.

The most intriguing rumor of police complicity, reported in one of Nigeria's tabloidlike newspapers, concerned the kidnapping of the eight-year-old son of a prominent doctor in Owerri, Darlington Amamasi (Nwachi 1996, 6). The story reported that Dr. Amamasi's son had been kidnapped, with police approval, in retaliation for the doctor's refusal to let 419 men take the body of the father of one of Nigeria's richest industrialists from the mortuary at his hospital. The 419 men, the story went, wanted to steal the body of the rich industrialist's father in order to ransom it back to him for millions of naira.[8]

Abure, like everyone interviewed by the judicial commission, denied any culpability in the events related to the Owerri riots. The police had investigated all credible reports of kidnapping, he said, and no one had ever brought any complaints about 419 men to him (Emerole 1996, 1, 3). Perhaps because Nigerians routinely experience police intimidation and so many people have firsthand experience with police corruption, the public did not find his testimony credible. Daily stops by armed police to demand money from drivers at checkpoints constructed every few kilometers on Nigerian highways, the police detention without trial of critics of the military, and countless experiences with unresolved (and seemingly uninvestigated) crimes have taught Nigerians to distrust and scorn the police. No one had complained to the police about 419 men, my friends said, because everyone knew they worked hand in hand *with* the police.

THE DEFENDANTS

As described above, when the eleven-year-old boy's headless body was unearthed at the Otokoto Hotel grounds, police arrested the hotel's owner and the entire hotel's staff. In the days and weeks that followed the riots, the hotel's owner, Chief Vincent Duru, became the primary suspect and the most pronounced public symbol of evil in the Otokoto saga. At the time of the riots, Duru's son was already in prison facing charges of child kidnapping and armed robbery. Police had arrested the younger Duru and several accomplices in one of the few cases of kidnapping in Owerri that had been solved. The known criminal activities of Duru's son and the fact that Ekeanyanwu worked for the senior Duru made Vincent a central suspect in the eleven-year-old boy's beheading. Indeed, popular accounts and media stories began to refer to Duru as "Otokoto."

In his testimony before the judicial commission of inquiry, Duru implicated another important political figure from his local government area, Chief Leonard Unaogu. Duru claimed that police officers had told him that Ekeanyanwu had confessed that Unaogu commissioned the killing (Imo State Government 1997). Duru's accusation that Unaogu masterminded the ritual killing led to Unaogu's arrest and appearance before the judicial commission of inquiry. Unaogu's arrest was particularly intriguing because his junior brother, Laz Unaogu, was a federal minister in Abacha's military regime.

In the report that resulted from the judicial commission of inquiry, the Imo State government recommended that both Duru and Unaogu be charged for the eleven-year-old boy's murder. Though their respective indictments represent two completely different theories of the crime, both men were held in prison to be charged with murder. That Unaogu was left in prison and charged, despite the fact that his brother was a federal minister, indicates how concerned the military government was over the Owerri riots and the potential for additional violence if someone was not brought to justice. The Nigerians I know normally expect that those with such powerful connections are immune from prosecution, no matter the enormity of their crime.

Although one military administrator, one police commissioner, and one traditional ruler came under great popular criticism and some formal sanctions for their association with and support for 419 men, the institutions of military and traditional rule remained strongly entrenched in the wake of the Otokoto saga. Though the political and military elite felt threatened by the Owerri riots, public outrage was ultimately focused on a few corrupt individuals who skirted the obligations of patron-clientism rather than on the institutional structures of a political economy dominated by highly hierarchical patronage networks. While symbols of corruption were violently attacked in the Owerri riots, the main mechanisms for corruption were not threatened, and the Nigerian public's ambivalent participation in the processes that reproduce corruption and inequality was not fundamentally altered.

CORRUPTION IN THE POPULAR IMAGINATION

From popular discourse, national and international media, and also personal experience through which people see firsthand the vast inequalities of their society, Nigerians take it as common knowledge that the police, the military, and the country's politicians collaborate to loot the treasury. Plenty of evidence suggests that 419 men often operate with official tolerance, if not outright collaboration (Apter 1999; Bayart 1999); however, no strong evidence uncovered in the aftermath of the riots suggested that any of the 419 men targeted by the mob, or any of their alleged government collaborators and protectors, actually practiced ritual murder. The only obvious link between 419 men and ritual murder was the purported discovery of the roasted human corpse at the compound of Damaco, about which many contradictory versions of events circulated. But the popular imagination in Owerri and among the many Nigerians who followed the story never let go of the belief that these 419 men and their official collaborators *did* engage in ritual murder. Accusations of occult practices served to explain, but also to brand as evil, the shadowy methods through which some people in society got so rich at the expense of the majority. The kidnapping of a child for the purpose of ritual murder was essential to the social construction of public outrage that led to the riots.

Perhaps the most intriguing and illuminating aspect of the events unfolding in the wake of the Owerri riots was the tremendous proliferation of related rumors and stories that dominated Nigerian popular discourse. Many of these rumors and stories focused on the causes and consequences of the Owerri riots. Spectacular tales circulated about the ostentatious behavior of Owerri's 419 men. Popular accounts reported that more than a dozen bodies had been unearthed at Otokoto Hotel. Rumors were passed around that a huge cache of body parts was found in Vincent Duru's freezer at his village home. An ever-mutating range of conspiracy theories linked military, political, and religious leaders in the web of ritual murder. As detailed below, these rumors often made their way into daily newspapers and weekly magazines.

Just as interesting, the Otokoto saga seemed to trigger a spate of child kidnappings, beheadings, and ritual murders across the nation, or more accurately, a rash of stories alleging these happenings. Almost weekly, for several months after the Owerri riots, the media reported such incidents across Nigeria, usually unsubstantiated. And in village communities—certainly in the semirural Igbo community where I lived—stories about local practices of black magic in the pursuit of fast wealth were produced and reproduced in community gossip, spurred by the events in Owerri. The public, it seemed, was inspired to talk about and condemn corruption and its associated inequalities through the idiom of the occult.

It is important to examine the meaning of the fantastic tales that circulated in popular discourse after the Owerri riots. When they are exaggerated, and even when they are seemingly completely apocryphal, these stories tell truths. They place in the arena of popular discourse "public secrets" (Taussig 1997) that cannot be exposed directly without fear of reprisals from those who control the means of punishment. They also provide a window into the ways in which the Nigerian public makes sense of issues like corruption, economic inequality, and political exclusion.

As Luise White (1997, 328) writes in a piece about the traffic in human heads in southern Africa, "These histories or stories are being told in, or through, or with heads (rather than the histories being about heads)." In other words, if one looks beyond the apparently outrageous and grotesque nature of the stories, it is possible to see that they are "physical descriptions of the reconstitution of politics and power" (334). As Birgit Meyer (1998) advises with regard to tales of satanic riches in southern Ghana, the fantastic stories that circulated in the wake of the Owerri riots have to be taken seriously as political statements. And yet the content of these political statements made through accusations of magic wealth focus public ire on inequality of a particular type and origin—that which flouts the traditional obligations of kinship-based patron-clientism. Such critiques preserve certain kinds of inequalities even as they challenge others.

The popular rumors, the newspaper articles chronicling the world of the occult, and the ever-mutating conspiracy theories about 419 men and their highbrow collaborators in ritual murder offer a version of reality that Karin Barber (1987, 9–12, 34–40) has called "the unofficial." Through these rumors and stories people are able to make some sense, in unofficial discourse, of the structures of power that shape social inequality. Using only a few of the myriad of rumors and stories that I heard or read in the months after the Owerri riots, I try to show how these tales allow people to grapple with issues of corruption and inequality. As political statements, these stories are both empowering and disempowering. They are empowering in that fantastic narratives permit people to criticize the military and its civilian political collaborators using the language of rumor and metaphor. It is hard for those in power to affix blame or mete out punishment for such fantastic forms of popular criticism. Yet these forms of discourse are also disempowering because the structures that sustain the inequalities are protected from overt assessment and condemnation since the ultimate source of inequalities remains mysterious, hidden, and possibly unknowable.

For many Nigerians, the 419 men embody ambition for wealth and power gone out of control. They are the ultimate symbols of corruption. Popular stories about their excesses emphasized their lack of respect for their fellow people. As one of Nigeria's daily newspapers reported, "Such affluent people terrorized the inhabitants [of Owerri] with their wealth" (Obibi 1996, 11). Among the more widely circulated genre of stories were narratives about how 419 men traveled. Several people told me that 419 men moved in convoys of fancy vehicles with armed escorts and blaring sirens—exactly how the country's top military officials moved about. A newspaper account about the 419 men and their wealth reproduced some of this imagery:

> The result is that big designer and exotic cars were bought, huge magnificent mansions and castles were built in villages for rodents and insects, because their owners were always either in Lagos or overseas. A new class of " *Nouveaux Riche*" emerged. They moved in convoys of about six cars on the largely untarred roads. The first, usually a jeep, often a Nissan Pathfinder followed by another jeep (this time either a Mitsubishi Pajero, Izuzu Rodeo or the America Cherokee), then the man in the Lexus brand of car followed by an American Limousine (carrying wife and children where he is married), escorted by two V-Boot Benz cars. Husband and wife were usually light skinned people, not gifted with too many words. Whenever they spoke money was splashed. (Udegbe 1996, 6)

It is worth noting the references to the 419 men as "always either in Lagos or overseas" (that is, neglecting their communities and kinfolk), traveling on "untarred roads" (that is, wealth squandered on individuals while the public infrastructure suffers), and usually "light skinned people, not gifted with too many words" (that is, trying to be what they are not, and lacking the talent or intelligence to have earned their status legitimately).

One of the most revealing stories I heard described how, when stopped at a police checkpoint, one of these 419 men slapped a police officer for not recognizing him, the implication being that he was an untouchable—someone protected by the powers that be. Interestingly, one of the most widely, if discreetly, reproduced stories about then military head-of-state Abacha alleged that when he was a young colonel, he shot dead a police officer who delayed him at a checkpoint. Popular critiques of the excesses of 419 men were, I think, not coincidentally similar to more quietly shared discontents over the excessive venality of the country's military rulers ("quietly shared" because overt criticisms of Abacha were much more dangerous than telling stories about 419 men).

People said these 419 men used their ill-gotten wealth to get access to all kinds of luxuries and commit numerous immoral acts, even when they were behind bars: stories circulated that imprisoned 419 men had comfortable beds, televisions, VCRs, and cellular telephones with which they were able to continue to direct their nefarious activities. For an average Nigerian, prison is a place of hunger, disease, and inhumane treatment. To many people, the most aggrieving symbol of the 419 men's excesses behind bars was a rumor that an arrested child kidnapper had impregnated a prison guard.

Many of the stories circulating after the riots focused on the behavioral excesses of the 419 men in terms of their conspicuous consumption, ostentatious displays of wealth, and ill-mannered and irreverent treatment of fellow citizens. Other stories embellished and exaggerated the extent of evidence of kidnappings, ritual murder, and black magic uncovered after Ekeanyanwu was discovered with the severed head. Rumors, stories, and media reports wildly exaggerated the numbers of bodies unearthed at the Otokoto Hotel. Newspapers carried reports of eight, nine, eleven, and eighteen bodies dug up. A front-page story in a national daily newspaper reported two days after the riots that "over 20 human heads have been discovered at various spots in the town by angry demonstrators" (Curfew 1996, 1). One of the more sensational newspapers led with an article saying that two hundred human male organs were found in a goat's belly stored in a freezer in Otokoto's (Duru's) village house (Two hundred male organs, 1996, 3). The police claimed, and the government report concluded, that only the boy's body was found (Imo State Government 1997, 17).

Perhaps these "unofficial" airings of "public secrets" are only possible (or at least only safe) using the tools of the imagination. It is important to emphasize that despite their fantastic elements, these stories refract reality—a reality, during the Abacha regime, of extrajudicial executions, the detention of political opponents without trial, and the massive looting and expatriation of the country's oil revenues. Given the rapid and massive accumulation of wealth by the military and its civilian collaborators, the use of violence, and the ever-present threat of violence to retain power, the imaginative leap to evil occult rituals and murderous magic is understandable.

In regard to the Otokoto saga, numerous conspiracy theories spread and mutated in each telling, linking local, regional, and national political figures to ritual murder and the trade in body parts. Some stories even linked the spree of child kidnapping to international sources, saying that children were sold as slaves in Saudi Arabia or that people's body parts were harvested for sale for organ transplants in Western countries. These images show how the nature of rumors and fantastic tales are situated in the context of Nigeria's political economy, including Nigeria's place in the global system. One newspaper account compared the cases of Otokoto and the Belgian Marc Dutroux, who had recently been arrested for a spree of child molestation and serial killings. Top Belgian government officials were implicated for their lack of attention in pursuing the Dutroux case (Emelumba 1996, 13). References to child molesters, serial killers, and the politics of scandal in the West, and to international trade in humans and human body parts, point to the transnational circulation of ideas about corruption, violence, and social ruin. While stories of cannibalistic 419 men who pursue wealth by murdering children are clearly drawn from traditional African ideas, they are equally influenced by globally circulating stories about political deception and scandal, organs for sale, pedophiles, serial killers, and the fabulously rich.

OTOKOTO REDUX: A PLAGUE OF RITUAL MURDER?

As mentioned above, in the aftermath of the Owerri riots, Nigeria seemed to be plagued by recurring incidents of child kidnappings, beheadings, and ritual murders. Daily newspapers and weekly magazines were filled with stories of Otokoto-related happenings across the country. Headlines included: "Roots of Ritual Killers: Across the Land, Innocent Civilians Are Being Killed and Their Parts 'Harvested' for Ritual Sacrifice" (Maduemesi 1996, 18); "Another Severed Head Found in Imo" (Ofou 1996, 1); "Ritual Murder Spreads" (Chukwurah and Alofetekun 1996, 1); "Ritual Killings: Onitsha on Fire" (Ehirim 1996, 7); and "Ritual Killers on the Prowl" (Ohakah 1996, 14). These and many other stories reported cases of kidnapping and killing believed to be perpetrated in the pursuit of wealth and power. While most of these incidents were categorically claimed by the police and other government authorities to be fabrications and rumormongering, their popular currency attests to their symbolic power and the lack of credibility of the authorities responsible for investigating such crimes.

Much of the Nigerian public genuinely feared the apparent epidemic of ritual killing. To assert that Nigerians used images of kidnapping, ritual murder, and trade in body parts as a way to think about, make sense of, and criticize corruption and the structures of power and inequality that support it, should *not* be taken to mean that people only thought of these stories metaphorically. While some Nigerians clearly saw these rumors and stories as untrue, many others perceived these threats as very real. In the context of Nigeria's ruthless and rapacious military government, perhaps it should not be surprising that stories of disappearances and killings should have such currency, or that evil acts should be interpreted as a means to attain wealth and power. These stories should be read, I think, as expressions of people's recognition and fear of the capricious nature of power and the massive corruption that underlies inequality in Nigeria.

But the power of the social critique embedded in these popular accounts is more subtle and complex than a simple expression of discontent over corruption. I have argued that the rumors and stories circulating after the Owerri riots preserve certain structures of inequality even as they challenge others. Along these lines, many of the tales produced in local communities seemed to implicate common people themselves in producing their own fate. As I have emphasized repeatedly, it is impossible not to be struck by what keen critics Nigerians are of their own society. Further, while Nigerians are quick to condemn their leaders and criticize the state of their society, they are also acutely aware of their own complicity in producing the leaders they have and making their society what it is. Some of the most interesting stories I collected in my village field site after the Owerri riots contained and illustrate this element of self-criticism.

The first of these stories I heard one evening in our village compound several weeks after the Owerri riots. Fourteen-year-old Obiageri was returning from a nearby stream where she had gone to fetch drinking water. After setting down her bucket, she told us that she had heard horrifying news from the other teenagers at the stream. She then narrated the story. A young man in a neighboring village was said to have died in his uncle's house. He perished vomiting money. The uncle, people said, had hired a juju man (a sorcerer or witch doctor) to help him get rich. The juju man instructed the uncle to give one of his family members a special medicine. If a family member ingested the medicine and the man observed the prescribed rituals, he would become rich, the juju man promised. The man picked a nephew who lived with him and locked the boy in a room, feeding him food that included the juju man's medicine. The man was not told that his nephew would be killed or exactly how he would become rich. The man was horrified when his nephew died, and he realized he could do nothing to stop the corpse from vomiting money.[9]

Many other people repeated versions of the story in the coming days, and almost always people commented on the consequences of selfish greed. The man did not set out to kill his nephew. But because he was so selfish and greedy, he did not bother to consider or ask what the consequences of the medicine would be for the person who ingested it, or how he would get rich. An important lesson of the story, in addition to the obvious message that too great a love of money is bad, is that the results of one's selfish acts often have repercussions for one's kin—and thereby, recursively, for oneself. How would the man explain this to his sister (the mother of the dead nephew)? people asked. The consequence of such a selfish act for one's kinship relations was a central moral of the tale. The fact that it was purported to have happened "just next door," using a local juju man, made the immoral act seem more familiar, and its lesson more applicable to local people than the horror of the beheading in Owerri. And yet the underlying message and the social tensions that gave rise to the act were essentially the same as in the stories surrounding the Owerri incident. The story told Igbos in this semirural community that conflicts between individual aspirations and obligations to one's kin group and community could lead to analogous horrors in their midst.

Another story with a similar message circulated in the village shortly thereafter. In this one, three traders (recall that Igbos are renowned in Nigeria for being businesspeople and traders) desperately wanted to become rich. They visited a juju man and asked for help. The juju man offered to help the traders become rich, but in order to do so they would have to be transformed into vultures for three days (vultures, as scavengers that eat dead carcasses, are often negative symbols in Igbo folklore). The traders agreed to the juju man's requirements and were turned into vultures for three days. When they came back to the juju man after three days and were turned back to human beings, they found that their businesses flourished. They were getting rich.

Two of the men returned to the juju man some weeks later and asked how they could become richer still. The third man refused to go back, saying he was already wealthy enough and did not like being turned into a vulture. The juju man told the two traders that they would have to be turned into vultures again, but this time for two weeks. The two traders eagerly agreed. They lived as vultures for two weeks and thereafter returned to the house of the juju man to be converted back into human beings. When they arrived at the juju man's compound they found a funeral underway. The juju man had been killed in a car accident a few days earlier. There was no one to change them back to human beings. The story ends by saying that if one goes to the market stalls of these two businessmen, one will see vultures sitting on the zinc-pan roofs looking on as their shops make lots of money that they can never eat. (Indeed, there are always vultures on the metal roofs in Nigeria's outdoor markets waiting for something to scavenge.)

These two stories, told in a semirural village community, express symbolically what Nigerians regularly discuss and debate explicitly—namely, their own culpability in sustaining the venality that plagues Nigeria's political economy. The 419 men and their murderous collaborators implicated in the Otokoto saga committed crimes that the average person found horrific. In terms more familiar to common people, the temptations and greed portrayed in these local tales present the conflict between individual aspirations and obligations to one's kin and community. The 419 men represent the consequences of corruption unleashed from the obligations of kinship and patron-clientism. The actions of the characters in these village stories acknowledge that some of the same desires that motivate 419 men also present conflicts and contradictions in the lives of ordinary people.

OKIJA: KILLER SHRINES AND 419

The Otokoto riots happened almost a decade ago, but the idiom of the occult continues to be one of the primary modes through which Nigerians interpret and criticize the endemic corruption that contributes to creating and exacerbating the country's dramatic inequalities. On August 4, 2004, scores of police in Anambra State raided the *Ogwugwu* shrines in the community of Okija. In the "evil forest" surrounding the shrines they reportedly found dozens of unburied human corpses in various stages of decomposition as well as large numbers of human skulls separated from their torsos. The Okija story dominated Nigerian media headlines and popular discourse for several weeks, and many accounts drew explicit parallels to the Otokoto saga of 1996. In particular, accusations swirled that ambitious politicians and greedy fraudsters used the shrines to advance their quests for power and their 419 moneymaking schemes.

The *Ogwugwu* shrines, and many similar ones throughout Igboland and in the communities of other ethnic groups in Nigeria, are described by most Nigerians as legacies of traditional religious practices—practices that in heavily Christian southeastern Nigeria, many people regard with disdain. The shrines are dedicated to deities believed to guard and influence various aspects of human affairs. The shrines are administered by priests whose role is to serve the deities, and act as mediators between the deities and the people who come to the shrines seeking assistance. One of the *Ogwugwu* deity's principal functions is to mediate disputes. When two parties cannot resolve a conflict, they can approach the shrine seeking mediation. In past times, disputes typically focused on land claims; nowadays, settling disagreements over money is more common. In most cases, the shrine priests, for a customary fee, are able to negotiate a settlement. But where arbitration is not possible, each party is required to swear an oath to the deity. The common belief is that calamity, and even death, will befall a party that attempts to deceive or defy the deity. In addition, when someone who had sworn an oath is "killed" by the deity, it is expected that that person's body and all their possessions related to the case must be deposited in the evil forest in order to remove the deity's curse from the kin of the deceased.

When the police raided the Okija shrines in 2004, they arrested thirty priests and charged them with murder. In media interviews the priests defended themselves, claiming that only the deity itself can kill, and that the bodies around the shrine had been brought there by the relatives of the deceased in conformity with tradition. Although the Okija shrine raid generated debates about religion, culture, and ethnicity, the dominant discourses focused on issues of power and corruption. The debates centered on whether people resorted to deities as a last means of seeking justice in a society so corrupt that the police and courts could be bought by the highest bidders, or whether the shrines themselves had become institutions of 419, wherein fraudsters and politicians sealed their nefarious deals in sworn oaths, with the shrine priests themselves collaborating in 419. In press accounts and conversations I heard among friends and acquaintances in the aftermath of the scandal, those who supported or sympathized with people's continued appeals to such shrines concentrated on the impossibility of getting justice through the formal institutions of the state. The words of Raymond Arazu, a Christian pastor interviewed in one of Nigeria's weekly newsmagazines, represent one strain of popular opinion that circulated in the wake of the raid:

> So you have to look for the basis of this kind of thing. Some people have said that you cannot get justice from the police. And you cannot also get justice from the law courts. Even then, the cost is exorbitant. . . . But at the shrine, there is justice which people are seeking for. And the person who is aggrieved, whether he has money or not can get justice at the shrine. That is why people are going there.
>
> There are so many people who are aggrieved, and before they realize it, the person who wronged them will invite the police just because they have money. Sometimes they are even locked up by the police for a week or so, and when they come out, they end up going to beg the same people who wronged them. . . .
>
> The modern system is not just. Once we have a police institution that is above board, that does not intimidate people and does not collect money from the rich to subvert justice, people will not patronize the shrine. (Our justice system 2004, 22–24)

Nevertheless, much more common than the defense of the shrines was the popular consensus that the traditional shrines had themselves become corrupt. Newspaper and magazine stories suggested that some of Nigeria's economic, political, and military elite had used the shrines to cement their corrupt bargains to rule and loot the nation. Headlines included captions such as "Okija Shrine Revelations: Panic Grips Politicians, Top Generals Worried" (cover for Our justice system 2004), "The Patrons of Okija Shrine: Full, Authentic List of Politicians, Churches" (Ojuwale 2004, 14–15), and "Okija: Those Who Fed Fat on the Shrine" (Eze 2004, 4). Most of the headlines were not substantiated by evidence. When the registers of shrine clients apparently recovered during the raid were released, the press and the public seemed disappointed that there were not more big names. Not surprisingly, many people suggested that the real lists were suppressed or edited. Whether or not Nigeria's economic, political, and military elite frequented Okija and other shrines in any great numbers, the Nigerian public wanted to believe they did. Rumors of dirty deals and sinister partnerships thrive in popular discourse about Nigerian politics. As in the Otokoto case, corruption is interpreted and implicitly criticized through accounts that explain the mechanisms that maintain inequality in the idiom of the occult.

The Okija shrine scandal erupted a little more than a year after the attempted godfather's coup in Anambra State, described in chapter 4. The two scandals were quickly intertwined, and parties on both sides of the conflict between Governor Ngige and his erstwhile godfather, Chris Uba, tried to use the Okija incident to their advantage. Long before the raid on the shrines, stories had circulated that Ngige and Uba had sealed their deal with a blood oath. In the wake of the Okija episode, Uba's supporters in Anambra State issued statements that Ngige himself initiated a visit to the Okija shrine to swear his loyalty to Uba and his clique. In widely published accounts they also suggested that the raid on the shrines had been masterminded by Ngige to destroy the shrines because he feared the consequences of his failure to live up to his oath. Other accounts hinted that Ngige's current troubles were the work of the deity, punishing him for reneging on his oath of allegiance to Uba. Ngige, for his part, had testified in a public hearing long before the Okija scandal that he had been forced to swear an oath by Uba and his operatives. But in his statements after the Okija revelations, he claimed that he never actually entered the shrine and that he had carried a Bible with him, implying that this indicated his true beliefs and immunized him from the consequences of any magic contamination suggested by his visit to Okija. His supporters claimed that it was Uba and his sycophants who engaged in occult rituals to secure their greedy aims. These public battles between the governor and the godfather over the role of the shrine in their conflict only deepened public suspicion that politicians resorted to charms, oaths, magic, and other forms of witchcraft to advance their political ambitions.

The popular consensus that all Nigerian organizations, even traditional institutions like the *Ogwugwu* shrines, are plagued by corruption was reinforced by stories suggesting that young people in Okija had hijacked the shrines and used them to extort money from clients. Accounts remarked that "what was once a revered ancient practice in Okija has recently become a money making venture among youths" (Eze 2004, 4). Rogue priests purportedly "killed or visited stage-managed misfortune" on clients to instill fear and extract money from them or their kin (Eze 2004, 4). Not only did Nigerians believe that elites were using the power of traditional rituals to facilitate their corrupt grabs of money and power, they suspected that even these traditional institutions had been infiltrated with 419.

Although the dominant public response to the Okija scandal was further cynicism about the intractable nature of corruption in the country, in their inimitable style Nigerians also managed to deploy the Okija incident in critical humor. People joked about the kinds of pacts Nigerian politicians made among themselves and suggested that the deities just might still have their revenge. A letter written to the editors of *Newswatch*, one of Nigeria's weekly newsmagazines, illustrates the popular capacity for wit. The writer observes that having more of the country's leaders swear at the shrine might be a good idea.

As it is, we should approach the matter from this angle; now that no solution has been found to the increasing wave of corruption in Nigeria for the past 44 years and the people who plunder the nation's resources are Christians and Moslems against biblical or Quranic injunctions "Thou shall not" we should take solace in Okija as the last option in the fight against corruption. . . .

A branch office/shrine of Okija should be established in the F.C.T. Abuja, preferably in the Three Arms Zone extending to the Federal Secretariat and the NNPC Building. Our defective constitution should incorporate the shrine and . . . the Village Head/Grand Commander of Aso Rock and his 152 Aides, the 469 members of the National Assembly and the more than 40 ministers should be made to swear by Okija; Those who presided over the 2003 Election Petition Tribunals; members of the Nigerian navy on off-shore operations, The Police, SSS, the Customs, Immigration and Prison Services should also swear; Member of Federal Government parastatals like NRC, NPA, NAA, BPE, NNPC, Ajao-kuta Steel Mill etc. should take their turn.

And finally, those at INEC and SIECS should swear for the 2003/2004 elections and against 2007 election "that all they did and are still doing are for the best of the ordinary citizens of this country." (Letter 2004, 4)

The litany of people and institutions in need of a visit to the shrine reads like a catalog of corruption that is familiar to all Nigerians. While the writer presents this proposal tongue in cheek, most Nigerians would sympathize with the sentiment that a deity capable of holding leaders accountable for corruption might be just what the nation needs. But many people would also add more humor, suggesting that the author, and by implication all ordinary Nigerians, should have to swear that he is not corrupt.

Class Consciousness, Kinship Connections, and Popular Critiques of Corruption

The Otokoto saga in Owerri and the Okija shrine scandal in Anambra are two prominent examples of a much larger production and circulation of stories about magic schemes to achieve wealth and power. Whether they are rumors or real events, practices such as child kidnapping, ritual murder, or swearing an oath to a deity provide insight into Nigerians' understandings of the mechanisms behind the corruption that underlies structures of inequality in their society. Stories of evil rituals and occult practices in the pursuit of wealth also point to tensions and ambivalence as people experience corruption in the context of the complex entanglements between emerging social classes and continuing ties of kinship. People recognize that in the present period of rapid social change, individual desires increasingly conflict with widely shared values of social obligation.

While some forms of corruption can be motivated by the obligation to share the fruits of one's position with one's people, much more troubling are instances where those who loot the state do so solely for their own benefit. The new economic elite in Owerri and the politicians who allegedly patronized the Okija shrine stood accused in popular discourse of using evil supernatural means to achieve their ends. Politicians and 419 men were depicted almost like modern witches, with their fraud and rapacious looting serving purely selfish purposes.

In the Africanist literature, witchcraft accusations have been widely linked to tensions produced in kinship relations marked by the volatile mixture of intimacy and inequality (Geschiere 1997; Meyer 1995). With increasing urbanization, the penetration of a capitalist market economy, and postindependence opportunities for the Nigerian elites to enrich themselves by looting the state, inequality has reached unprecedented levels. Yet ties of kinship, community, and ethnicity remain extremely powerful (Geschiere and Gugler 1998; Geschiere and Nyamnjoh 1998), and in the context of growing inequality, these ties produce tremendous tensions as well as productive cooperation. Peter Geschiere (1997, 11) has called witchcraft "the dark side of kinship." Birgit Meyer (1998, 19) has associated stories of satanic riches with "the dark side of modernity." Central to understanding the power of stories of the occult and accusations of witchcraft in contemporary Nigeria is recognizing the incredible strains placed on individuals in modern Nigeria by the contradictory pressures of increasing individual ambition and continuing obligations to kin and community, all in a context of economic insecurity.

But one of the most striking things about the stories of child kidnapping, ritual murder, and the trade in body parts that characterized the Otokoto saga was the *lack of relatedness* between the 419 men and their victims. Indeed, the impersonal, anonymous, and random nature of the evil acts these people allegedly perpetrated was perceived to be one of the most troubling aspects of this "new" brand of occult practice. The beheaded eleven-year-old boy could have been anybody's child. He had no kinship ties to Ekeanyanwu, Duru, or any of the 419 men implicated in public assignments of responsibility for the spree of child kidnapping and ritual murder purportedly plaguing Owerri. A fifty-five-year-old Presbyterian minister, who was the dean at a local theological seminary and with whom I discussed the Otokoto saga, said to me, "We Africans have a long tradition of sacrificing human life to seek power or wealth. But in the past, one always had to kill a kinsman. You could not just kill any stranger. This imposed limits and costs to taking a human life. It is not so easy to kill your relation. But now these people kill anybody to satisfy their greed. We are in trouble." He did not mean to imply that he accepted ritual killing in any form; he clearly saw all such acts as horrific as well as un-

Christian. But his dismay over the loosening of ritual killing from its moorings in the ties of kinship points to changes in the nature of power and inequality in contemporary Nigeria that are central to understanding the Owerri riots and the proliferation of stories about ritual killing. In particular, the focus on 419 men as the symbolic evil actors highlights popular discontent with inequalities and power relations that are no longer securely rooted in kinship-based patron-clientism.

In their violation of a moral economy rooted in kinship, patron-clientism, and reciprocal obligation, the 419 men implicated in the Otokoto saga are similar to and may stand metaphorically for the military that ruled Nigeria so ruthlessly for most of the years since independence. What worried people most was that the military ignored the obligations of patron-clientism rather than that it failed to uphold a Western notion of bureaucratic transparency. They deplored the military not so much because it looted the state (as indicated earlier, many Nigerians will tell you that civilians are just as bad, or worse) but because it kept everything for itself. Military officers were terrible patrons. Owerri's 419 men behaved similarly in that they were perceived to flout obligations to kin, community, and society in the way that they celebrated themselves without sharing with others.

As Jean-François Bayart notes (1993, 233), "A man who manages 'to make good' without ensuring that his network shares in his prosperity brings shame upon himself and acquires the reputation of 'eating' others in the invisible world." It is not coincidental, I think, that these people who so blatantly ignored their obligations to their extended family and community networks were accused of kidnapping and killing innocent children with whom they had no ties. Even in the world of the occult, such actions broke all the rules.

The focus of accusations on 419 men, the specific targeting of their property in the Owerri riots, and the stories that circulated about important people who patronized the Okija shrine all represent popular discontent with changes in the structure of inequality in Nigeria—specifically the increasingly individualized character of greed, corruption, and aspirations for power. The stories Nigerians tell acknowledge the degree to which common people themselves share in the very desires that they condemn and participate in the very transformations they find so troubling. The Otokoto saga suggests that the emergence of class polarization and class consciousness in Nigeria cannot be disentangled from the structures of patron-clientism. Nigerians clearly recognize the injustices of inequality. Witchcraft accusations have long been tied to the volatile mixture of intimacy and inequality that characterizes kinship relations (Geschiere 1997), but contemporary changes that have encouraged individualism and heightened inequality seem to have made the burdens of kinship obligations all the more difficult to negotiate. Yet the Owerri riots, the Okija scandal, and the stories that surrounded these events indicate that while Nigerians are ambivalent about these burdens, they prefer them to a world in which people wield wealth and power without reciprocal obligations.

"They Became the Criminals They Were Supposed to Fight": Crime, Corruption, and Vigilante Justice

EARLY ONE MORNING in July 2001, I was driving with a friend to a village near where I work in Abia State, just a few miles from the town of Umuahia. As we made our way down a sandy unpaved road, negotiating deep gullies created by recent rains, two vehicles carrying about fifteen men came up quickly from behind. The blue pickup truck in front flashed its lights, and the young man riding shotgun waved a weapon at me, beckoning us to pull aside. At first I thought it was the police. But as the two vehicles passed, and several young men waving guns and machetes scowled angrily at me and my friend, I realized it was the Bakassi Boys, a well-known vigilante group in southeastern Nigeria. They were all dressed in black; several tied red bandanas around their heads; most wore dark glasses, even though it was just after dawn; and they each tied amulets to their bodies to signify that they were protected by *juju* (again, magic charms). None looked over the age of thirty, and all carried weapons of one sort or another.

To our horror, instead of speeding on to a distant destination, the vehicles stopped just fifty yards ahead of us, and the Bakassi Boys descended with a speed and movement that resembled a commando raid. At first I thought they were coming back for us, but they quickly circled a house on the side of the road. Shots rang out, and at that moment fear overwhelmed curiosity. I told my friend that we had better turn back and I shifted my rusty little 1983 Toyota Corolla into reverse, attempting to back up the hill to a place where we could turn around and flee. In my haste, I entered a large gully, and within seconds we were stuck. I tried to rock the vehicle out but to no avail. More shots rang out. Soon the Bakassi Boys were coming back to their vehicle, pushing and hitting a young man who was the target of their operation. He had not been shot but looked badly beaten. As the Bakassi Boys reentered their vehicles with their prisoner and turned around, I realized that we were blocking the road. They approached again, lights flashing and guns waving, and then stopped in front of us. I got out of my car, afraid, but hoping they would not shoot me simply for blocking the road. I explained that my car was stuck and asked if they could help push us free. Somewhat reluctantly, the apparent leader shouted to others to come push my car. After the car was free, the leader then asked me in English, "Where do you stay?" With great hesitation, I told him I lived in Ubakala and added quickly in Igbo, "I am your in-law, my wife is from Ubakala." I was relieved that my time-tested strategy worked in this case as well. The leader came as close as he dared to smile (a cold and fearsome affect is among the crucial elements of the Bakassi Boys' aura) and asked me, "Has anyone been disturbing you?" I answered that everything was fine. He then offered, "If anyone bothers you, let me know. We will deal with them." They entered their vehicles and sped away.

This was my first personal encounter with the Bakassi Boys, but I had seen them in the towns of Umuahia and Owerri over the previous two years, and stories about them often made headlines in the press and circulated regularly in popular discourse. By the time I met them that morning, they had grown from a local group into a nationally known and extremely violent vigilante force.

VIGILANTISM AND THE DISAPPOINTMENTS OF DEMOCRACY

For many Nigerians, optimism that democracy would promote economic growth, advance political reform, and curtail corruption has given way to frustration over the extent to which politics continues to serve the interests of a few at the expense of the many. Perhaps nothing symbolizes the disappointments of democracy more than an all-consuming popular perception that violent crime is rampant and out of control. The intense sense of insecurity that pervades Nigeria builds on and exacerbates larger anxieties about economic deprivation, political uncertainty, and the injustices associated with pervasive corruption. In popular discourse, the rising wave of crime is portrayed as both a cause and a consequence of the venality plaguing the state and society.

Responding to and capitalizing on public anxiety, violent vigilante groups emerged in many parts of the country in the late 1990s and operated with widespread popular support (Gore and Pratten 2003; Ikelegbe 2001). The O'odua People's Congress in the Southwest (Human Rights Watch 2003), the Egbesu Boys in the Niger Delta, and the Bakassi Boys in the Southeast (Human Rights Watch 2002; Harnischfeger 2003; McCall 2004) are among the most notorious of many vigilante groups to appear in recent years. These vigilante groups ascended in a context of widespread perceptions that the police, the courts, and other institutions of the state were too corrupt to curtail crime.

But vigilantism is much more than a popular response to crime. It operates at the intersection between the state and society, and lies at the center of popular understandings of the roots of inequality, injustice, and corruption in Nigeria. Public support for vigilantism builds on notions of local sovereignty, people's ambitions and frustrations with regard to participation in Nigeria's nascent democracy, and a sense that inequitable access to resources controlled by the state undermines traditional mechanisms of reciprocity associated with long-standing systems of patron-clientism. Indeed, vigilante groups in Nigeria were for several years extremely popular among ordinary people because they represented a brand of "people's justice" in the face of the corruption associated with politics and state institutions. But popular vigilantism in democratic Nigeria has also been co-opted by politicians, resulting in a growing disillusionment with vigilante groups because they are perceived as becoming political and therefore corrupt.

This chapter examines the case of the Bakassi Boys, arguably the most notorious of all the vigilante groups in Nigeria. It explores the complex intersections between corruption, violence, vigilantism, and the state. In analyzing these interconnections, I consider the relationship between postcolonial state practices, inequality, and ordinary people's perceptions of and responses to perceived injustice. On the one hand, both vigilantism and the widespread popular support for it can be read as a reaction to the failures of democracy to deliver expected political and economic dividends. As I will show below, vigilantism was extolled in local discourse as an indigenous alternative to the corruption of the state. On the other hand, vigilantism must also be read as an expression of discontent with regard to more traditional structures of patron-clientism as they play out in an era of centralized state power and heightened inequality, particularly in a population that is younger, more educated and urbanized, and full of frustrated ambitions. Popular support for vigilantism drew on dissatisfaction with the supposed democratic state, but also on critiques of traditional patronage structures that were voiced, partly, in the language of democratic ideals.

The rise of violent vigilantism, particularly youthful urban-based vigilante groups like the Bakassi Boys, is not unique to Nigeria. Similar phenomena have occurred in Cameroon (Argenti 1998), Kenya (Anderson 2002), South Africa (Haysom 1990; Baker 2002a), and elsewhere, suggesting a wider relevance of some of the connections in Nigeria between youth, vigilantism, and popular understandings of inequality in a period when the promise of democracy is belied by the ineptitude of the state and the willful injustices perpetrated by its leaders. Indeed, Ray Abrahams (1996, 1998) has demonstrated many historical and cross-cultural parallels in the relationship between vigilantism and the state, suggesting that vigilantism is a common response to ambiguities and ambivalence regarding state authority. The role and authority of the state seem to be particularly problematic and provocative for Nigerian youth, who are both inspired by the promises of democracy and frustrated over the way that state institutions continue to be manipulated by powerful politicians. As elites utilize state institutions to turn traditional patron-client structures into mechanisms for massive individual enrichment, the anger of youth is double-edged. Young people have been disappointed both by patron-clientism and the mechanisms of the neoliberal state.

The irony of the Bakassi Boys is that although they ascended to popularity based on perceptions that they were incorruptible crime fighters, they were eventually discredited precisely because they came to be seen as corrupt. Although violent vigilantism expresses the anger of youth about inequality and injustice in Nigeria, ultimately vigilantism can serve to deflect or obscure the role of political elites in perpetuating the conditions that produce crime and corruption. Rather than targeting elite politicians who might be said to be most responsible for inequality and injustice, or working to reorganize Nigeria's complex political economy in ways that better benefit the young and the poor, vigilantism channels frustrations against ordinary criminals, who are themselves as often victims as perpetrators.

The Emergence of the Bakassi Boys

In late 1998, in the commercial southeastern Nigerian city of Aba, shoemakers and traders, angry over the extent of extortion and violent robberies perpetrated by an increasingly powerful group of criminals, organized a vigilante force that became known as the Bakassi Boys.[1] Initially made up of young traders and other young men paid with contributions provided by the traders' association, the Bakassi Boys embarked on a mission to rid Aba's main market of violent criminals, publicly executing dozens of alleged offenders. These executions, dubbed "instant justice" in popular discourse, typically took place in prominent public spaces such as major intersections or market centers, attracting large crowds of observers. The Bakassi Boys killed these alleged criminals with machete blows, dismembering their bodies and then burning them at the site of the execution.

The original Bakassi Boys vigilante group in Aba probably numbered no more than a few dozen men, but over the next several years, as the Bakassi Boys expanded their coverage to include other cities in the Southeast, their ranks increased to perhaps several hundred. The Bakassi Boys were typically between the ages of eighteen and forty, and while some of the leaders were married men with families, most of the rank-and-file vigilantes were single young men. They appeared to be from relatively poor backgrounds. Almost all were recruited from urban areas, and when the Bakassi Boys eventually lost popularity, many local people observed that there seemed to be little difference in the overall profile between the Bakassi Boys and the criminals they fought. My own impression was certainly that the Bakassi Boys and the criminals had a great deal in common in terms of background, with the violence of each fueled by anger and frustration over unfulfilled expectations in contemporary Nigeria. Indeed, when the Bakassi Boys were disbanded in 2002, many people speculated that the erstwhile vigilantes resorted or returned to lives of crime.

But initially they were quite favorably received. As news of their successes in combating criminals in Aba spread, the Bakassi Boys quickly grew into a regional vigilante force. By 2000, they operated in several cities in three states across southeastern Nigeria. Their exploits were widely reported in the media, and their fame extended well beyond the Southeast. Local politicians seized on their popularity, providing them with legitimacy and support. In both Abia and Anambra, home of the major cities where the Bakassi Boys operated, the state governors offered official backing to the vigilantes, giving them formal names (Abia State Vigilante Services and Anambra Vigilante Services), funding, vehicles, and political cover.

A State of Insecurity

Local explanations for the emergence of vigilante groups focused on the extremely high rates of violent crime that plagued Nigeria's cities in the late 1990s. In commercial southeastern cities such as Aba and Onitsha, reports of armed robberies, often resulting in the deaths of the victims, were weekly and sometimes even daily occurrences. Nightlife had virtually ground to a halt as people scrambled home to beat the darkness: "The robberies had the effect of forcing residents into a self-imposed curfew after 7 p.m., with many women and children taking to sleeping in churches" (Baker 2002b, 225). By nightfall, many parts of cities such as Aba and Onitsha were considered no-go areas, and even in the smaller state capitals such as Enugu, Owerri, and Umuahia, city streets emptied quickly after dark. In contemporary urban Nigeria, the wealthy enclose their compounds with high fences topped with razor wire or glass shards designed to deter criminals. One cannot sleep in well-off residential areas in southeastern cities without being wakened hourly by the clanging and drumming of night guards aiming to demonstrate to their employers (and presumably to the criminals) that they are awake and vigilant.

While high rates and great fears of violent crime provide an obvious context for understanding the rise of vigilantism in Nigeria, they are not a sufficient explanation. The youthful vigilantism of the Bakassi Boys and the massive popularity they initially enjoyed reflect the complex and contradictory ways in which ordinary Nigerians experience and understand inequality. To oversimplify a bit, Nigerians juggle two seemingly irreconcilable idioms of accountability—one grounded in a moral economy of reciprocal patron-clientism rooted in ties to kin and community of origin (and reinforced by notions that the ultimate sanctions for immoral human conduct are supernatural), and another adopted with the emergence of the modern nation-state, and tied to Weberian and neoliberal ideals about bureaucracy and democracy (Ekeh 1975; Comaroff and Comaroff 1999b; Gore and Pratten 2003).

Of course, in reality these systems are intertwined. Ordinary Nigerians fashion their understandings of inequality in a social world where politicians must prove, or pretend, that they are both good democrats and good patrons. As I have shown in previous chapters, common folk simultaneously condemn the corruption of politicians and cultivate corruption in their own patrons as the only means by which their interests are served. These contradictions produce popular ambivalence and frustration, and a sense of insecurity that is exacerbated, but also powerfully symbolized, in fears about crime. Anxieties about crime crystallize people's collective sense of insecurity. They also mobilize violence against these perceived threats, in ways that both lash out against inequality, and sadly, reflect and reproduce some of the ways violence has been inflicted on the wider population by the state. Vigilante violence is both rooted in and a rejection of state violence and corruption. To understand this apparent contradiction, it is necessary to examine Nigerians' experiences with and collective representations of state-controlled violence in the pursuit of corruption, primarily by the police and the military.

INSTITUTIONS OF INJUSTICE

Popular experiences with the Nigerian military and police normalized perceptions that the most powerful institutions of the state were instruments of corruption and perpetrators of injustice rather than protectors of the people. Nigerians commonly believe that the state is not only incapable of combating crime but is often complicit in its commission. During the thirty years the military ruled the country since independence in 1960, Nigerians experienced numerous forms of everyday violence that accompanied and supported the massive looting of state coffers. Arrests, imprisonment, and extrajudicial executions of political opponents were widely reported in the national and international press. Over the years, many ethnic and political demonstrations and riots have been put down through violent military responses, in which many hundreds of citizens have been killed. While high-profile cases such as Abacha's execution of Saro-Wiwa in 1995 symbolized the capacity of the military to impose its will through violence, it is more everyday forms of state-sponsored brutality that have both normalized violence and created an expectation that violence is an acceptable means to deal with threats to the social order.

Though Nigerians often lament the violence of the state, many people also participate in discourses that construct certain kinds of violence as ethical and necessary for the maintenance of an otherwise unruly society. This is quite evident in the way many Nigerians have welcomed new military regimes and constructed nostalgic memories of previous ones. As discussed in chapter 4, nostalgia for military rulers such as Muhammad, whose reign was cut short by assassination, and Buhari, who implemented the famed War against Indiscipline, represents a prevalent strain in Nigerian popular consciousness that stemming corruption and indiscipline in Nigerian society requires strict and harsh leadership. The comments of my friend Chudi, a forty-two-year-old businessman, as we walked down a crowded street in the city of Owerri in 1991, link the pervasiveness of corruption to the need for stricter governance:

> See, see, see. We cannot even pass this road without soiling ourselves in garbage. Look at the way that bus driver has almost run over those people in his rush to park near the market and load passengers. That idiot policeman is too busy collecting his cigarette money to notice anything but the weight of the naira in his dirty pocket. No one even bothers that the roadside has become a public toilet. And every building has painted on the wall "This house is not for sale" because fraud is so extensive that 419 men will sell your house to unsuspecting buyers. Just imagine! It was not so during Buhari. You dare not piss on the street. Nigerians, hah! We are an impossible people. We need to be ruled by an iron hand.

This kind of nostalgia is common; so is Nigerians' self-representation of themselves as unruly and undisciplined. Such perceptions contribute to explaining people's readiness to accept and applaud violent vigilante groups like the Bakassi Boys.

In contrast to the military, about which Nigerians seem to have ambivalent feelings, popular perceptions of the police are overwhelmingly negative. In addition to widely shared experiences of extortion at the ubiquitous roadside checkpoints, the police are perceived to be unconcerned about investigating crime, quick to unleash violence on uncooperative citizens (even when they have committed no crime except resisting police extortion), and even complicit in the very epidemic of violent armed robbery that gave rise to the Bakassi Boys. Stories about corruption in the ranks of the police are legion in Nigeria. Particularly galling to ordinary citizens is the treatment they receive when they are the victims of crime. The case of Athan Obioma, a friend whose home was attacked by armed robbers, illustrates some of the typical experiences.

In the middle of the night Athan, his wife, Nkiru, and their four children were awakened by pounding on their front door, accompanied by gunshots. Athan and his family lived in a relatively remote area on the outskirts of the town of Owerri, in housing provided by the agricultural development project for which he worked as an accountant. They had few nearby neighbors. The armed robbers shouted that Athan should open the door, threatening that if they had to gain entrance themselves they would shoot everyone inside. Rather than risk this Athan ushered his wife and children into one bedroom, asked them to lock the door, and then went to the front door and opened it for the thieves. One of the armed robbers hit Athan and told him that he better give them everything or he would lose his life. When Athan asked what they wanted, they said they needed the keys to his car and all the cash in the house. He gave them the keys and all the money in his wallet. The thieves said the money was not enough, that they wanted it all. Athan tried to assure them there was no more money. At that point they demanded to know where his wife and children were, shouting that they would shoot Athan if they did not come out. Fearing the worst, Nkiru opened the locked bedroom door. The thieves told the children to remain inside and then pinned both Athan and Nkiru on the floor, holding guns to their heads. The apparent leader told Athan that if he did not bring out more money, they would rape Nkiru and then kill them both in front of the children. Nkiru told them where she also had some cash hidden, but they were still not satisfied. They hit Athan again several times demanding more, but he pleaded that there was none. Finally they left, taking Athan's car.

Thoroughly terrorized, Athan reported the robbery to the police. The police expressed sympathy but explained to Athan that they had few resources. In order to file a report he would need to provide money for a pen, paper, and funds to open a file for the case. Aggravated, but realizing that the amount was minimal, Athan complied. Once the police had taken his statement, they then explained that the investigation would require transportation and that their office did not have adequate transportation. They requested a larger sum to be able to conduct the investigation. Athan was annoyed but had no choice. He thought the police were his only hope of recovering the car.

In the first week of the investigation the police detained and beat up Athan's driver, though he was not among the armed robbers. They said they suspected an "inside job" and that the driver had likely led the thieves to Athan's relatively remote house. The driver was poor, and although they never extracted any confession or evidence from him, the police demanded a large sum to "bail" him. Athan and Nkiru felt guilty that their poor driver had been beaten and jailed when they had little reason to believe he was involved, and in the end they put up a good deal of the "bail" money to get him out (in Nigeria, bail money is a permanent payment to the police; one does not eventually get it back).

Several weeks into the expensive but unsuccessful investigation, the police informed Athan that they had some leads, but that it was often the case that it was easier to recover stolen cars if money could be provided to key informants who know the circles in which these car thieves move to dispose of their stolen vehicles. Athan agonized over what to do. He knew other Nigerians who had, in fact, recovered their cars by paying the police such sums. On the other hand, he worried that it was just one more way for them to eat his money. In the end he decided to give them the money they asked for, an amount that was equal to almost a fifth of the value of the car. In a few days, the head of the investigation informed him that they had recovered the car, though they had so far been unable to apprehend the thieves. Relieved to recover the car, Athan paid a few more "fees" to get the car released from police custody.

This story, and many others like it, contribute to the popular perception in Nigeria that the police are hopelessly corrupt. Even when the police arrest alleged criminals, Nigerians have little faith that the judicial system will deliver justice. The common perception is that people of means can pay their way out of prison. The courts, like other state institutions, are seen as corrupt. Political power and the capacity to pay bribes are more likely to determine winners and losers before the bench than is the impartial weighing of facts—at least this is the widely held belief among ordinary Nigerians. For poor people, the courts are seen as yet another mechanism through which elites can oppress citizens of lesser means, because it is only those with money and political connections who can prevail. Though Nigerian judges have occasionally stood up to egregious conduct on the part of political leaders, more commonly the courts have rubber-stamped the policies of military and civilian rulers. Even in the local government magistrate courts where average Nigerians can pursue land cases, inheritance disputes, or other civil suits, it is well-known that money talks. In a context where the main institutions of justice are perceived to be corrupt, and in a society where state violence has long been associated with the maintenance of order, violent vigilante groups like the Bakassi Boys find a receptive public.

CRIMINALS AND SOCIAL CLASS

Criminals in southeastern Nigeria operated in ways that made Nigerians feel vulnerable in many arenas. The attacks in markets struck at the heart of people's livelihoods. In addition, armed robbers entered homes at night and committed carjackings in broad daylight on major highways. Each time I visited Nigeria in the late 1990s and early twenty-first century, friends reported having been the victims of armed attacks. More than a score of people I know personally had their cars stolen at gunpoint. Several others had their homes robbed, like Athan and his family, by groups of young men who come late at night wielding guns and knives. Fear of such crimes is exacerbated not only by the fact that criminals will often wound and sometimes kill their victims but also by the kinds of stories that circulated in the Otokoto saga of kidnapped children as well as traffic in humans and their body parts. These criminals behave in ways that deeply violate a shared sense of moral behavior, and the criminals' behavior has come to stand for wider transformations in the structure of inequality. Understanding how these attacks are represented and interpreted in this way is crucial to making sense of the initial support for the Bakassi Boys and vigilantism more generally.

It is a truism that robbers attack victims who they think have something worth taking. People who have their cars stolen are people who can afford to own cars—a small proportion of Nigerian society. Yet violent crime is not popularly understood in class terms that one might easily predict. Several factors contribute to the complicated shape of class consciousness about violent crime. First, the structure of inequality in Nigeria, in which the affective and moral obligations of kinship intertwine with the inequalities and reciprocities of patron-clientism, tends to link rather than oppose the haves and the have-nots (Joseph 1987; Smith 2001b). When a relatively wealthy man has his car stolen in town, his rural kinfolk and other people in his sphere of influence feel genuine sympathy. In addition to affective sentiments motivating their sympathy, they often have more instrumental reasons to be concerned about his welfare because he may serve as their patron.

Second, while it is certainly true that some types of violent crime, such as carjackings, target an elite sector of society, most violent crime affects more ordinary people. In 2002, for example, late one night in his modest flat, armed robbers attacked James, a friend who is a low-level civil servant in the town of Owerri. One of the robbers held a gun to the head of James's four-year-old daughter and demanded that he give them whatever cash was kept in the apartment. The robbers hit this apartment as part of an "operation" in which they swept through several blocks of apartment buildings. While the truly rich are able to protect themselves with high fences, razor wire, dogs, guards, and personal armaments, more ordinary folk such as James feel vulnerable. As is true in U.S. society, the reality of crime in Nigeria is that the elite's sense of vulnerability is exaggerated in relation to actual patterns of crime in which the poor victimize other poor.

Whatever the facts may be with regard to the rates and demographic distribution of violent crime in Nigeria—and to the best of my knowledge no such data exist—the circulation of specific stories personalizes risk and also contributes to a sense of widespread vulnerability. A number of particularly brazen and deadly attacks on public transportation, mainly night buses traveling from the Southeast to Lagos, Nigeria's commercial capital in the Southwest, have captured media and popular attention over the past several years (Baker 2002b). Prior to the founding and regional expansion of the Bakassi Boys, attacks on these night buses resulted in scores of deaths, including several cases where armed bandits killed more than twenty passengers. Attacks on public transportation have similar symbolic consequences as do attacks on the market; both places are vital to the economic and social fabric of society. The reality of attacks on ordinary folk and on markets and mass transportation produces a sense of public vulnerability that obscures some of the political and economic roots of crime, and creates a willingness to embrace vigilante groups and their brand of instant justice.

Perhaps most intriguing with regard to the social imagination about violent criminals in Nigeria is a kind of symbolic inversion that characterizes Nigerians' perceptions of criminals and the causes of violent crime. This inversion is simultaneously an astute commentary on politics and inequality *and* part of a process that deflects attention from the structures and dynamics that underlie the corruption and inequalities people find so troubling. Nigerians widely believe that the most violent armed robbers are children of the elite—sons of politicians and wealthy families. Most often they are popularly represented as university students who have become criminalized (Bastian 2001; Gore and Pratten 2003). These young criminals are described as having been spoiled by their parents' wealth and tainted by their privilege. They are depicted as having no will or incentive to do something productive for society, and are seen as lacking the moral character to care about their fellow human beings. Almost every Nigerian I know aspires to wealth along with a university education for their children, yet wealth and university education are often portrayed as having the potential to produce morally and socially ruinous outcomes.

University campuses in Nigeria are in fact plagued by secret cults in which young men murder members of rival groups (Adekeye 2002; Bastian 2001; Oriji 2003). Capturing extensive media attention, dozens of lives have been lost in university cult clashes, and major Nigerian universities have often been closed in the wake of cult violence (Adekeye 2002). Like armed robbers, university cult members are popularly portrayed as coming from the most elite sectors of society. Uzoma, a twenty-two-year-old student in Owerri, expressed an opinion that I heard from many people: "The guys in the cults are the children of politicians and rich businessmen. They have too much time on their hands. While most of us struggle to pay school fees and worry about how we will eat, these guys drive around in the latest Mercedes-Benzes and wear designer clothes. Daddy pays for everything. They rob, rape, and kill for the thrill. They think they are untouchable. Nigeria na war-o!"

Media accounts over the past few years have occasionally presented cases of armed robbers who have been caught and who were allegedly cult members and children of the elite. No empirical evidence is available regarding the proportion of violent crimes committed by university cult members and children of the elite. I suspect they are few. Yet the perception that children of the elite are criminals reflects not only a popular understanding that the elite are exploiting (and robbing) the poor but also a widely shared sense that the traditional kinship-based patron-client relationships that maintained a moral obligation between the haves and the have-nots are breaking down. As young people seek more modern and urban lives, they frequently challenge their obligations to their rural communities and extended families. Representations of elite university students armed and out of control, while grounded only partly in reality, are symbolically powerful because they resonate with larger concerns about the changing structure of inequality and fears about the disintegration of traditional mechanisms of accountability.

VIGILANTES AS SUPERNATURALLY POWERED SUPERHEROES

Against a history in which the police and the state are viewed as ineffective, corrupt, and even complicit in violent crime, but in a society where supernatural judgment is often perceived as the ultimate mechanism of accountability, and where violence by the state has been normalized and even celebrated as an ethical and effective response against disorder, the Bakassi Boys were not only well received, they were constructed as heroes. Their hero status seemed to blind the public to clear early signs of the risks that vigilantism posed to achieving justice, including the possible loss of innocent individual life and the misuse of extrajudicial "prosecutions" and executions to settle personal and political scores. In the rush to celebrate the apparent curtailment of violent crime, most people were initially impervious to evidence that the Bakassi Boys were being co-opted by politicians and manipulated in political, ethnic, and sectional disputes. In addition, for almost three years, the public largely overlooked indications that the Bakassi Boys themselves seemed increasingly to resemble a criminal gang as much as a supernaturally inspired vigilante force. Before examining the relationship of the Bakassi Boys to politicians and the state, it is important to analyze the processes through which the Bakassi Boys achieved hero status, particularly the belief that they had supernatural power.

Initially, most people in southeastern Nigeria believed that the Bakassi Boys were an effective anticrime force—a view reproduced even in scholarly literature: "There can be no doubt about the dramatic impact of the Bakassi Boys on crime rate. From the time of their inauguration in July 2000 until January 2002, there were practically no armed robberies anywhere in Anambra state" (Baker 2002b, 227). While such claims are perhaps based more on popular accounts than on empirical data, in the years 2000–02 public and private sentiments about the Bakassi Boys were overwhelmingly positive. The comments of Emmanuel, a fifty-one-year-old trader in Umuahia's main market, are typical: "Before Bakassi we did not sleep. Everyone lived in fear. People rushed home after work. The armed robbers had taken over. It was too much. But Bakassi has shown them fire for fire. The criminals know that they will be dealt with mercilessly. They did not fear the police because even if they were caught, with enough money they would be released the next day. The police are useless. Now there is instant justice. With Bakassi we sleep through the night."

The Bakassi Boys' popularity is only partly explained by their apparent reduction of crime, however. Once the Bakassi Boys were formed, they represented themselves and were represented in the media and popular discourse in ways that fueled their symbolic status as heroes enforcing an idiom of accountability tied to the supernatural. The Bakassi Boys' physical appearance—their black attire, dark glasses, amulets, and weapons as well as the feel of their facial expressions—contributed to their image of invulnerability. They looked dangerous and intimidating. Further, the aura of invincibility surrounding the Bakassi Boys and the popular imagery of them ridding society of armed criminals was promoted by various forms of media attention, in newspapers and magazines, but especially through popular media like videos and posters. In 2001, I purchased a three-part series of home videos produced in Nigeria called *Issakaba*. Issakaba is, almost, Bakassi spelled backward. These films, in the genre of docudrama, presented fictional stories that drew on the real-life exploits of the Bakassi Boys, and they were very popular (McCall 2004). In them, the Bakassi Boys are represented as vigilantes protected by charms that enabled them to avoid injury from criminals' bullets and detect innocence or guilt through the magic use of their machetes. Similar depictions of the vigilantes appeared in widely circulating cartoonlike posters. The ability of the Bakassi Boys to magically determine a suspect's innocence or guilt was ironically dubbed in popular discourse a "lab test" (Harnischfeger 2003).

Adding to this image, the Bakassi Boys also adopted personal nicknames that contributed to their supernatural superhero status. These names played on an Igbo tradition of naming to signify accomplishments, most noteworthy in Igbo systems of title taking (Henderson 1972). But the use of these names also served to distance the vigilantes (and those who

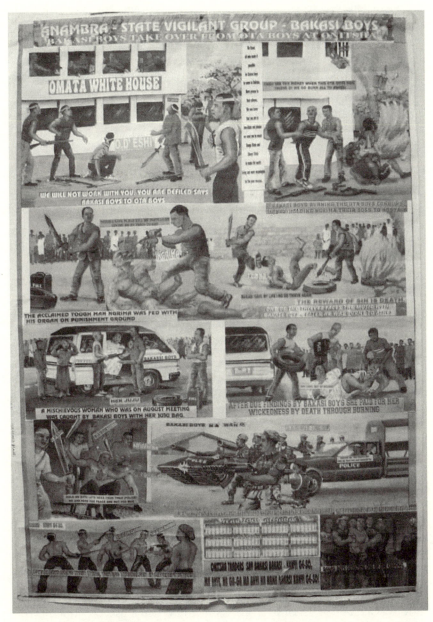

Figure 8. Many variations of posters such as this one, depicting the violent exploits and special powers of the Bakassi Boys, were produced and widely displayed in southeastern Nigeria from 1999 to 2002 (photo by author).

cheered them on) from culpability for their actions. The nicknames included those drawn from U.S. action movies such as "the Terminator," "Rambo," and "Schwarzenegger" as well as Igbo names that translate into phrases such as "God Forbid," "No Mercy," "the Nail," "Final Burial," and "the People's Machete." The superhero image enabled the Nigerian public to justify vigilante executions without empathizing with the executioner or the victim. The experience of witnessing these public executions was not infrequently described as "free film," a poignant and troubling reference to the gratuitous violence prevalent in the U.S. action videos and, increasingly, locally made videos that are popular in Nigeria (Haynes 2000; McCall 2004).

The belief that the Bakassi Boys had supernatural powers was vital to the public confidence in their abilities to catch criminals and distinguish the innocent from the guilty. In a detailed analysis of the case of the Bakassi Boys' extrajudicial execution of Eddy Okeke, a Christian "prophet" widely suspected of using ritual murder to attract followers and magically increase his own wealth, Johannes Harnischfeger (2003) argues persuasively that the Bakassi Boys asserted their legitimacy by demonstrating their capacity to fight not just ordinary criminals but the evils of the occult. Indeed, Ray Abrahams (1996) maintains that the capacity to fight "witches" is part of what gives many vigilante groups legitimacy that the police and other state law enforcement agents lack. Put another way, the Bakassi Boys appealed to and tried to prove their worthiness in an idiom of accountability that in the minds of many ordinary Nigerians, trumps that of the state. In this idiom of accountability, incorruptibility is backed by supernatural power, but supernatural power is only proven by incorruptibility. Each is easily undermined when doubts emerge about the other. As experience with the Bakassi Boys grew, doubts about both their incorruptibility and their supernatural powers emerged.

The importance of the association of incorruptibility and supernatural powers surfaced in many ways. Two or three occasions when members of the Bakassi Boys were reportedly killed in battles with criminals (and later with police) challenged their supernatural status. These stories evoked great debate: some people dismissed the accounts as untrue; others opined that those killed were likely not "real" Bakassi; while a few suggested that the Bakassi Boys were not, in fact, protected by charms. In June 2001, I found myself unexpectedly caught in the middle of a demonstration by several thousand people in the city of Owerri over the launching of a vigilante service by the Imo State government. When I asked people in the crowd what the protest was about, I was surprised when they told me that they were demonstrating against the launching of the Bakassi Boys. It took several more conversations to discover that the anger was not over the Bakassi Boys or vigilantism per se. Instead, it was over a widely shared suspicion that the vigilante group being introduced was not the real Bakassi Boys but rather a group sponsored by the state's increasingly unpopular governor. "These ones are fake," one young man in the crowd told me, "Let us see if their bodies can resist bullets. If not, they are not real Bakassi." The idea that the Bakassi Boys were supernaturally endowed with extrahuman capabilities helps explain not only the confidence people placed in their capacity to combat crime but also the initial lack of public concern about the possibility that they were killing innocent people.

VIGILANTISM, POLITICS, AND THE STATE

As magically empowered superheroes combating violent criminals and evil forces that the corrupt police were unable or unwilling to apprehend, the Bakassi Boys became attractive to politicians who seized on their popularity and attempted to co-opt their vigilante activities for political gain. When news of the "success" of the Bakassi Boys in combating crime spread from Aba to other Igbo-speaking cities in the Southeast, traders' associations and other citizens' groups in Onitsha, Nnewi, Awka, and Umuahia clamored for similar anticrime vigilantism. The governors of Abia and Anambra states responded by inviting the Bakassi Boys to fight crime in major cities under their jurisdiction. The news media reported that state governments were providing vigilante groups with funds and vehicles, and in Anambra, the government passed a law officially creating the Anambra Vigilante Services (Baker 2002b). So close were the ties between the governor and the Anambra Vigilante Services that the latter had an office inside the Government House, the official compound of the state governor.

On May 29, 2001, the Bakassi Boys in Onitsha slaughtered more than thirty alleged criminals in a mass public execution. May 29 is a public holiday in Nigeria, designated as "Democracy Day" to mark the transition to civilian rule in 1999. This mass execution, the timing of which was perhaps calculated by the Bakassi Boys to emphasize their power in Anambra State politics and society, drew in blood some of the fault lines between the federal, state, and local authorities that had emerged in the transition to democracy. The creation of the Anambra Vigilante Services by Governor Chinwoke Mbadinuju, mentioned above, is particularly illustrative for a number of reasons: Anambra went farthest in legally enshrining the Bakassi Boys through the passage of a law creating the Anambra Vigilante Services; the most widely publicized accusations that the Bakassi Boys were themselves agents of corruption, used to intimidate and assassinate political opponents, occurred in Anambra; Anambra's commercial capital Onitsha, reputed to have one of the largest markets in West Africa, was perceived to have the highest level of violent crime in southeastern Nigeria prior to the introduction of the Bakassi Boys, and experienced by far the greatest number of executions carried out by the vigilantes; and federal government attempts to crack down on the Bakassi Boys were most pronounced in Anambra.

The vigilantes were first invited to Anambra by local leaders in the commercial city of Nnewi in April 2000. As a Nigerian newspaper reported,

> The Chairman of Nnewi North Council, Mr. Amobi Chikwendu, tagged the operation "Nnewi Environmental Sanitation Exercise." . . . No fewer than 105 suspected robbers in the town are said to have been killed in extrajudicial execution and security situation in the area has consequently improved. Armed robbers are now fleeing from the zone. . . . The success of the Bakassi Revolution in Aba and Nnewi prompted the Anambra State Governor, Chinweoke Mbadinuju to give a tacit approval to the "sanitation exercise" and recommends it as a panacea to the rising tide of armed banditry in the State since an "unconventional problem calls for an unconventional solution." (Bakassi Boys 2000, 1)

Indeed, by late June 2000, barely two months after the Bakassi Boys "cleansed" Nnewi, Governor Mbadinuju invited them to extend their services to the entire state. Announcing the governor's decision, a prominent daily newspaper reported:

> As the security situation in Anambra state continues to worsen by each passing day, Governor Chinwoke Mbadinuju has approved the operation of the dreaded Aba-based Bakassi Boys vigilante group to take charge of security in the state. . . . Mbadinuju who visited Onitsha over the alarming crime wave in the commercial town Tuesday, formally announced the state government's order on the dreaded Bakassi Boys to extend their services to every nook and cranny of the state. . . . The governor also directed citizens of the state to kill instantly, any confirmed robber in their midst, saying such people were enemies of the society. . . . Mbadinuju who reacted to recent criticisms by some human rights groups and legal bodies over the modus operandi of the Bakassi Boys, said these bodies should rather condemn armed robbers who maim and kill innocent civilians. . . . The governor who was received by a mammoth crowd who chanted "we want Bakassi, we want Bakassi," promised them full government support. (Edike 2000a, 1)

The widespread sense of insecurity and high rates of violent crime created a climate in which a populist rhetoric that called on people to take back the streets appealed to the public. In the wake of the first wave of killings in Anambra in 2000—in which scores, and perhaps hundreds, of alleged criminals were executed—some federal authorities expressed concern. In late July, a spokesperson for the Federal Executive Council announced that it had instructed the Nigerian police to halt the activities of the Bakassi Boys in Onitsha:

> The Federal Executive Council (FEC) yesterday in Abuja directed the Nigerian Police Force (NPF) to stop the activities of the Bakassi Boys, who were invited to contain armed robbery in Onitsha. Announcing the directive after yesterday's FEC meeting, Minister of Economic Matters, Mr. Vincent Ogbulafor, said the council has directed NPF, through the Minister of Police Affairs, to flush out all Bakassi Boys from Onitsha immediately. He said the FEC's decision followed reports that the Bakassi Boys, who were invited by the Governor of Anambra State to put a check on the mayhem perpetrated by armed robbers in the commercial city, had taken "laws into their hands and were killing innocent people." According to him, the Bakassi group had been infiltrated by "bad eggs" who were being used to perpetrate havoc on innocent people who fell victim in the process of settling scores. (FG asks police 2000, 1)

Several things are striking about the initial announcement authorizing the police to intervene. First, in choosing Ogbulafor, an Igbo-speaking minister from the Southeast, to make this announcement, the government clearly recognized the potential for the ban to be interpreted as an anti-Igbo decision. Second, Ogbulafor's assertion that bad eggs had infiltrated the vigilante group was a tactical move not to challenge the public faith in the efficacy of the "real" Bakassi Boys. Third, and most significant, the crackdown never occurred. Local public reaction to the federal government's announcement was swift and strong, with public opinion in the Southeast clearly favoring the preservation of the Bakassi Boys. Sentiments expressed by residents in Onitsha, as reported in a newspaper story, are representative of similar comments I heard from people in Owerri and Umuahia as these events unfolded:

> A cross-section of the people who spoke on the development express dismay over the decision of the federal government to flush out the Bakassi Boys whom, they now regard as their "messiah." Ogbuefi Okonkwo a trader in Onitsha told *Vanguard* that "The federal government appeared to be unfair to the people of this area, otherwise how can one ever think of exposing the citizenry to armed robbers who have laid siege on the state recently." Okonkwo wondered why the government kept quiet all these while that men of the underworld were terrorizing innocent citizens in the state, saying it was completely wrong for government to order the police to flush out the Bakassi Boys when adequate security arrangement has not been made for the state. He stated that since the Bakassi people came to Onitsha, the town has been crime-free and asked the federal government to try to feel the pulse of the people. (Edike 2000b, 1)

Why the federal government failed to follow through with its plans is not clear. Harnischfeger (2003) reports that rumors (almost certainly false) circulating in Onitsha claimed the Bakassi Boys repelled federal forces at the outskirts of the city. Whatever the reality, Governor Mbadinuju represented the government's inaction as the outcome of his personal lobbying of President Obasanjo: "I have sufficiently explained to President Obasanjo about the activities of the Bakassi Boys and he has lifted the ban and this presidential approval of Bakassi Boys was received with joy by people of Anambra State" (Onwubiko 2000, 1). Although the governor's version of what transpired was obviously politically inspired, it is nonetheless true that in Anambra, as well as in Abia and Imo states, the federal government never made any attempt to check the activities of the Bakassi Boys until the crackdown in August and September 2002.

The federal government's tolerance of the Bakassi Boys reflected its reluctance to challenge powerful local idioms of accountability when its own legitimacy seemed so precarious. The Bakassi Boys' popularity and the success with which politicians in the Southeast cast vigilantism in populist terms meant that disbanding them would have potentially destabilizing political repercussions. From the federal government's perspective, the populism expressed in vigilantism was most dangerous precisely because of its potential to exacerbate already powerful cleavages in the Nigerian polity. Federal authorities faced a dilemma. Allowing such groups to exist posed the risk that they could be mobilized for political purposes, but banning them might stoke the very ethnic and regional polarization they hoped to avoid.

ETHNIC MILITIAS AND RELIGION

While politicians in the Southeast did everything possible to represent the Bakassi Boys to the federal government in nonethnic terms, representation of them as an Igbo organization was powerful in local discourse. Igbos took pride in the national reputation of the Bakassi Boys as a "dreaded force"—dreaded by criminals, but also inspiring great fear in the larger society. In the aftermath of Nigeria's civil war from 1967 to 1970, in which Igbos lost their bid to secede from Nigeria and create the independent state of Biafra, they have continuously decried their marginalization in Nigerian politics and governance. Letters and editorials lamenting this marginalization appear in newspapers almost daily, and everyday political conversation in the Southeast inevitably turns to the issue. Local discourse about the Bakassi Boys frequently cited the success of indigenous vigilantism as an example of how much better Igbos could do if they were left to govern themselves.

The statement of my friend Ikechi, a fifty-six-year-old man who ran a small provisions store, exemplifies similar comments I heard from many people: "The police do nothing. Their only interest is lining their pockets with our money. They do not care about the welfare of our people. When the Igbo man works hard to earn a living they simply blackmail us into subsidizing their lives. Crime was ruining business. The Bakassi Boys have taken back the market. We are the ones who know how to deal with these problems. If the Igbo man were given a free hand in Nigeria there would not be so many problems." The fact that the Nigerian police are a federal force is a significant part of the story. Police officers are usually deployed away from their places of origin, and police commanders in the Southeast are most often non-Igbos. A corrupt federal police force believed to tolerate and even collude in crime reinforces the local sense that people are not in control of their own governance, and for Igbos this is exacerbated by the legacy of Biafra. Among ordinary Igbos, the Bakassi Boys' popularity was fanned by a collective sense of political marginalization.

Despite their obvious appeals to Igbo pride, the Bakassi Boys denied having any political ambitions or affiliations. To stave off federal intervention, local politicians worked hard to avoid any perception that the Bakassi Boys were an "ethnic militia." Indeed, compared with the O'odua People's Congress in the Yoruba Southwest or the Egbesu Boys in the Niger Delta, organizations that had explicit political and ethnic agendas, the Bakassi Boys seemed much less politically and ethnically oriented. Yet local support for the Bakassi Boys and the initial federal decision to disband the vigilante group produced strong regional and ethnic sentiments that contributed to the popular resistance to federal intervention. In Onitsha, for example, thousands of traders marched to the Government House to express solidarity with the Bakassi Boys.

Igbo support for the Bakassi Boys, however, is only partly attributable to regional interest and ethnic pride. Popular justification for the Bakassi Boys also incorporated a religious dimension that reflected the increasing role of religious difference as a polarizing force in Nigeria, albeit in ways that intersect with ethnic and regional divisions. Since the transition to civilian rule in 1999, many mostly Islamic northern Nigerian states have instituted sharia law, asserting their right to do so under Nigeria's ostensibly decentralized federal system. Just as the mostly Christian population in the Southeast justified the Bakassi Boys as a means to fight crime in a society where the state's institutions of justice are corrupt, many Nigerian Muslims justified the need for sharia law on similar grounds. The federal government's hands-off approach to sharia in northern Nigeria was motivated by political calculations similar to their initial tolerance of the Bakassi Boys. Intervention would involve considerable political costs. The parallel between sharia law and vigilante justice existed not only in calculations of government officials. I heard many Igbos discuss the Bakassi Boys as the Igbo alternative to sharia. The words of Ferguson Nwoke, a fifty-two-year-old unemployed Catholic, are similar to several statements I collected about the parallels between them: "Crime in Nigeria was out of control. The Hausas instituted sharia law to restore order. That's their justice. They cut off people's hands when they steal and stone to death adulterers. Bakassi is our sharia. The Bakassi Boys have restored sanity to the society. If government allows the North to have sharia, why should we not have Bakassi?"

In fact, no one has actually been stoned to death under sharia law in northern Nigeria, despite high-profile sharia court rulings ordering such punishment. While Igbos and Christian southerners generally are apt to condemn sharia as primitive and barbaric, the Bakassi Boys were far more violent and deadly than anything that has resulted from sharia law. Nonetheless, the parallels that many Igbos drew between sharia and the Bakassi Boys' justice reflect the degree to which vigilantism was justified and federal intervention was resisted in the name of local rights as well as idioms of accountability that rejected crime and corruption, and called on regional, ethnic, and religious identities.

"THEY BECAME THE CRIMINALS THEY WERE SUPPOSED TO FIGHT"

I witnessed the Bakassi Boys in action several times during my fieldwork in 2000–02. Twice in the town of Umuahia and once in Owerri, I happened to be in or near the main market when the Bakassi Boys swooped down on an alleged criminal. Each time, they descended in groups of fifteen to twenty men to capture their quarry. Crowds gathered quickly to see these free films. I saw alleged criminals bleeding from machete blows to their bodies, their limbs bound and most of their clothes stripped. Twice, the Bakassi Boys bundled their prisoners into a vehicle and sped off, reportedly to sites on the outskirts of town where they conducted "trials" and carried out executions of those found "guilty." On the third occasion, the execution took place at the scene of the purported crime. I watched for a few minutes as the crowd grew, but I left before the trial (an event that can be completed in a matter of minutes) and execution. I had long since concluded that the crowds and the popularity of instant justice increased the incidence of these events. If I watched, I felt I would be complicit.

Though I did not witness any executions, on several occasions I saw the results: dismembered burned corpses that had yet to be removed from the streets. Many people I know in southeastern Nigeria witnessed executions conducted by the Bakassi Boys. While some expressed horror at the brutality of what they saw, such discomfort mixed fluidly with stories told laughingly of the Bakassi Boys playing soccer with the decapitated heads of their victims. I am unable to document or estimate accurately the number of people killed by these vigilantes. Amnesty International (2002) estimated over one thousand extrajudicial executions; Human Rights Watch (2002) claimed to have confirmed well over a hundred killings in Onitsha alone. Reading Nigerian newspapers and listening to popular stories of widely discussed executions—those where many alleged criminals were killed at once—leads me to believe that the number is at least in the hundreds.

The executions that received the most publicity and were documented in greatest detail in Human Rights Watch's (2002) extensive report were cases in which the people killed were high-profile public figures. One was a politician and former local government chairman who was an outspoken political opponent of Anambra governor Mbadinuju; another was the previously mentioned Okeke, the popular Christian prophet who promised miracles to his followers (Harnischfeger 2003), but who was accused in popular rumors (and on widely circulated posters) of being involved in ritual murder. The executions of these men by the Bakassi Boys created much publicity, in part because they demonstrated both the extent and potential abuses of the Bakassi Boys' powers. The brutal murder in 2002 of Barnabas Igwe, president of the Anambra chapter of the Nigerian Bar Association and a leading critic of the Anambra State government's role in supporting the Bakassi Boys, seemed to catalyze the federal government's decision to disband the vigilante group. Igwe had been a leader in a growing chorus of criticism of violent vigilantism by Nigerian civil liberties groups. He and his wife were assassinated in a barbaric murder in which the killers repeatedly ran over the victims' bodies with the Igwes' own car. It was widely suspected that Igwe was executed by the Bakassi Boys, perhaps on the orders of their political patrons, in retaliation for his prominent role in criticizing the vigilantes and the politicians who used them.

These high-profile cases likely contributed to the federal government's decision to intervene. But in order to understand the gradual change in popular sentiment about the Bakassi Boys that made government intervention politically feasible, one needs to examine the perpetration of corruption and violence by the Bakassi Boys on the very public that had supported them. Although they invoked and relied on an idiom of accountability tied to the supernatural, their legitimacy was ultimately destroyed by their involvement in the same corruption and crime they ostensibly fought.

The media documented the names of only a few of the victims executed by the Bakassi Boys. Most remained nameless even after their deaths—a fact that belies the popular representation of criminals as children of the elite. While public support for vigilantism hinged in part on a construction of criminals as elites, government tolerance of extrajudicial killing almost surely depended on the fact that the powerless were the ones who were actually executed. Yet in the end, the realization that the Bakassi

Boys served the interests of politicians and used their power to exploit rather than rescue the public led to the erosion of popular support. Stories began to circulate that personalized the accumulation of everyday violence and injustices perpetrated by them. Gradually, some of the dead became real people with names, mothers, families, and communities.

Several friends told me that the Bakassi Boys abducted young men in their communities as alleged criminals, only to demand ransom for their release. Many people were directly affected by the levies the Bakassi Boys imposed on businesses of every size—fees increasingly viewed as protection money. Stories of poor petty traders being beaten by the Bakassi Boys for failing to pay their levies exemplified public displeasure with the Bakassi Boys' exploitation of their powerful position. Numerous accounts circulated that the Bakassi Boys were being hired to intervene in local disputes, not as impartial judges, but as paid muscle for one side over the other. These stories all undermined the image of the Bakassi Boys as incorruptible superheroes dedicated to eradicating crime. By the morning of August 3, 2002, when I witnessed the police occupying and destroying the Bakassi Boys' headquarters next to my tennis club in Umuahia, my friend Levinus Okeh, who once extolled the virtues of vigilantism, said, "Good riddance to the bastards. They became the criminals they were supposed to fight."

The Legacy of the Bakassi Boys

In August and September 2002, on orders from the federal government, Nigeria's Mobile Police Force attacked the Bakassi Boys in the main cities in the Southeast where they operated. The police killed an untold number of the Bakassi Boys and detained scores of others. Federal government spokespersons asserted that the vigilante group was banned, and for a period of time, they seemed to disappear from the scene. The Bakassi Boys had undermined their own popularity through their collaboration with politicians, availability as thugs for hire, and extortion of the very public they proclaimed to protect. Nevertheless, the idea of vigilante justice and the dream of a society in which criminals of all stripes (be they armed robbers or corrupt politicians) are subject to popular accountability remain extremely powerful among the masses.

In the run up to Nigeria's elections in April 2003, many politicians in the Southeast called for the reinstitution of vigilantism—albeit always arguing for real vigilantes. Since the elections, newly elected officials have promised to revitalize groups like the Bakassi Boys, and local traders in Onitsha have apparently formed a new vigilante force to protect the market. Chris Ngige, the embattled governor in Anambra State, was reportedly protected by vigilantes, often described in the press as the Bakassi Boys, when his federal security force was withdrawn. Most recently, in September 2005, newspapers in Nigeria reported that twenty-seven people were found dead in the city of Aba in a small detention center apparently run by a revitalized vigilante force described as the Bakassi Boys. Whether these new incarnations of the Bakassi Boys include many of the same individuals as the earlier groups or whether they are simply representing themselves or being labeled in the media using the familiar name remains unclear.

Continued distrust of the police and other institutions of state justice has also led to other innovative and potentially dangerous forms of extrajudicial accountability. For example, in Aba, a novel type of "street justice" has recently emerged. If a criminal is caught in the act of stealing, if a car accident occurs, or if two individuals' disagreement escalates to the point where onlookers take notice, "people's courts" are constituted immediately, the cases are "tried," and sentences are passed and carried out. Seemingly random onlookers and passersby become lawyers, judges, and juries (and in the most disturbing cases, executioners). While the consequences of some of these cases of street justice seem innocuous enough—for example, a car driver is made to pay the hospital costs of a motorcycle driver he collided with—the opportunities for injustice, including extrajudicial execution, abound. Indeed, the couple of incidents I witnessed myself, both of which resulted from traffic accidents, seem to suggest that the force of individual characters who were protagonists in these unfolding dramas determined the outcome as much as any principles of justice.

But the popularity of these forms of people's justice in places like Aba is unmistakable, attributable largely to people's sense of disappointment with corruption plaguing the institutions of the state. When I was in Aba in June 2003, I asked numerous local people their reactions to the demise of the Bakassi Boys. By far the most common response was illustrated in the words of a textile trader in Kent Market, who said, "Now the whole of Aba is Bakassi." What he meant, and what many others expressed, was that the people have taken the task of assuring public safety and punishing criminals into their own hands. Just as the police and the state could not be trusted, neither could the Bakassi Boys. The irony is that it is people's expectations for—as well as their disappointments with—the promises of democracy that have created a situation where opportunities to do injustice in the name of justice have multiplied.

The popularity of violent vigilantism in Nigeria must be understood as part of a complex intertwining of people's experiences of everyday corruption and violence, and the particular political structures and symbolic systems that both produce these experiences and provide the means to interpret them. Vigilantism in Nigeria responded to public perceptions of injustice that projected onto violent crime popular understandings of the roots of poverty, corruption, and inequality. Ironically, the symbolic construction of vigilantism obscured its entanglements with the state and the political processes that reproduce the injustices that gave rise to the Bakassi Boys. The way in which discourses of democracy and notions of civil society were deployed both in public interpretations and politicians' manipulation of vigilantism should give pause to any simplistic conclusions about the relationship between civil society and the state in Nigeria's postmilitary democracy. The Bakassi Boys were both antagonistic to the state and co-opted by it. Their ambiguous relationship to the state mirrors a dualism that characterizes Nigerians' experiences of politics. Ordinary Nigerians are simultaneously conciliatory and antagonistic to the state (Gore and Pratten 2003, 218–19). The deep entanglements of the state and civil society produce tremendous ambivalence, creating a climate where competing idioms of accountability at once contradict and complement each other.

In order to understand the popularity of violent vigilantism, it is necessary to see this popularity as an act of political imagination—one that simultaneously expresses condemnation of the realities of crime and corruption that underlie inequality in Nigeria while also distancing people from them. Understanding the complex confluence of political processes, symbolic meanings, and everyday experience that can make some forms of violence popular offers the best hope for constructing alternatives. The resurgence of ethnic nationalism and the burgeoning popularity of born-again Christianity in southeastern Nigeria, phenomena examined in the next chapter, offer different, but equally complex examples of how Nigerians have responded to their frustrations and discontents with corruption and its associated ills.

CHAPTER 7

Anticorruption Aspirations: Biafrans and Born-again Christians

NIGERIANS ARE BOMBARDED every day with state propaganda about government efforts to combat corruption. Soon after the transition to democracy in 1999, with great fanfare, President Obasanjo created the Economic and Financial Crimes Commission along with the Independent Corrupt Practices and Other Related Offences Commission, promising that these offices would put teeth into anticorruption efforts that were lacking in the late General Abacha's hypocritical "Not in Our Character" campaign. Many Nigerians suspected that these new bureaucracies would go the way of their predecessors, providing lip service to the ideals of government accountability and transparency, but offering little in the way of real action. Indeed, more than a few of my friends and associates cynically suggested that the new offices would simply create additional layers of bureaucracy through which politicians and high-level civil servants could pad their fortunes.

Achille Mbembe (1992), Jean François Bayart (1993), and others have demonstrated the ways in which postcolonial African states exercise power by manipulating the fictions of a liberal democracy to further enable rapacious corruption and an obscene accumulation of wealth. Average Nigerians are well aware of the hypocrisy and corruption of their leaders, and recognize the tragicomic nature of state efforts to implement anticorruption programs. As I have shown in previous chapters, ordinary citizens are also cognizant and critical of their own participation, recognizing that as they seek favors from and put pressure on their own patrons to deliver a share of the national cake, they are sometimes contributing to the perpetuation of corruption.

Although Nigerian citizens are skeptical and often contemptuous of official anticorruption efforts, passionate popular aspirations for a less corrupt society are powerfully expressed in unofficial idioms. Corruption is frequently interpreted and challenged through the lenses and languages of ethnicity and religion. Resurging ethnic nationalisms and burgeoning participation in popular religious movements, in both the mostly Muslim North and the predominantly Christian South, have created cultural spaces in which ever-larger numbers of citizens interpret and challenge corruption and inequality in contemporary Nigeria. In southeastern Nigeria, these trends are manifest in a revival of Igbo nationalism and a spectacular growth in the popularity of Pentecostal and other forms of charismatic and evangelical Christianity. Both can be characterized, in part, as anticorruption movements. Ethnic nationalism and religion offer ordinary citizens the frameworks through which to interpret the struggles and contradictions of everyday life, the language with which to express their frustrated aspirations, and the social communities through which some of their ambitions can be pursued. Corruption is, of course, only part of what inspires ethnic nationalism and religious revivalism. But to the extent that discontents about corruption parallel broader frustrations and aspirations associated with the trajectories of social change in Nigeria, and in many postcolonial settings, examining the anticorruption aspects of these phenomena is illuminating. The results of resurgent Igbo ethnic nationalism and burgeoning Pentecostal Christianity in southeastern Nigeria beg the question of whether these trends are hopeful or discouraging.

CORRUPTION, MARGINALIZATION, AND ETHNIC NATIONALISM

Since the Igbo Southeast lost its bid for independence in Nigeria's civil war from 1967 to 1970, the prevailing popular political discourse in southeastern Nigeria has been that of marginalization. In columns written by Igbo writers in newspapers and magazines, letters to editors, comments made through call-in programs on local radio and television stations, and most of all, everyday conversations, the Igbo preoccupation with their marginalization in postwar Nigeria is profound. Igbo complaints about their marginal status in Nigeria take many forms, including claims that federal government resources are channeled disproportionately to other regions, that rules for appointments to civil service positions and entrance into government secondary and tertiary educational institutions are deliberately weighted against Igbos, and that official information and state data collection exercises such as census taking are purposely designed to undercount Igbos and thwart their rightful share of political representation as well as government revenues.

While Igbo complaints about marginalization are manifold, Igbo discontent is most powerfully expressed in their perceived exclusion from three institutions: the presidency, the military, and the NNPC. Igbos have been appointed to some of the highest posts in the federal government (for instance, in the current Obasanjo administration Igbos head both the Ministry of Finance and the Central Bank), but since the civil war there has been no Igbo military head of state and no Igbo civilian president, and Igbos have occupied few of the highest posts in the military or the NNPC. Exclusion from these institutions is more than symbolic; in Nigeria's military and oil-dominated postcolonial history, controlling the center has translated into controlling the preponderance of the nation's wealth and power.

Discerning the relative marginalization of Igbos is a political project beyond my scope. I am interested, though, in how Igbo discourses about marginalization and the resurgence of Igbo nationalism that has occurred since the transition to civilian rule in 1999 are closely intertwined with Igbo understandings of corruption. On the one hand, cries of marginalization—particularly the focus on Igbo absence in the highest offices in the federal government, the military, and the oil industry—must be read as an expression of dissatisfaction over being excluded from the mechanisms of corruption through which most people believe that the national cake is shared. Igbos are angry, in part, because they believe they are not getting their share of the national patrimony. On the other hand, ethnic nationalist rhetoric builds on and stokes anger and discontent over the very system of corruption itself. Ordinary Igbos who support or at least sympathize with the idea of independence from Nigeria express both the desire for a bigger share of the patronage pie and the aspiration for a less corrupt and more equal society.

The resurgence of ethnic nationalism is happening in many other parts of Nigeria as well. The O'odua People's Congress represents one strain of Yoruba nationalism in the Southwest. Multiple groups in the oil-producing Niger Delta articulate desires for autonomy or independence, expressing popular discontent over the extreme corruption, exploitation, and inequality created in the management of Nigeria's oil industry. While ethnic nationalist organizations exploit frustrations about corruption to build support for their causes, interpreting corruption and inequality in a language that highlights ethnic discrimination, these same groups are themselves targets of charges of corruption. The prominence of corruption as both a justification for nationalist movements and a critique to undermine them illustrates both the extent of discontent about corruption and Nigerians' cynicism that anyone can rise above it.

BIAFRAN DREAMS AND CORRUPTION DIALOGUES

On May 22, 2000, Ralph Uwazurike led a symbolic hoisting of the Biafran flag in the city of Aba in southeastern Nigeria and declared the intention of the Movement for the Actualization of the Sovereign State of Biafra (MASSOB) to lead a revival of the Igbo quest for independence from Nigeria. Known among MASSOB followers as the "Aba Declaration," Uwazurike's speech marked the birth of the most vocal and organized Igbo nationalist effort since the civil war. Although only a few hundred people attended the ceremony, in Igbo communities across Nigeria the renewed call for Biafra and the possibility of independence from Nigeria sparked the popular imagination. While many Igbos do not support the idea of secession from Nigeria, and while most Igbos I know seem to view the possibility of an independent Biafra in the immediate future as an unrealistic dream, the emergence of MASSOB triggered a torrent of discussion, debate, and critical commentary.

Much of the popular discourse about MASSOB and a new Biafra amplified long-standing Igbo complaints. Many of the reasons people offered in justifying the call for independence focused on the evils of corruption in Nigeria, particularly as it functioned to exclude and divide the Igbo. Independence would free Igbos from Nigeria's corrupt hold, the supporters of MASSOB asserted, and they would thrive as a result. In the years following the creation of MASSOB, such views have circulated commonly in ordinary conversations and are regularly reproduced in the media. The following excerpt from a column in one of Nigeria's major daily newspapers is illustrative.

> In the six years of the Obasanjo presidency, we continue to experience a skewered attention to the various parts of the federation. Igbo interests still do not count. New power stations for instance have been built in Ondo and Ogun states, the entire infrastructure of the Nigerian oil industry has been strategically appropriated by Obasanjo and his kinsmen, from oil production to oil pricing. A new multibillion-naira terminal is being constructed at the Lagos airport, the Gateway Cargo airport is currently under construction by the federal government in Ogun state, the largest LNG project is slated for Ondo, and all these are good things. They should be built in those places. What the Igbo ask is: "where is our own?" What is the Igbo stake in Nigeria worth? The Nigerian commonwealth has treated the Igbo, especially, and our minority neighbours shabbily. The Obasanjo government continues a relentless pattern of subjugation. Eastern roads are no longer the issue. The complaints are to no avail.
>
> The other devil on the Igbo shoulder thus is the Nigerian state itself as it is currently constructed. I have written that Nigeria is a burden to the Igbo. Left alone, the Igbo would soar to the stars. Nigeria has almost destroyed the Igbo dream and ability to transcend the conditions of coloniality. (Nwakanma 2005)

The references to the investments in airports and petroleum-related projects in southwestern states imply that major government investments are made on the basis of a corrupt system in which the president steers money to his own region and ethnic group. Having never held the ultimate reins of power since the civil war, most Igbos believe that they regularly lose out in the sharing of the biggest pieces of the national cake.

While Igbos generally believe that the interests of their region have been neglected since the civil war, not all who share this sense of marginalization see independence as desirable or feasible. Among people who think that independence will not happen, corruption is put forward as a major reason. In one view, Igbo independence would be too threatening to Nigeria's corruption machine, and elites in the rest of Nigeria would never allow it to happen. An independent Biafra would be too close to the country's oil reserves and might even lead the peoples of the Niger Delta to embark on similar paths toward independence. The rest of Nigeria would fight to save the national patrimony—the oil. During one of the regular debates about Biafra that occurred at the club where I played tennis in Umuahia in 2004, Dr. James Ifediora argued with his friends who asserted that Igbo independence is the best solution to the current economic hardship. Rebutting several interlocutors who echoed the sentiment in the above newspaper column—that left on their own the Igbo would thrive—he said: "Not as long as there is oil. You think they will let us go and take the oil? No way! They went to war with us once already to protect the oil and they will do it again. What is the struggle to sit on top of Aso Rock [the name of the presidential villa in Abuja] if not to control the oil? That *is* Nigeria. If you create Biafra with no oil, what would we be but another little landlocked African country with no resources? It will never happen. Without the oil we are nothing. If we want the oil they will kill us first."

Ifediora's position reflects not only a widely held conviction that the larger Nigeria would fight hard to hold onto the oil-producing regions but the memory that at least one reason Biafra lost the civil war was that Nigeria managed to convince populations in many oil-producing areas that they would be better off with Nigeria than with the Igbos. Although some oil is produced in Igbo territory, the bulk is pumped from smaller minority communities south of the Igbo region and in waters offshore from these minority communities. While minority groups in the Niger Delta (for example, the Ogoni and the Ijaw) are deeply dissatisfied with their treatment in Nigeria, few would welcome becoming minorities in an Igbo-dominated Biafra. Many Igbos agree with Ifediora that Nigeria will never allow secession as long as there is oil money to steal and share.

Another prevalent position about the relationship between corruption and the possible revival of Biafra is the complaint that Igbos themselves are too corrupt to engineer their independence. Igbo leaders, this view suggests, have long proven their willingness to betray collective interests for personal gain. Even people with pro-Biafra positions sometimes lament the disunity sown by corruption. One of the main mechanisms through which pro-Biafran propaganda is disseminated is the shortwave radio broadcasts of the Voice of Biafra International, which airs every Wednesday and Saturday nights from 10:00 to 11:00 p.m. local time. The station apparently transmits from somewhere outside Nigeria, and is managed and financed by Igbos living abroad. Even some of the station's pro-Biafra propaganda emphasizes the consequences of Igbo corruption and the willingness of ordinary Igbos not only to tolerate elite corruption but to facilitate it. Excerpts from a Voice of Biafra International broadcast on November 27, 2004, exemplify common Igbo concerns about their participation in and tolerance for corruption.

> Since the end of the Biafra-Nigeria war in 1970, several Igbo criminals have been doing things to completely destroy Igbo society. First you had traitors who called themselves Ndigbo [the Igbo plural for Igbos], then joined the enemy to slaughter and starve to death millions of Ndigbo. The war ended and they just walked back into Igbo land to share kola nut, food, and drinks with the same people they just planned to murder. The Igbo did not ask any questions. Igbo did not protest or take action against these murderers. After watching how these traitors were received a new group of criminals emerged. They took money meant for contract jobs like providing electricity, pipe-borne water, roads, and bridges for the Igbo. They took the money and did not do the job. The Igbo made them chiefs and gave them big titles. The Igbo did not protest. Igbo did not ask questions. Igbo did not punish them. The next group of criminals watched and learned.
>
> The new group was no longer satisfied with just stealing the money meant for development projects for the Igbo, they actually shut down institutions like schools, hospitals, courts, and the civil service meant to serve the people. Not only did the Igbo not ask any questions, the Igbo gave them titles. The Igbo called them big names like "Oderaa" [the honorary title of the former governor of Anambra State, Chinwoke Mbadinuju, who became a symbol of politicians' venality] and worshipped them. The Igbo did not fight back, they merely protested meekly. Other criminals watched and learned. Now there are new kids on the block, the new criminals. Since the Igbo never fight back the new criminals have a new program for the Igbo: First they will take over the government and its apparatuses including governor, commissioner, police, everything. Then they will take over institutions like schools, courts, [and] hospitals, and use them as their private property. They will give themselves the right to use them or destroy them as they wish. Finally they will deal ruthlessly with anyone who opposes their wish to do whatever they like. They will kill, maim, burn, rape, you name it and they will do it. Once they arrive at this point the society goes into [a] coma and needs intensive care to survive.
>
> Ndigbo! Ndigbo!! Ndigbo!!! It is time to take your society back.

The various groups of "criminals" referred to in the broadcast are familiar to all Igbos—they are the Igbo leaders who collaborated with Nigeria during the war, the Igbo economic and political elite of the 1980s and 1990s who accepted contracts and payoffs from the military in exchange for political support, and the Igbo politicians and their godfathers in the post-1999 democratic dispensation who have turned public offices into private empires. Indeed, the final passages of the broadcast are obviously a direct reference to the recent crisis in Anambra State. Venality, in this widely shared view, has been the Igbos' undoing. Critical commentary about corruption features prominently in the collective discourse about Biafra, whether it is to promote independence or deride its feasibility.

Okada Drivers' Debates

In southeastern Nigeria and the larger Igbo diaspora across the country and around the globe, support and skepticism regarding a Biafran revival extend across socioeconomic boundaries. Debates about the desirability and viability of Igbo independence occur among the rich and the poor, among the highly educated and the illiterate, and in urban neighborhoods and village hamlets. A good deal of the most visible pro-Biafra propaganda is produced by Igbos living abroad, particularly in Great Britain and the United States. In addition to the Voice of Biafra International, several popular Web sites and many e-mail listserves are maintained by Igbos abroad who support the proposition of a new Biafra. The vocal support for Biafra in the Igbo diaspora is something of a luxury that those at home in Nigeria cannot always afford, either because they are too busy struggling for economic survival or because of the risks of state-sponsored intimidation and detention. The Nigerian government has been inconsistent in its reaction to MASSOB, sometimes tolerating its actions, and at other times cracking down violently and arresting its members for various alleged crimes, including treason. While Igbos in Nigeria seem to have little fear of engaging in boisterous debates and discussions about Biafra, participating in overt political action to implement an independence agenda carries many more risks, and the numbers of people willing to face violence, imprisonment, or death in the name of the revival of Biafra remain few.

Although the most ardent proindependence activists seem to be Igbos abroad, within Nigeria it is relatively poor men in urban areas who are the most vocal proponents and interested interlocutors in the public debates about reviving Biafra. During my fieldwork over the past several years, two groups in particular have stood out for the verve with which they engage in arguments, discussions, gossip, and rumors about the possibility of Igbo independence: the small armies of motorcycle taxi (okada) drivers in Nigeria's cities, and the masses of young men who work in Nigeria's sprawling markets as merchants, apprentices, or hawkers. In the idle time when business is negligible, these people can spend hours circulating the latest news, debating the truth or merit of various points, and arguing over the best way forward in a society where nearly all agree that corruption has enriched the elite and relegated the poor to suffer the injustices of inequality.

To most urban residents in southeastern Nigeria, okada drivers symbolize the dangers of urban life but also the ruggedness of ordinary Nigerians in the face of urban poverty. Okada drivers have a reputation for being reckless, rough, and prone to rioting. Accidents involving automobiles and motorcycle taxis draw scores of supportive okada drivers in a few minutes. The motorcyclists frequently intimidate and demand compensation from automobile drivers. During the reign of the Bakassi Boys, okada drivers made up a large portion of the most enthusiastic audiences for extrajudicial executions, and in the street trials that have taken place in Aba and other cities after the demise of the Bakassi Boys, okada drivers are frequently active participants. Even the police are careful in how they deal with okada drivers; the Nigerian press has carried many accounts of deadly clashes between the two groups.

Okada drivers are highly organized and politically engaged. During the last two elections in 1999 and 2003, Governor Orji Uzo Kalu of Abia State garnered significant urban support (and recruited a small army of potential political thugs) by pledging and then creating a program to provide okada drivers with new motorcycles on credit. Although they have been recruited and co-opted by mainstream politicians such as Governor Kalu, okada drivers are among the most ardent supporters of the new Biafra movement. They spend hours at newsstands in towns across southeastern Nigeria, discussing the country's ills, debating the best solutions to the problems of corruption and inequality, and sharing the latest political rumors, including those about MASSOB and Biafra.

My experience with the political discourse of okada drivers began because I stopped regularly at newsstands to peruse and purchase Nigerian newspapers and magazines. The size of the assemblies of okada drivers at newsstands has definitely increased over recent years—a fact attributable to both the growth in the absolute numbers of okada in virtually every city and town, but also perhaps to a freeing of political discourse and an enlivened press since the transition to civilian rule in 1999.[1] The crowds of motorcyclists can be intimidating. Okada drivers typically wear hats, dark glasses, and various jackets, sweaters, or sweatshirts purchased in the used clothing markets, which most urban poor rely on for their wardrobes. The okada drivers' sartorial style is mostly functional—meant to protect them from the sun, the rain, or the perceived cold of morning and night— but their appearance is rugged and menacing. Urban Nigerians frequently refer to okada drivers as ruffians. Although at first I tried to avoid them in my visits to the local newsstands, the more I overheard the intensely political nature of their conversations, the more interested I became in their perspectives on politics, corruption, and whatever current event captured the popular imagination at the moment.

Okada drivers are mostly young; over the years many have told me that they resent the work they are forced to do to survive. Young motorcyclists who have finished or dropped out of secondary school but cannot find other jobs make up an increasingly large proportion of the profession.[2] They commonly attribute their struggles to the corruption of elites and the failures of the Nigerian state to act on behalf of the masses. A good deal of okada drivers' anger over state corruption has been channeled into an ethnic nationalist discourse in which poverty and inequality are explained in terms of Igbo marginalization. Though most okada drivers are too young to remember the actual events of the civil war, they have become primary agents through which collective memories are revised and recirculated.[3] Leaders of MASSOB normally distribute their leaflets and posters at these newsstands, not only because they are places to read news but because okada drivers are renowned for their role in sharing information with each other and their clients. Given their relatively marginal economic position, they play a disproportionately large role in political discourse.

Over the past few years, I have spent dozens of hours at Nigerian newsstands listening to and occasionally participating in the okada drivers' discussions and debates. Their conversations span the full range of social issues, from the role of "indecent" female wardrobes in the HIV/AIDS epidemic to whether it is realistic for the Igbos to strive for the Nigerian presidency in 2007. Okada drivers' debates offered some of the clearest evidence I collected regarding the connections in collective consciousness between corruption, inequality, and ethnic nationalism. A dominant opinion in conversations about MASSOB and Biafra was that Hausas and Yorubas (the two other "majority" ethnic groups in Nigeria, along with the Igbo) used the mechanism of political and administrative corruption to rig Igbos out of the highest political offices and steer economic resources to other regions. Silas, a twenty-eight-year-old motorcyclist in Umuahia, the capital of Abia State, said in July 2003 during a discussion about the recent elections: "The Hausas and the Yorubas are afraid of the Igbo man. They use the power of government to frustrate us. They rig the elections, steal the oil, and eat all the money from the big contracts. Everyone knows that we are being punished for Biafra. Corruption is the weapon they use to kill us. The Igbo man cannot get his children into school; he cannot get a federal job; he cannot win a government contract. But God is in charge. One day we will have Biafra and justice will be restored."

While okada drivers seem to be more fervent in their faith in the possibility of Biafra than the larger Igbo population, not all point the finger of blame at non-Igbo corruption. Echoing the kind of sentiment about intra-

Figure 9. Following the launching of MASSOB in 2001, calendars, leaflets, and posters such as this one were circulated extensively in southeastern Nigeria (photo by author).

Igbo corruption expressed in the Voice of Biafra International broadcast quoted above, Chidiebere, a thirty-two-year-old cyclist, responded to Silas: "No doubt Obasanjo and his allies use their power to frustrate the Igbos, but the evil is also within. Why is the road through Onitsha to Lagos like a track road [dirt path]? How many Igbo men have been awarded the contract? Is it not our brothers, the so-called godfathers, who finance the sale of our elected offices to people who will play ball? Before Igbos will succeed we must confront the evil within us." Such debates are the daily fare among the okada drivers at newsstands in southeastern Nigeria and in the sections of cities throughout the country where Igbo migrants congregate.

While okada drivers are among the most vocal supporters of a resurgent Igbo ethnic nationalism, they are by no means alone. The huge markets that dominate collective urban space in Nigeria are vital centers of discussion and debate about politics, corruption, and other contemporary issues. They are also centers for the production and circulation of revealing rumors. A trip I made to the huge automobile spare-parts market in the commercial city of Aba was particularly illuminating.

MARKETPLACE RUMORS

The 1988 Nissan Bluebird I bought in Owerri in 2004 had a badly rusted pipe running to the fuel tank, and thus every time I tried to pump gasoline, half of it spilled to the ground. The pipe was too rusted to be welded, and the replacement part was unavailable in Owerri or Umuahia, so one morning I recruited my regular mechanic in Umuahia to accompany me to Aba, known as the spare-parts hub of the Southeast, to acquire the part. Unless one has visited a place like the Alaorji spare-parts market in Aba, it is hard to fathom the size of such a specialized marketplace. Several acres of real estate are occupied by merchants selling nothing but every imaginable motor vehicle spare part, mostly used parts bought in Europe and Asia. As we entered the market, the car was swamped by young men asking what I needed and directing us to follow them. Fortunately, Coleman, my mechanic, knew exactly where to go. After I parked the car, we agreed that Coleman would go in search of the part and I would wait—in an attempt to avoid being charged an *onyeocha* (white person) price.

Within seconds of Coleman's disappearance down a narrow lane, one of the nearby vendors offered me a chair by his stall. As I sat down, several other merchants and their apprentices gathered around. After polite greetings, they asked which country I was from, what I was doing in Nigeria, how I liked the country, and of course, whether I eat *akpo*. As we talked the crowd grew, until eventually there were at least twenty-five men around me, most between the ages of twenty and forty-five. I noticed a couple of them arguing with each other in Igbo about whether they should ask me, but I could not catch what it was they were referring to. I said they should ask any questions they had. At this, one of them shouted that everyone should be quiet; they had some important questions for me.

One of them began by explaining about MASSOB and the hope for an independent Biafra. I listened and said that I knew about MASSOB. Finally, they got to the pressing question. "Is it true," I was asked, "that Biafra now has an embassy in the United States and that America is prepared to recognize an independent Biafra?" Twenty-five faces looked on in eager anticipation. But my response was clearly disappointing. I told them that Biafra had no embassy in the United States, and that probably what they were referring to was the opening in 2001 of "Biafra House" in Washington, DC—a facility that had been opened by the same mostly diasporic group of pro-Biafra Igbos who finance the Voice of Biafra International and the most popular Biafra Web site. Clearly, the skeptics in the group felt vindicated. "You see," they said. But others pressed me further. "Would America support an independent Biafra?" I responded with my own best guess, which was that the United States would not support Biafran independence because of its twin interests in the uninterrupted flow of oil and maintaining the stability of the nation-state system. The United States, I explained, was as self-interested as any other nation.

My answers, which were probably given more weight than they should have been, sparked extensive discussion about whether the leaders of MASSOB were as corrupt as the leaders of Nigeria (and as corrupt as those of the United States, one young man chimed in). There was a collective fear that perhaps they were being deceived by the promises of proindependence politicians. Someone even mentioned a rumor I had heard before—that in an earlier period Ralph Uwazurike, the MASSOB leader, had actually converted to Islam in order to garner favor with the northern generals then ruling the country. Given the intense Christianity of most Igbos, and the connections between rising ethnic nationalism and Christian-Muslim polarization in Nigeria, this was a damning accusation. But most in the group dismissed it. While the conversation included a fair amount of condemnation of Igbo leaders for selling out their people, none of this seemed to dampen the enthusiasm for a future Biafra; it only injected a note of realism about the intractability of Nigeria's corruption and the obstacles it posed to Biafra, or any other project that would bring greater equality and justice for ordinary people.

As Coleman returned with the spare part, one of the older men in the gathering said to the group, "Oga is going now, so if you have any other questions ask them now." One man said that he did have one more question. "Is it true," he inquired, "that if the leader of an independence movement survives for thirty years after the start of that rebellion that the United Nations will automatically recognize that people?" Clearly the question referred to Emeka Odumegwu Ojukwu, the Igbos' leader during the civil war. Ojukwu had recently run unsuccessfully as a candidate in the 2003 presidential elections. Once again I had to be the bearer of bad news. "No," I said, "I am not aware of any such provision." As I entered my car to go back to Umuahia, the men thanked me and wished me a safe journey. Looking in my rearview mirror I could see that the discussion continued.

The All Progressives Grand Alliance, Ojukwu, and the 2003 Elections

As the former leader of the defeated Biafran army, Ojukwu is probably the most powerful living symbol of Igbo independence. Following more than twenty years in exile, Ojukwu was officially welcomed back to Nigeria in 1992. Though well-known for his outspokenness, Ojukwu remained a cautious figure after his return, sometimes even angering his former followers with his apparent support for Nigeria's military government. But in 2003, Ojukwu ran for the presidency under the banner of the All Progressives Grand Alliance (APGA) party. The APGA and Ojukwu had national ambitions, and participation in Nigeria's elections implied a de facto acceptance of "one Nigeria." But Ojukwu's candidacy symbolized ethnic pride for many Igbos, even among those who did not necessarily support MASSOB or the notion of Igbo independence. According to the many people I spoke with in 2003 and 2004 about the 2003 elections, Igbos across the country voted in large numbers for Ojukwu. In addition, AGPA candidates for governorships in Igbo-dominated states garnered significant support, especially in Imo and Anambra states, where many people believe the PDP governors won only through rigging. The rigging that apparently marred the 2003 elections further convinced Igbos that the machinery of the Nigerian state was manipulated against them, tightening the perceived connection between official corruption and ethnic marginalization. In the wake of the 2003 elections, the APGA became a symbol for thwarted Igbo interests and Ojukwu's place as an Igbo icon was rejuvenated.

Many friends in Owerri told me that they witnessed blatant forms of ballot box stuffing and stealing in the Imo State elections, mostly designed to ensure PDP victory and discount the votes for Ojukwu and the APGA governorship candidate. In the wake of the unfolding crisis after the Anambra governorship elections, especially President Obasanjo's revelation in his public letter that Governor Ngige and his erstwhile godfather, Uba, admitted that Ngige had not really won the election, most people believed that it was the APGA candidate, Peter Obi, who had been rigged out. One pro-Biafra Web site complained:

> Nothing shocks Nigeria any more. Nigeria watched and accommodated the egregious fraud and evil unleashed by Obasanjo and PDP all this time, without any audible outcry. In fact, many joined him and PDP to share the loot.
>
> It was the obsession of Obasanjo-PDP-Nigeria to defeat Biafra by specifically defeating Ojukwu, the living symbol of Biafra, in Anambra, Ojukwu's home-State and quintessential Biafra, during the same elections, which drove Obasanjo-PDP-Nigeria to the sort of recklessness that has resulted in the Anambra debacle of today. And, we have not seen the end of it yet; Waterloo looms large against Obasanjo-PDP-Nigeria. (2004: The Year of Biafra identity 2005).

Another columnist, writing in response to the revelation in Obasanjo's public letter about the Anambra crisis, cleverly connects the date of the 2003 presidential elections to 419.

> I am neither amused nor shocked by the unrefined contents of General Olusegun Obasanjo's letter. The revelation is not out of his volition. The spirit of Nigeria is fighting against all of them. Obasanjo knew that the date of the election says it all 4–19 (April 19). This was considered by the evil genius among them before they scheduled the elections. How could some people expect Obasanjo to hand over Uba and Ngige to Police when the date of the elections indicated that the elections were predetermined? Which Police are they going to handover Uba to? Is it the Police under corrupt Tafa Balogun who is part and parcel of the riggings? How would they expect Obasanjo to invite the Police when he himself was a beneficiary of the robbery in all the states that he was declared the winner, including Anambra and my State, Ogun?
>
> Because Obasanjo knew his instructions to Abel Guobadia [head of the supposedly Independent National Electoral Commission (INEC)] and the rest [of the] resident electoral commissioners, nothing in Obasanjo's letter wonders how Uba could have rigged without the collusion of his staff in INEC (Banjo 2004).

While ordinary Nigerians of all ethnic groups experienced the 2003 polls as a process of corrupt and predetermined "selection" rather than democratic election, Igbos coupled the experience of electoral corruption with their perception of marginalization based on ethnicity. Even Ojukwu, who appears to have cast his lot with Igbo politicians who see the most realistic road to power as within Nigeria rather than in separation from it, spoke of the 2003 rigging as an anti-Igbo plot. When MASSOB called for all Igbos to stay at home on August 26, 2004, in order to express their unity with the Biafran cause, Ojukwu's expressions of support got him in trouble with the government.

August 26, 2004

For at least a couple of weeks prior to the MASSOB stay-at-home order, communities in southeastern Nigeria were abuzz with anticipation about whether the de facto one-day Igbo strike would be successful. In my in-laws' semirural community of Ubakala, people speculated not only about the level of adherence to the order but about the federal government's response. People passed around the flyers calling for the action and relayed summaries of the most recent broadcasts on the Voice of Biafra International, which was heavily promoting the work stoppage. Even among people who were skeptical about or plainly opposed to the MASSOB vision of an independent Biafra there was considerable sympathy for the stay-at-home strike. The words of Okechukwu, a fifty-two-year-old man who makes a living selling timber, were typical of the sentiment among people who were not necessarily ardent Biafra revivalists: "Biafra is a dream. I do not see it happening in my lifetime—maybe in the far future. But I will stay at home on August 26 and I will instruct my wife and children to do the same. Perhaps this will show Obasanjo and his government that we know what they are doing. Do they think that when they rig all the elections and eat all the money nobody is aware? We know what they are doing and one day they will see, if not in this world then in the next. We will stay at home."

In the days prior to the one-day Igbo strike, federal and state government officials issued statements urging Nigerians to go to work. Despite the government appeals (or perhaps partly because of them), on the appointed day the stay-at-home action was widely observed. In cities and towns throughout southeastern Nigeria, offices and markets were shuttered, schools remained closed, and most people simply stayed at home. Some people complied mostly out of fear that pro-MASSOB supporters or government security forces would foment violence. The almost ubiquitous compliance with the one-day sit-down strike certainly could not be read as an indicator of vast support for MASSOB, but it was an expression of almost universal Igbo dissatisfaction with the poverty, inequality, and corruption that has continued to plague postmilitary Nigeria.

The success of the strike—all the cities in southeastern Nigeria were largely shut down, and even some of the major Igbo-dominated markets in places like Lagos and Kano were closed—was covered not only in the local media but also on BBC World Service radio broadcasts. For Biafra supporters, the one-day strike buoyed emotions.

In the days after the strike, conversations about possibilities for Biafra swelled. The stay-at-home strike was not followed by any other events, however, and the fact that the strike passed without violence probably contributed to the speed with which it receded from the public consciousness. I do not know whether the federal government was purposely passive, but if so, it appeared to be the right strategy for minimizing any catalytic effects. Indeed, the one aftershock from the strike came in the government's response to a statement by Ojukwu.

Shortly after the strike, Ojukwu said in an interview that he supported the aspirations of the Igbo people for an independent Biafra—the closest he had come to expressing outright support for MASSOB and its secessionist goals. In response, the federal State Security Services (SSS) sent Ojukwu a one-way air ticket to Abuja, directing him to come in for questioning. Ojukwu responded by going public with his "invitation," and implying that the fact that the SSS sent him a one-way ticket meant that they did not plan for him to return—they planned either to imprison or kill him. Ojukwu's one-way ticket story sparked vociferous public discussions. Igbo leaders of all stripes called for the government to keep their hands off Ojukwu, eventually leading to a statement from the SSS denying that the one-way ticket implied any of the sinister motives that circulated in the popular rumors. The SSS simply wanted to "talk to" Ojukwu. But Ojukwu never went to Abuja, and the SSS never compelled him to do so. While Igbos are by no means united about another Biafra, the leader of their failed attempt at independence remains something of a sacred symbol, and the SSS was probably wise to leave Ojukwu alone.

IGBOS AS JEWS AND NIGERIA AS EGYPT

Enthusiasm for the revival of Biafra and resentment over perceived marginalization, even among the majority of Igbos who see another attempt at independence as unrealistic, is fueled by perceptions that the corrupt machinery of the federal government runs against the interests of the Igbo people, and funnels resources away from the Southeast as punishment for the failed secession attempt more than thirty years ago. The language of ethnic nationalism and the rhetoric of complaint about marginalization and corruption frequently take on a religious tone, the more so as polarization between Nigeria's mostly Christian South and its mostly Muslim North has intensified. An enthusiastic e-mail sent to the Biafra nation Web site just after the August 26 stay-at-home strike exemplifies the religious metaphors that are increasingly prevalent in Igbo discourse:

Fellow Biafrans,
To you all, Biafrans, young and old, those at home and those abroad, fellow Jews in Israel, America, Great Britain even at France. I thank you all especially members of Biafra Foundation, Ekwenche and to all Great Massobians all over the world. God our Father bless you all, Amen.

May I gladly and excitedly inform you all from my own report that the "SIT-AT-HOME—EXERCISE" programmed by the authority of Massob on Thursday being 26th August 2004 was "ONE HUNDRED AND FIFTY PERCENT" (150%) observed by Biafrans all over Egypt—called and addressed as Nigeria which has been by false. This event forced the entire so called Nigerians to join, as the Easterners observed in totality. It was successful in observation and in compliance.

We want the world to know that we willingness to sacrifice for the actualization of Biafra State where we'll not be oppressed, deprived, denied and intimidated and kill at will and deprived at will, a place for the free world of speech and free from fraud and corruption, which has been instituted and legalized in Nigeria, further more a place where the house of our God will not be pulled down at will and worshippers young and old killed at will. (Result of our sit-at-home 2005)

The idea that Igbos are one of the lost tribes of Israel has circulated in popular discourse for many years, even generating a small literature of supposedly scholarly books to make the case (Ononuju 1996; Alaezi 1999). In the Igbo collective consciousness, the parallels between the Igbos and the Jews are many. Each group is well-known for entrepreneurial migration and business acumen; each was persecuted for its faith and ethnicity in places dominated by other ethnic and religious majorities; and each has struggled for an independent homeland. While serious scholars, including serious Igbo scholars, reject any real historical connections between Igbos and Jews, the currency of this idea in contemporary Igboland is worthy of intellectual attention. With the resurgence of Igbo nationalism, the comparison of Igbos in Nigeria to Jews in Egypt has taken on a renewed salience.

In addition, as Pentecostal and evangelical Christianity have become increasingly popular throughout southern Nigeria, and as more radical forms of Islam have taken hold in northern Nigeria, a growing amount of the rhetoric of Nigerian politics is conducted in religious idioms. Discontents about corruption, frustration over perceived marginalization, and aspirations for a more equal and just society are expressed in religious language. This is among the most significant and potentially explosive trends in contemporary Nigerian society.

"GOD IS IN CHARGE": THE POPULARITY OF PENTECOSTAL CHRISTIANITY

For two weeks prior to the event, scores of colorful banners and massive signboards placed throughout Umuahia and its surrounding communities advertised a five-day religious crusade to be led by Reinhardt Bonnke, a German Pentecostal evangelist famous in Nigeria and across Africa for his miracle-promising ministry (Gifford 1987). On Friday, October 22, 2004, I joined dozens of my in-laws and neighbors to attend an all-night crusade. Tens of thousands of people, in a greater urban area of perhaps a quarter million, participated in Bonnke's Umuahia crusade, mostly during over-night vigils over the weekend. The night vigils included inspired preach-ing, testimonies from the healed and the saved, and countless collective prayers for people coming forward to receive their miracles, all supple-mented with an impressive audiovisual system that included live bands and jumbo-sized video screens. The crowd included not only members of the region's many Pentecostal and evangelical churches but countless numbers of Catholics and mainline Protestants with varying positions re-garding Pentecostalism. The crusade was a cultural spectacle as much as a religious ritual.

Whereas my many in-laws, friends, neighbors, and other acquaintances in southeastern Nigeria expressed a considerable diversity of views about the prospect of an independent Biafra, people shared an almost universal belief in Christianity and an overwhelming faith that God is in charge. Christian beliefs are diverse, and it would be wrong to paint Nigerian or Igbo Christianity with one broad brush. But in the last two or three de-cades, the dramatic rise of Pentecostal and other evangelical and charis-matic churches—what Nigerians commonly refer to as born-again or "new-breed" churches—has been one of the most striking social phenom-ena of the era, affecting not only people who join these newer churches but also members of Nigeria's older congregations.

The fact that so many people in and around Umuahia flocked to Rever-end Bonnke's crusade illustrates the extent to which Nigeria's Pentecostal Christian movement connects followers in a circuitry that spans the globe. The "globalization" of Pentecostal Christianity has received considerable scholarly attention in anthropology and related disciplines (Robbins 2004; Coleman 2000). Much of this work has pointed to the popularity of born-again Christianity among the poor and the disenfranchised. Along with Latin America, Africa has been in the vanguard of burgeoning Pentecostalism (Meyer 2004; Corten and Marshall-Fratani 2001; Gifford 1998), and Nigeria is one of the countries with the greatest participation, both in absolute numbers and in terms of the relative proportion of the population involved (Marshall 1991, 1995; Marshall-Fratani 1998).

Bonnke's crusade was the biggest of many revivals, retreats, and reli-gious camps that were widely attended in and around Umuahia during my most recent fieldwork. Several other events involved U.S. or European evangelists. Further, elite Nigerian members and leaders of these new-breed churches take regular trips overseas to attend various trainings, con-ferences, or crusades. But the global connections of Nigeria's born-again movement should not lead to the erroneous conclusion that it is driven

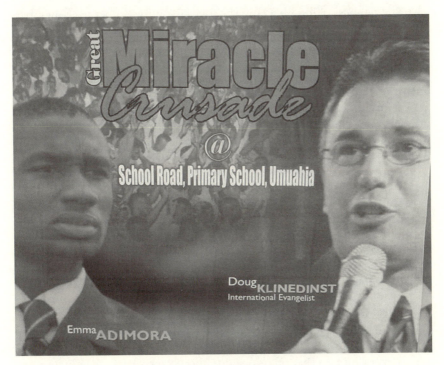

Figure 10. Many of the Pentecostal churches popular in Nigeria promise prosperity and offer miracles in return for faith (photo by author).

primarily by extra-Nigerian forces. Quite to the contrary, the leadership in most new-breed churches is wholly Nigerian, the flavor of religious ritual is "African," and even the efforts to seek and build global connections are motivated largely by local interests and concerns.

The capacity of Pentecostalism to incorporate its adherents into a seemingly homogenizing worldwide religion that makes followers feel a part of something much bigger than their local world, but also integrate local cultural traditions has been hypothesized to be one of born-again Christianity's great appeals (Robbins 2004; Casanova 2001). Explanations for the popularity of Pentecostal Christianity have included: that it offers a new and ritually dense system of social organization and cultural meaning for the urban poor as well as other populations who feel increasingly frustrated by the failures of the state, or alienated by the demands and obligations of traditional kin and community groups (Robbins 2004); that it promises hope and eternal rewards for people whose lives are marked by poverty, inequality, and injustice—the signboards for Bonnke's crusade announced boldly "Come and receive your miracle" (Meyer 2004); and that the richness of its rituals and the social life it fosters between members blur the lines between religious worship and leisure (Robbins 2004). In addition, scholars have suggested that Pentecostal Christianity's globalizing pull is part of a larger process in which poor people in non-Western societies are socialized to become more modern subjects, ritually recruited into the capitalist global economy, or in more optimistic versions, prepared for modernity and democratization. In Nigeria, each of these explanations contains elements of truth. In addition, and of primary interest here, for millions of Nigerians, Pentecostal Christianity is a lens through which they can interpret, criticize, and justify the social inequalities that are so readily attributed to corruption.

As with the popular fantasies that the Bakassi Boys were supernaturally powered vigilantes, the modern versions of witchcraft allegations that occurred in Owerri during the Otokoto saga, the rumors and stories that swirled in the wake of the Okija shrine scandal in Anambra State, and the resurgence of Igbo nationalism, I believe that the tremendous appeal of Pentecostal Christianity can be better explained by taking into account its relationship to Nigerians' experiences with and understandings of corruption. This is not to say that the rise of Pentecostal Christianity should be understood primarily as a response to corruption. Clearly, the factors underlying the burgeoning of new-breed churches in Nigeria, and elsewhere, are multiple and complex. But considering born-again Christianity and corruption together offers insights about each that are productive and well warranted, especially given the way in which Nigerians themselves perceive the relationship between the two.

CRITIQUES OF CORRUPTION AND PROMISES OF PROSPERITY

In the conclusion to his insightful analysis of the "moral economy" of corruption in Africa, Jean-Pierre Olivier de Sardan (1999, 48) suggested the possibility that Pentecostalism and other similar religious movements offer one imaginable route out of the morass of corruption: "Hence the general feeling of helplessness in the face of an infernal mechanism. And hence this hypothesis, which is also a risk: the development of movements of a 'puritanical' tendency, intended to bring about reform of public morals (which can assume, in Islam as in Christianity, a fundamentalist hue) may be among the ultimate means, in the absence of improbable self-reformation of the political elites, to attempt to change the present course of affairs. Any 'anti-corruption' policy must face up to these realities." Scholars of Pentecostalism in Africa have also noted the role of the born-again movement in criticizing corruption and pushing for the influence of religious morality in the public spheres of politics, civil society, and state governance, though I will suggest below that the influence of Pentecostalism on morality seems to have recently taken a different trajectory. Ruth Marshall (1995, 251–52), a leading anthropological scholar of Pentecostalism in contemporary Nigeria, has documented the growing involvement of Pentecostalists in the public sphere, and shown that their agenda sometimes includes fighting corruption and its associated injustices.

> One can see in the Pentecostal circles the beginnings of the creation of a kind of "public space" in which the critique of government and social ills connected with misgovernment are organized through interdenominational interest groups. Pentecostal lawyers' groups, bankers' associations, women's fellowships, students' and Youth Corps groups, to name a few, are all involved in the project of the redemption of their respective fields. Attacking corruption, exploitation, illegal practices, and "spiritual degeneration" in the institutions of what others have called "civil society," the Pentecostal movement not only debates civic virtue, but is attempting to bring it into the civic sphere of the nation.

Certainly my many friends and acquaintances who belonged to Pentecostal or other similar charismatic churches widely believed that they held themselves to a higher standard of moral accountability than people who were not born-again. Several friends who founded local NGOs consciously marketed their outfits as more accountable and transparent because of their born-again credentials. In recent local government elections, a group of born-again university students in Ubakala organized themselves into a sort of coalition that promoted the examination of candidates' credentials in terms of their capacity to fight corruption—an assessment that implicitly included a judgment about whether the office seeker truly accepted Jesus as their personal savior. One of the bright young men, Emeka, who engineered the youth coalition said to me: "Everyone knows that our politicians seek office with one goal—to enrich themselves. Nigeria, even Ubakala, rewards people who steal money, build big houses, drive Mercedes-Benz, share government contracts with their friends, and buy fancy chieftancy titles with big praise names. I am not saying that no Christians are involved. Even some so-called born-agains are corrupt, but people who have really accepted Christ are more humble. They have more integrity. They fear God."

The youth coalition won meetings with several candidates for the local government chairmanship and councillorships as well as proclamations of strong Christian faith and fear of God. In the end they did not endorse one particular candidate, and even the most ardent members of the coalition agreed that corruption plagued the election and continues to characterize the operations of the local government administration. But Emeka remained adamant that religion would one day win out: "All the selfishness and greed of our politicians is because they do not fear God, but one day justice will prevail and the words of Jesus will come to pass, if not in this world, then in the next."

The forms of Pentecostalism that became popular in Nigeria beginning in the 1970s tended to attract mainly the poor and the dispossessed. They preached ascetic "holiness" doctrines that condemned the pursuit of riches in this world and promised all rewards in the hereafter. Members of these churches, with names such as Deeper Life, dressed conservatively. Women were forbidden to wear jewelry. Moral codes were puritanical. Few people in the middle and upper classes participated. But over the last fifteen to twenty years, and especially over the last decade, a new brand of Pentecostalism has swept Nigeria and other parts of Africa, preaching a gospel of prosperity (Gifford 2004; Meyer 2004). Known in some academic parlance as the Faith Movement (Robbins 2004), the prosperity gospel promises health, wealth, and success in this world. Faith in Jesus is framed as the key to fulfilling this-worldly ambitions. The prosperity churches have attracted large numbers of the middle class and the wealthy, for whom the new religious doctrines provide meaningful foundations for their economic privilege. These churches also have also drawn massive numbers of poor people, especially the urban poor, young people, and women, all of whom have growing social and economic aspirations. The prosperity churches offer their converts the promise of fulfilling these aspirations as well as new communities of ritual and social interaction that affirm their modern ambitions.

The number of prosperity churches is huge, with entrepreneurial pastors starting new churches seemingly every day. Several prosperity churches have become megachurches, with international memberships and enormous congregations. A quintessential example is Winners' Chapel, started in Lagos in 1983 (Gifford 2004, 56–61). It has spread to thirty-eight African countries, has over four hundred branches in Nigeria, and boasts an auditorium in Lagos that holds over fifty thousand worshippers. As in all the prosperity churches, the emphasis is on success, particularly economic prosperity. Paul Gifford's (2004) study of Pentecostalism in Ghana, where Winners' Chapel has attracted one of its biggest followings outside Nigeria, documents in detail the kind of language common in Winners' sermons and rituals. Statements and promises such as: "Financial hardship is an insult to your identity, your location, your position, your kingdom"; "Within thirty days from today your life will be dramatically changed. By the end of this week your crisis will be gone"; and "As you depart here today, you will be receiving phone calls, for a new job, a new business, new opportunity" are common, and mark the emphasis on the connections between the savior of the spirit and material success (Gifford 2004, 57). While Winners' Chapel is exceptional in its success, it represents the general ethos of the prosperity gospel. All over Nigeria one can observe bumper stickers, greeting cards, advertising slogans, and framed biblical quotations that suggest the path to prosperity is through Christ.

Services and rituals in these new-breed churches are lively, combining music, singing, and dancing with inspired preaching, testimonies about the miracles that Christ has brought to coverts' lives, and extensive tithing. The wealth and success of members, and of the pastors themselves, is celebrated as evidence of the blessing of the Lord. Birgit Meyer (2004, 448), in her review of contemporary African Christianity, describes "flamboyant leaders of the new mega-churches, who dress in the latest (African) fashion, drive nothing less than a Mercedes Benz, participate in the global Pentecost jetset, broadcast the message through flashy TV and radio programs, and preach the Prosperity gospel to their deprived and hitherto-hopeless born-again followers at home and in the diaspora" (see also Marshall-Fratani 2001). The growth of prosperity churches has been dramatic, and though only a relatively small number of new-breed church founders, leaders, and pastors have become fantastically wealthy, the perception that people are getting rich by starting churches led to the critical humor mentioned at the beginning of chapter 3: that the best ways for unemployed graduates to make money in modern Nigeria are to start their own churches or form their own NGOs. Mainline churches and even the more ascetically oriented Pentecostal churches have been forced to modify their messages to compete with the popular prosperity churches, which seem to be setting the Christian agenda in contemporary Nigeria.

The growing predominance of prosperity churches has complicated the role of Pentecostalism in the criticism of corruption. The large numbers of middle-class and elite Nigerians who belong to these prosperity churches are able justify their wealth and success in religious language, even though many have clearly acquired their wealth through various mechanisms of corruption. The contradictions created by a born-again doctrine that promises prosperity to the faithful in a society where many, if not most, rich people come by their money through some form of corruption has resulted in two interesting trends. First, although many wealthy Pentecostalists justify their success as God-given, countervailing accusations that elites have acquired their riches through devilish or satanic means are voiced in Pentecostal discourse. As the Pentecostal lens has come to dominate popular religious interpretations of contemporary events in much of southeastern Nigeria, the idiom of the occult has been recast in terms of a battle between God and Satan, and between true believers and others. The realm of the supernatural is preserved as the province in which interpretations of inequality and criticisms of corruption are expressed, but in the language of Pentecostal Christianity.

Second, the powerful moralism of Pentecostal Christianity has become increasingly domesticated, moving attention away from the public sphere. Personal behavior in the domestic arena, such as being a good spouse or parent, eschewing alcohol, gambling, and extramarital sex, praying in the home, and not allowing one's children to dress indecently or act disrespectfully, are emphasized in church sermons, collective gossip, and individuals' assessments of their own morality. I know numerous businesspeople and politicians who are devout born-again Christians and who maintain strict codes of personal behavior even as they participate in election rigging, the overinvoicing of contracts, and the outright looting of government coffers. Of course, I also know people who pretend to observe strict codes of personal behavior but actually do differently, yet such hypocrites are less interesting in terms of what has happened in the relationship between Pentecostalism and corruption. It is the born-again Christians who really try to live by their churches' teachings regarding personal and intimate behavior, and yet still participate in public actions that perpetuate corruption, who encapsulate the complexity of the relationship between religious morality and corruption. The domestication of Pentecostal moralism, focusing attention on sexuality, marriage, and family, has enabled the prosperous to live piously even as they loot the state and society.

Occult Powers and Satanic Riches

One of the reasons commonly offered for explaining the rapid global proliferation of Pentecostal and charismatic Christianity is the capacity of born-again worldviews to incorporate traditional cultural beliefs even as they offer believers a position from which to understand and adapt to the dramatic changes associated with modernity (Robbins 2004; Smith 2001a). In contemporary Nigeria, Pentecostal understandings of the supernatural have become a primary idiom through which ordinary Nigerians interpret the injustices and inequalities of the country's political economy. The venality that underlies the competition for wealth and power is implicitly criticized in the litany of stories that circulate about the involvement of elites in witchcraft and other occult rituals (now glossed as devilish or satanic) designed to secure their ambitions.

Popular awareness of the hypocrisy in official state anticorruption and prodemocracy rhetoric is exemplified in the widespread belief that powerful people use potent supernatural magic to attain and maintain their positions at the top of the political, economic, and social hierarchy. The branding of such practices as satanic in Pentecostal discourse both condemns these behaviors and affirms their efficacy (if only until the Kingdom of God prevails). Ruth Marshall-Fratani (1998, 304) explains common

Nigerian perceptions of the connections between official power and the supernatural:

> The official discourse about government is seen as mendacious and unconvincing to most people since it fails to address those issues which are central to the idioms that make up popular consciousness—in particular the unseen world of spiritual forces. The popular press is full of stories of witchcraft, "money medicine," and evil spirits such as "Mammy Wata"; in urban centres, rumour and panic about uncontrolled spiritual forces abound (such as the missing genitals' scare of 1990, where people were lynched after having "spirited" away the private parts of others by casual contact). In Nigeria, power is itself evidence of strong spiritual connections; all "big men" that have "eaten well" are understood to have links to secret and occult forms of power.

The most electrifying and enduring rumors and stories of the occult usually have important public figures as protagonists, highlighting popular discontent over the role of leaders in Nigerians' suffering. Even in cases where there is not much concrete evidence of elite involvement, such as in the beheading of the eleven-year-old boy in Owerri in 1996 or in the names on the shrine registers at Okija in 2004, the public appetite for accounts that attribute events to grand satanic conspiracies among elites inevitably produces rumors of involvement "higher up." While these stories place considerable blame for corruption and inequality on the evil acts of rapacious leaders, even in Pentecostal discourse ordinary Nigerians implicate themselves. Nonelites who join Pentecostal churches commonly give testimony of their own past evils, including incredible stories about pacts with the devil or previous lives lived in parallel satanic worlds.

In 1996, a young Pentecostal pastor, who was not rich or powerful by any measure, told me a two-hour story about his past allegiance to Mammy Wata, a mermaidlike spirit who is a common figure in Nigerian tales of the occult (Bastian 1996). He described a whole life he had lived in an underworld before becoming born-again—a life characterized by material riches, obscene sexuality, and cannibalism. Such conversion stories are part of demonstrating one's born-again credentials, and they are recounted in public testimonies by many converts, regardless of their social class. On the one hand, these testimonies are another idiom through which ordinary people recognize and criticize their own participation in the forms of corruption they find so troubling. On the other hand, critiques of corruption and inequality that rely on accusations of satanic or occult practices serve to obscure the political and material roots of inequality. Although these stories can be interpreted as expressions of discontent about corruption and inequality, like the domestication of religious morality, they reconfigure political issues as morality tales.

THE DOMESTICATION OF RELIGIOUS MORALITY

Each morning in Uche Nkem's house, the family gathers at 6:00 a.m. in the parlor for morning prayers. Uche, his wife, and four children sing and pray together for about twenty minutes. A couple of nights a week they attend fellowship meetings with other members of their Assemblies of God congregation. On Sundays, they attend church services that can last five or six hours, and frequently also participate in Bible study classes that take another hour or two. At his workplace, Uche and other born-again Christians gather once a week in a prayer group. Before any long journey, Uche exhorts fellow travelers to pray together for Jesus's journey mercies. Everyday conversations are sprinkled with allusions to the Bible.

Uche is remarkably devoted to his wife and children. Unlike my perceptions regarding many of my relatively elite Nigerian married male friends, I am quite sure that Uche is steadfastly faithful to his wife. He speaks quite movingly about how his and his wife's shared faith in Jesus has deepened their marital bond, and the degree of obvious affection he demonstrates for his wife, in front of his children and in front of visitors to his home, is striking. His playful affection for his children is equally apparent, even as it intertwines with a strong sense of moral authority regarding their personal conduct. Uche expects that his children will work hard in school, avoid premarital sex, and express deference and courtesy to their seniors and all guests. He and his wife reinforce their moral authority by inculcating a strong sense in their children that it is faith in God that requires, but also assists them in maintaining a high level of personal ethics. Uche's teenage daughters, who I have come to know well over the years, ask me lots of questions about the United States, and while they have great curiosity and would like to visit, they also often express a fear that mine is a society of great sin, where personal morality is waning and faith in Jesus is weak.

I know the family well enough to argue with them about religion—something I often refrain from to avoid offending people I know less well. Uche and his family like me despite my lack of faith, but also justify our friendship with their belief that one day I will "know Jesus." In fact, they often tell me that I am a servant of God—I just do not know it yet. Most of my born-again friends seem to see me this way—as a convert in waiting. Whenever I stay at Uche's home I am reminded of the positive aspects of religious faith, which frankly, I have a tendency to ignore in my eagerness to apply a secular academic lens to discern the more sociological functions and dysfunctions of religion.

I know many people in southeastern Nigeria whose lives have been transformed in various ways by their conversion to born-again Christianity. It is not only the elite, such as Uche and his family, who are so committed to Pentecostal Christianity. In semirural Ubakala, as in many typical Igbo communities, large numbers of poor people are flocking to these new churches. Many of my friends and in-laws in Ubakala, who are not elites by any measure, express strong conviction in the capacity of Christ to transform their lives. In the sermons at Sunday service and the conversations that occur every day in the community, concerns over personal morality feature prominently. In a society where so many suffer and struggle in order to survive, it is hard to begrudge people anything that offers help, hope, and solace. But the focus of Pentecostalism on personal morality obscures the ways in which it is more political behavior that is often at the root of people's suffering. By privileging personal morality, Pentecostalism can both justify corruption in the public domain and hide the larger social and political structures that underlie inequality.

This domestication of religious morality, in which individual conduct in the spheres of family, sexuality, and everyday religious observance are emphasized to the exclusion of attention to political and civic behavior, enables elites to participate in corruption while still viewing themselves as ethical people. It deflects the attention of ordinary citizens away from the political and toward the personal when they imagine the causes of Nigeria's social ills. My friend Uche, for example, has been involved for several years in a business relationship with an important politician, in which the politician funnels some of his stolen wealth into a legitimate business that Uche runs on the politician's behalf. In exchange for laundering the politician's money, Uche gets 10 percent of the profits and a significant amount of access to and clout with his political patron. Uche seems to justify this relationship through a combination of rationales, including that his political patron is also born-again, and that reality (the Nigerian factor) requires these kinds of alliances in order to succeed in Nigeria. But mostly, he seems to separate his civic and political behavior from his strong religious beliefs and personal ethics.

Among the poorer converts to Pentecostalism, who far outnumber the more elite followers such as Uche, the domestication of religious morality averts attention from the more political dimensions of material inequality. When the focus is on philandering men, alcohol abuse, promiscuous young women, youthful disrespect of their seniors, failure to pray, or absenteeism from church, it means that attention is less attuned to the state, and to the political and economic structures and practices that actually produce poverty and inequality. The focus on morality in people's private lives both deflects attention from questions about political morality and fills the vacuum of amorality that Nigerians associate with their state, and the politicians and their cronies who dominate public life.

CORRUPTION IN THE CHURCH

The Pentecostal discourse in Nigeria is a crucial part of an even larger popular perception that personal immorality and public amorality plague the country, and manifest themselves in all kinds of problems. Although Pentecostal Christianity has achieved its tremendous following in Nigeria in part because it offers such appealing critiques of contemporary morality, including some forms of corruption, the depth of popular cynicism, and indeed the pervasiveness of actual corruption, has meant that Pentecostal churches are also the object of corruption allegations and the subject of corruption scandals. Even as Nigerians join new-breed churches in droves, they widely suspect that many of these churches are moneymaking enterprises for their founders and leaders.

Newspapers and magazines regularly feature stories about corruption in churches, sometimes exposing even the most popular churches. For example, the cover of the July 19, 2004, edition of one of Nigeria's leading newsmagazines, *Newswatch*, announced in a bold headline, "Scandal Rocks Winners' Chapel." The article described a dispute over fifty thousand dollars that was required to be remitted annually from a Ghanaian branch of the church to the headquarters in Lagos. The opulent lifestyle of many of the leaders of Nigeria's new generation prosperity churches is frequently tied to insinuations of materialism and corruption. Nigeria's huge video industry includes numerous films where the corruption of pastors is a favorite plot (Haynes 2000; Meyer 2004). While the media and popular gossip are the most common venues for these accusations, a similar strain of criticism was aired in a Voice of Biafra International radio broadcast on December 4, 2004:

> Look at our Churches; bishops, priests, and pastors will gladly accept a bag of money from a man they know to be a criminal even if the money is still dripping with blood of the victim. They will put this person in the front seat in the Church, sing his praises and tell the congregation what a wonderful person he is. Because everyone knows that this person is a murderer and an armed robber the pastor will simply say, "Thou shall not judge, let God be the judge." What kind of nonsense is that? There used to be bishops and priests who had moral character and who would stand up for honesty, justice, and morality no matter who was involved.

As in other realms of public life, the corruption assumed to permeate religious institutions is often imaginatively connected to beliefs that access to wealth and power is facilitated by occult rituals. Because Pentecostal Christianity is so obsessed with condemning the occult, it is perhaps not surprising that successful church leaders who make such a nice living by preaching against witchcraft are sometimes accused of practicing it. Corruption scandals involving new-breed churches frequently include allusions to the hidden bargains that the beneficiaries have struck with spirits of the underworld. In Nigeria, every anticorruption movement is liable to be the target of accusations of corruption.

ETHNIC NATIONALISM AND RELIGION RECONSIDERED

A volatile mix of ethnic nationalism and religious polarization is commonly presented as one of the most obvious threats to the stability and continued existence of Nigeria. The violence that has occurred in the country in recent years in the name of ethnicity and religion is extensive. Thousands of people have lost their lives. But the tendency of analysts inside and outside Nigeria to attribute violence primarily to ethnic and religious differences obscures the degree to which these conflicts build on discontents about poverty, inequality, and corruption. When Nigerians kill each other over religion or ethnicity, it is largely because issues of material inequality and political power have been recast in ethnic and religious idioms. To recognize and understand the role of ethnicity and religion in the ways that Nigerians interpret, critique, tolerate, and participate in the political and social processes that perpetuate inequality does not minimize the importance of these symbolic domains. In fact, it draws attention to just how powerful they are.

Ethnic nationalism is commonly portrayed in Western media as the product of historical squabbles between primitive peoples. Religious revivalism is often viewed as a reversion from modernity. Yet the cases of resurgent Igbo nationalism and Pentecostal Christianity in southeastern Nigeria show how responsive these movements are to the most contemporary issues and events in Nigerian society. They provide some of the most direct and concrete examples of how Nigerians interpret and react to the realities of corruption and its associated inequality. Rather than being the legacy of some primordial past, ethnic nationalism and religious revivalism are much more accurately seen as expressions and outcomes of people's suffering in postcolonial Nigeria.

Ethnicity and religion are important spheres in which critiques of corruption are articulated. The focus on personal morality and loyalty to one's group, however—whether it is family, a church congregation, or an ethnic association—tends to deflect attention from the larger political structures that are most directly culpable in producing and reproducing social inequality. Nigerians perceive the world of politics and the realm of the state as operating without morality. Even as ethnic nationalism and Pentecostal

Christianity make morality such a prominent feature of Nigerians' responses to corruption, these new moralities often provide cover for continued corruption by turning attention toward personal ethics and away from issues of social class as well as the larger structures and strategies through which inequality is maintained.

IN THIS BOOK'S OPENING vignette about the Texas oil executive who was conned using the facades and formalities of Nigeria's state-controlled national petroleum corporation, I noted that the reactions of the audience to my friend AC's incredible story included a mixture of lament, cynicism, and resignation, combined with a sense of admiration for the creativity and sheer audacity of the perpetrators. In concluding this book, it would be disingenuous to fail to remark on the degree of approbation that accompanies certain forms of 419 in Nigeria, particularly stories that suggest Nigerians have hoodwinked wealthy Westerners or their own national elites. As the content of the notorious Nigerian e-mail scam letters indicate, and as the young scam-letter writers themselves attest, most 419 scams depend on the fact of already extant global inequality, corruption, and greed. In a world where corruption is so frequently wielded by the West as a simplistic and exculpatory explanation for global poverty and inequality, and for the failures of development and democracy in Africa and other poor countries, it is understandable that Nigerians might sometimes take a certain pride in an endeavor that is perceived as reversing some of the asymmetries of wealth and power. Nigeria's international identity is so intertwined with its reputation for corruption that it is no wonder that the skills required to execute some forms of corruption are occasionally the object of popular admiration.

Nigerians' pride about the capabilities associated with corruption is illustrated in national humor. Over the years I have heard many versions of the following joke about contractors:

> Three contractors were visiting a famous museum on the same day. One was from Nigeria, another from Germany, and the third from France. At the end of the tour, the guard asked them what they did for a living. When they all replied that they were contractors, the guard said, "Wow, we need one of the rear fences redone. Why don't you all take a look at it and give me a bid?" So, they all went to the fence to check it out. First was the German contractor. He took out his tape measure and pencil, did some measuring and said, "Well, I figure the job will run about $1,200–$500 for materials, $500 for labor, and $200 profit for me." Next was the French contractor. He also took out his tape measure and pencil, did some quick figuring, and said, "It looks like I can do this job for $1,000–$400 for materials, $400 for my crew, and $200 profit for me." Without so much as moving, the Nigerian contractor said, "$3,000." The guard, incredulous, looked at him and said, "You didn't even measure like the other guys!

How did you come up with such a high figure?" "Easy," he said. "$1,000 for you, $1,000, for me, and $1,000 for the guy we hire from France."

A similarly well-known joke about three pastors offers a comparable punch line:

> Three pastors, an Irishman, an American, and a Nigerian, were engaged in a discussion as to how they share the proceeds from offerings they received after each Sunday service. "I draw a big circle on the floor and toss all the money in the air," reported the Irish pastor, "the notes and coins that fall within the circle are for God and the ones that fall outside it are mine." The American pastor said, "Well, I draw a long line on the floor. The notes and coins that fall on one side of the line are for God and the ones that fall on the other side of the line are for me." "In my own case," the Nigerian pastor said, "I simply toss all the notes and coins in the air. The ones that God catches are his and the ones He allows to fall back to earth He leaves for my own welfare!"

Jokes like these are familiar to many Nigerians, and through them the global discourse about corruption, which tends to blame Nigeria and other poor countries for their plight, is reversed. Instead of corruption being depicted as a legacy of primordial traditions or a symptom of cultural backwardness, as it is so often represented in Western media, corruption becomes a contemporary skill in which Nigerians can match and indeed surpass people from the West.

But to overemphasize Nigerians' pride in certain aspects of 419 would reverse what I believe is the larger and more significant thrust of ordinary Nigerians' understandings and responses to corruption. While some stories about 419 contain a Robin Hood–like dimension, more often Nigerians associate 419 with the most egregious mechanisms of corruption through which elites exploit the masses. As the many examples presented in the preceding chapters suggest, for Nigerians, 419 has become a signifier for forms of corruption that exceed the boundaries of acceptable social morality, and stand for widely shared perceptions that amorality is a pervasive problem of postcolonial political and social life.

To understand forms of corruption that most Nigerians view as not only morally objectionable but also indicative of problematic social transformations, it is important to understand the kinds of corruption that are relatively acceptable. As I have shown, Nigerians find some forms of everyday corruption tolerable. Indeed, some acts are not seen as corruption at all in Nigeria, depending in part on one's social position vis-à-vis the particular behavior. Actions to assist family, friends, clients, and community are often undertaken out of a sense of social obligation that trumps a notion of civic duty tied to the state or the national polity. Obligations to kin and clients are rooted in a moral economy that privileges reciprocity, sharing, and interdependence. A politician who steals government money is not accused of 419 if he uses a substantial portion of the money to help his village. A mother who uses nepotistic practices help to her son get a job in her office or a man who uses political influence to help his niece get admission to an exclusive secondary school are not seen as perpetrating 419. Rather, they are performing as good kin and good patrons should.

The label 419 signifies a violation of the expected morality of patrons. In practices of 419, the perpetrators undertake actions to deceive others in schemes that ultimately benefit only themselves. The anger vented against the 419 perpetrators in the Owerri riots was not primarily a consequence of the fact that they obtained their money through criminal activities but that they used their wealth for their own self-aggrandizement, without care for their obligations to others. They violated norms of sharing and reciprocity associated with kinship and patron-clientism. The 419 men targeted in the riots were much like the military men who ruled Nigeria for so many years, and who treated the state as their personal property, without regard for sharing the national cake with the citizenry.

The classic practices of 419, as manifest in the e-mail scams, depend on a deceitful misuse of the trappings of formal institutions to perpetuate corruption. When Nigerians speak of government programs, NGO projects, and democratic elections as being 419, what they mean is that the formalities and appearances associated with these institutions have been manipulated as ruses by unscrupulous elites to consolidate wealth and power in their own hands. While an accusation of 419 is often an expression of disillusionment with the failures of the state to deliver the promises of democracy and development, it is also an indicator that established mechanisms of patron-clientism are no longer benefiting ordinary people. The most aggravating aspect of corruption to Nigerians is that elites are able to straddle and manipulate both the postcolonial state and longer-standing networks of patron-clientism in order to hijack each in ways that benefit a few at the expense of the many.

In recent years, the practices and discontents associated with 419 have cut across a much wider swath of social life than the nexus between citizens and the state. Everything from medical charlatanism to deception among lovers can be glossed in popular Nigerian discourse as 419. While some of the situations and behaviors to which the label 419 is applied appear to move quite far from any conventional notion of corruption, the examples presented throughout the book illustrate how the intertwining of corruption and social morality is central to explaining not only the idioms of Nigerian discontent about corruption but also a good deal of corruption's intractability. As a signifier of discontent that spans so many domains of social life, 419 highlights the connections between the perceived failures of the state and the experience of ordinary citizens as they navigate a political economy where it is presumed by all actors that the Nigerian factor is always present. Nigerians are quick to assume that their fellow citizens are apt to engage in various forms of corruption, including 419, because people share the experience that it is hard to survive, much less succeed, without participating.

The fact that so much popular criticism is leveled not only at elites but turned inward in discourses that implicate a broad breakdown in social morality raises again the question of whether or not this critical collective self-consciousness is constructive. The rise of Pentecostal Christianity in southeastern Nigeria is perhaps the most salient example. On the one hand, Pentecostal discourse has elevated and given powerful voice to popular discontents about injustice and inequality, and in some instances Pentecostalism seems to mobilize collective efforts to effect changes in civic life that could have a direct impact on corruption. On the other hand, the fact that much of the scrutiny of Pentecostalism has focused on personal and domestic behavior, in what I have called "the domestication of religious morality," seems to channel attention away from the public sphere and mitigate any effects that religious revivalism might have on the more political dimensions of corruption. Popular discontent about corruption creates multiple strands of cultural critique, and how these cultural responses affect the practices and trajectory of corruption in Nigeria is one of the key questions for the country's future.

CORRUPTION AND CULTURE

From the outset, I have emphasized that although Nigeria is notorious for corruption, an ethnographic investigation of corruption, in which the experiences of ordinary citizens are examined and privileged, makes it clear that the relationship between corruption and culture is multidimensional. One way to express this multidimensionality is to note, demonstrate, and explain that Nigeria's is as much a culture *against* corruption as a culture *of* corruption. Everyday life in Africa's giant is dominated by people's responses to corruption even more than by corruption itself. It is the level of discontent about corruption among ordinary Nigerians, and the tremendous influence these discontents have on the political imagination and social action, that served as the catalyst to write this book.

I am, obviously, attached to Nigeria in all kinds of ways—as a scholar and an anthropologist, as a friend and colleague to so many Nigerians, and of course, as a husband and an in-law. Writing an anthropological account about corruption posed considerable risks, with perhaps the biggest being that I would unintentionally reinforce misguided notions that corruption in Nigeria is rooted in some sort of primordial traditional culture. This risk is particularly large because corruption has become such a common explanation in the West for the failures of democracy and development in Africa. In contrast, it should be clear from the material presented here that the widespread prevalence of corruption in Nigeria can only be explained by taking into account Nigeria's integration in the world economy as an oil-producing country and a developing nation. Further, as the discontents about corruption (and 419) suggest, Nigerians are well aware that it is the manipulations associated with the institutions and symbols of democracy and development that are integral to the perpetration of the most egregious forms of corruption.

Nigerians do not view corruption as either a traditional or desirable feature of everyday life. The fact that so much of the most spectacular and aggrieving corruption occurs within the state, and in particular at the interface between the state and international institutions, demonstrates not only the global dimensions of the problem but the varying degrees of culpability for Nigerian corruption that extend well beyond Nigeria's borders. While the global obsession with corruption may have some long-term benefits, as it gives ordinary people discursive ammunition to resist elite domination, when it is turned against poor countries by the rich, blaming poverty and inequality on ordinary people and local cultures, these anticorruption discourses end up serving the interests of the powerful.

The distortions created and the inequalities perpetuated when corruption in Nigeria is explained based on reified and simplistic notions of African culture should be strongly contested. I hope that an account such as this one, which recognizes and portrays the tremendous discontent about corruption in Nigeria, and describes the countervailing cultural forces that this discontent both builds on and engenders, helps undermine explanations that simply blame the victims. But it would be irresponsible, from a scholarly point of view and politically, to shrink from confronting some of the troubling conclusions about the relationship between corruption and culture evident in this ethnographic account. When Nigerians speak of the Nigerian factor and everyone knows immediately that it signifies corruption, it suggests an embedded configuration of practices and cultural logics that cannot be explained without confronting questions about culture. It is impossible to absorb the prevalence of corruption and its discontents in Nigeria without concluding that corruption has become heavily implicated in Nigerians' views of their own culture.

Nigerians' ambivalence about corruption is explained by the realities they face. To the extent that ordinary Nigerians are participants in corruption, as well as critics and victims, it is because they are pragmatic: the stakes for individuals in Nigeria are tied ideologically and materially to the social groups to which they belong. Thus, when individuals make choices that one might describe in terms of corruption, they do so with a sense that their own failures to acquire resources will drag others down, and with the knowledge that their own success will be evaluated in terms of its contribution to the larger group. Further, people are well aware of the intense scrutiny they face from their families, communities, and other associates. Hence, when Nigerians speak of the Nigerian factor, they are referring not only to corruption per se but to the pragmatic choices that individuals must make in the context of their obligations to deliver to their people whatever share of the national cake they can capture.

From this perspective, corruption does not look so bad, and indeed, if this were all there were to corruption, I think Nigerians would be much less discontented than they are. But as the concept of 419 suggests, and as the many examples here have shown, corruption in contemporary Nigeria has far exceeded the boundaries that can be explained by ties of kinship, obligations of patronage, and duties to the communities and groups to which an individual belongs. Because 419 relies on deceptions that manipulate the facades of the state, the trappings of development and democracy, and the symbols of modernity, it stands for people's dissatisfaction with precisely these aspects of contemporary life in postcolonial Nigeria. As the institutions of kinship and patron-clientism have become increasingly stretched and strained with the rise of the state as the primary locus of national patrimony, and people can no longer reliably depend on reciprocity and sharing to deliver what they need, practices of 419 have become part of a pragmatic repertoire that ever-larger numbers of Nigerians use to exploit the contemporary political economic landscape. To ordinary Nigerians, the most troubling implication of the Nigerian factor is that 419 has indeed become a way of life.

Widespread cynicism about the ulterior motives of even seemingly well-intentioned endeavors permeates popular culture, with almost anyone or anything being a potential target for an accusation of 419. The joke I mentioned several times—that founding a church or starting an NGO is a promising career choice for recent graduates—is always told with an implication that many new churches and NGOs are 419, in the sense that they are fronts for their founders, designed simply to generate wealth. Churches and NGOs are supposed to be institutions in the service of the greatest good. The fact that they are often perceived to be frauds attests to the depths to which Nigerians believe things have fallen. In recent visits to Nigeria, I have heard people accuse civil rights leaders, anticorruption crusaders, and even outspoken individuals living with HIV as being perpetrators of 419, because they are suspected of manipulating appearances purely for their own gain. It is certainly true that in contemporary Nigeria, there are a whole host of charlatans, fakes, and other opportunists who are suitably described by the label 419. In Nigeria's insecure and unstable economic circumstances, for many people, 419 has become a common strategy.

But the fact that most Nigerians are so upset about, and even obsessed with the prevalence of 419 in their society suggests that countervailing moralities and life strategies are still dominant. The notion of 419 is itself an indigenous Nigerian critique of forms of corruption that the vast majority of Nigerians reject. I find it hopeful to recognize and emphasize ordinary Nigerians' condemnation of 419 and the problematic social transformations it represents. Unfortunately, the degree to which ordinary Nigerians point the fingers of accusation inward, quickly suspecting each other of 419, also deflects attention from the larger structural explanations for their suffering.

ASSESSING ANTICORRUPTION DISCOURSE

The sheer volume of anticorruption rhetoric in Nigeria is overwhelming. Whether it is the recent anticorruption efforts spearheaded by President Obasanjo, the daily editorials against corruption in Nigeria's vibrant press, or the multiple forms of popular cultural critique voiced in the idioms of ethnicity, religion, and other languages of social morality, public and private discourse is saturated with anticorruption argot. Why corruption remains so intractable, even as it is the object of so much venom, merits some final thoughts.

As I was completing the initial draft of this book, President Obasanjo announced the arrest of his minister of Education over allegations that the minister had bribed federal legislators to increase the budget allocation to his ministry. The president delivered a nationally broadcast speech calling for the resignation of several senators, stating in the boldest terms since his election his commitment to fight official corruption. Since then, a number of other top officials have been investigated, arrested, or sacked over allegations of corruption. While ordinary Nigerians would widely welcome a serious crackdown on official corruption, most Nigerians I know view the president's anticorruption crusade with considerable cynicism. In the minds of many Nigerians, official anticorruption efforts are simply tools that political elites use to please international donors, punish political opponents, and further bamboozle the public by pretending to combat corruption even as they loot the state. The vast majority of people in my social networks had little doubt that the minister of education bribed legislators, but wondered why he had been singled out when such practices are believed to be ubiquitous.

Nigerians' skepticism is well-founded. While the government's anticorruption agencies have conducted numerous investigations and even indicted a few former officials, few public figures have been convicted and imprisoned for corruption since the transition to civilian rule in 1999. The fact that politicians use anticorruption rhetoric for political purposes is not surprising, nor is it unique to Nigeria. When politicians and government officials benefit so handsomely from corruption, it is small wonder that their anticorruption initiatives have little bite. More important to explain is why the Nigerian public appears to tolerate the cavalcade of toothless reforms.

Even the explosion of media accounts about corruption and regular editorials supporting anticorruption initiatives seem to have little real effect. Nigeria has one of the most vibrant presses in all of Africa. Particularly since the transition to democracy, reporting has increasingly targeted specific cases of corruption. Yet little seems to change. People accused of spectacular scams frequently remain in office with no obvious consequences. The seeming impotence of media attention to stem corruption results from a combination of factors, including the fluid lines between fact and fiction in the Nigerian press, the stake that so many Nigerians have in specific acts of corruption, and the results of accumulated collective experience, which suggests that corruption is so endemic, all efforts to combat it are superficial compared with the real interests that sustain it.

Very rarely do media accounts of corruption include the level of documentation and detail that would assist in the prosecution of the alleged culprits. Indeed, probably more often than not, there is little real evidence in the press to substantiate the stories of corruption. Many times over the past fifteen years I have wondered whether the rumors about corruption I heard in popular discourse were generated through equally unsubstantiated newspaper stories, or whether the newspaper stories were themselves simply a reproduction of a widely circulating rumor that finally made it into print. When the media function similarly to rumors—giving voice to popular interpretations and discontents, rather than documenting evidence—they often become just another vehicle for the symbolic expression of frustrations about corruption, without offering any leverage to effect change.

As a medium to express and vent frustrations with corruption, the press participates in the larger problem, in which general frustrations with corruption are widespread, but particular accusations of corruption are always contested by those whose interests are threatened. Thus, in almost every case of alleged corruption that has risen to the level of extensive media attention in Nigeria, a political story emerges, in which those whose interests are attached to the fate of the allegedly corrupt official recast the accusation as a politically motivated vendetta. These political explanations are widely believed by the public, because the assumption is that in a society where corruption is perceived as ubiquitous, some other reason must account for who gets caught.

Corruption is so entrenched in Nigeria that no one can really imagine that anticorruption efforts are anything but political—often they are perceived as outright ruses. To the extent that ordinary Nigerians themselves are the voices and vehicles for the expression of anticorruption sentiments, a combination of dramatic inequality and the insidious ways that common people must depend on mechanisms of corruption simply to survive tempers the extent to which these anticorruption sentiments can translate into wider social transformations. Nevertheless, while Nigerians themselves are often quite glum about the prospects for change, the widespread discontents about corruption can also be seen as an indicator of Nigerians' capacities to craft alternative futures. As cynical as many people seem to be about official anticorruption efforts, the aspirations for change—indeed the expectations that things will one day be different—are palpable.

EXPECTATIONS FOR DEMOCRACY AND DEVELOPMENT

The striking twin to Nigerians' tremendous cynicism about their own society is a remarkable degree of self-confidence that they have what it takes to make things better. This self-confidence contributes to a collective expectation that the country can and should be great. Corruption and the failures it represents are galling to Nigerians because they believe so strongly that they have the natural and human resources to be a successful country.

In many respects, corruption in Nigeria seems truly intractable. Part of the goal of this book has been to show how and why people feel pressured and obliged to participate, even as most citizens also criticize corruption and recognize that in general terms, it is bad for them and their country. But by paying attention to people's ambivalence and discontents about corruption, and particularly to anger over the forms of corruption Nigerians label 419, I believe it is reasonable to conclude that the seeds of change are germinating, and that the very mechanisms through which 419 is perpetrated are part of a larger process in which expectations for democracy and development are cultivated.

The ironic consequence of the ways in which political and economic elites have manipulated the symbols of democracy and development for their own benefit is that even in their unfulfilled form, these ideals have created growing popular expectations that they be delivered in reality. In contemporary Nigeria, ordinary citizens are stretching their networks of kinship and patron-clientism as far as they can in order to obtain whatever share of the national cake that they can manage. The fact that Nigerians must rely on patronage for access to state resources contributes directly to corruption. But as these networks become less reliable (in part because elites use 419 to capture so many resources), people are looking for alternative mechanisms and idioms of accountability with which to secure what they need. Even as many of the endeavors of government to implement democracy and development are experienced by the Nigerian public as 419, the state is also creating expectations and providing the population with the discursive language with which to demand that these expectations be fulfilled. Nigeria may not have achieved either true democracy or adequate development, but ordinary Nigerians are well aware of these failures and their aspirations for change grow stronger every day.

Expressing discontent is the national pastime. Indeed, one of the most admirable characteristics of Nigerians is their willingness to criticize themselves when they analyze the state of their society. But they are self-critical to a fault. In my view, whether the growing expectations for democracy and development can be harnessed to create real change in ways that address the country's endemic corruption and the inequalities it perpetuates depends on the way in which ordinary Nigerians direct their cultural critiques. Will they evolve into truly political critiques that demand accountability from Nigeria's leaders, or will they further devolve into tirades about social morality that obscure the real roots of suffering?

THE NIGERIAN FACTOR RECONSIDERED

To Nigerians, corruption is such a common phenomenon that it defines the nation. *The Nigerian factor is corruption.* It is the variable that everyone, from ordinary citizens to elite politicians, takes into account in all interactions with the state, but also in many other arenas of political, economic, and social life. Expectations of corruption infuse everyday experience. Whether one is a motorist approaching a police checkpoint on a public highway, a businessperson looking to secure a contract, a parent anticipating a child's entrance into secondary school, a patient seeking treatment for an illness, a traveler applying for a foreign visa, or even an adolescent involved in a romance, the specter of corruption looms large. The very expansiveness of 419 as a descriptor for all things corrupt, whether political or personal, economic or moral, attests to the pervasiveness of corruption and its centrality as a metaphor for modern life in Nigeria.

Discourses about corruption take many forms and are expressed in numerous idioms. Stories about corruption dominate newspaper headlines, energize ethnic nationalist political propaganda, animate witchcraft accusations, enliven church sermons, spark marketplace debates, and stimulate village gossip. Whether they are in idioms of humor or complaint, politics or religion, neoliberalism or witchcraft, discourses about corruption saturate the popular imagination in contemporary Nigeria. Corruption is a primary discursive lens through which people interpret the experience of postcolonial citizenship and suffering in Africa's giant. No other issue so thoroughly captures popular attention and captivates the collective consciousness.

Through an ethnographic account, I have tried to explain the apparent paradox that ordinary Nigerians are at once active participants, vocal critics, and the principal victims when it comes to corruption. The explanation for this apparent contradiction offers a revealing perspective on the nature of social transformation in Nigeria, and in many other postcolonial contexts. Both Nigerians' participation in corruption and their constant complaints, including widespread collective self-criticism about their own involvement, demonstrate the complex and often contradictory social realities that ordinary citizens must navigate in order to survive. Corruption and the discontent it produces operate at the interstices between state and society, public and private, local and global, and pragmatic and moral. Moreover, as the many cases examined in the previous chapters have shown, corruption and its associated discourses of complaint cut across contrasting institutions and competing moral idioms.

Reduced to its simplest form, the story of corruption in Nigeria illuminates the struggles that unfold as people in postcolonial societies experience the transition from forms of social organization and shared moralities rooted in kinship and patron-clientism to those associated with modern nation-states and a capitalist global economy. The transgressions and discontents that these transformations produce seem to be integral to the ways that postcolonial states, and the elites who dominate them, utilize expectations of development and democracy to control national wealth and power. The ultimate question is whether ordinary Nigerians' paradoxical position as participants, critics, and victims will provide them leverage to facilitate a long process of positive transformation that gives rise to genuinely accountable institutions of democracy and development, or whether elites are able to continue to manipulate promises of democracy and development to keep wealth and power out of reach for ordinary people.

Appendix

Letter from Chief Audo Ogbeh, People's Democratic Party National Chairman, to Nigerian President Olusegun Obasanjo (reproduced from http://www.dawodu.com/ogbeh1.htm [accessed May 19, 2005]).

December 6, 2004
His Excellency,
The President, Commander-In-Chief,
Federal Republic of Nigeria, Abuja

RE: **ANAMBRA AND RELATED MATTERS**

About a month ago, the nation woke up to the shocking news of a devastating attack on Anambra State resulting in the burning down of radio and television stations, hotels, vehicles, assembly quarters, the residence of the state Chief Judge and finally, Government House, Awka. Dynamite was even applied in the exercise and all or nearly most of these in the full glare of our own police force as shown on NTA for the world to see. The operation lasted three days.

That week, in all churches and mosques, we, our party, and you as Head of Government and Leader of this Nation came under the most scathing and blithering attacks. We were singly and severally accused of connivance in action and so forth. Public anger reached its peak.

RECOMMENDATION

You set up a reconciliation committee headed by Ebonyi State Governor, Dr. Sam Egwu, and we all thought this would help calm nerves and perhaps bring about some respite. But quite clearly things are nowhere near getting better.

While the reconciliation team attempted to inspect damaged sites in Anambra, they were scared away by gun fire, further heightening public anger and disdain for us.

BOMB EXPLOSION IN GOVERNMENT HOUSE, AWKA

On Tuesday, the 30th day of November, 2004, another shocking development; a reported bomb explosion in Government House Awka. Since then, the media, public discourse within and even outside of our borders, have been dominated by the most heinous and hateful of expletives against our party and your person and government. It would appear that the perpetrators of these acts are determined to stop at nothing since there has not been any visible sign of reproach from law enforcement agencies. I am now convinced that the rumours and speculations making the rounds that they are determined to kill Dr. Chris Ngige may not be unfounded.

The question now is, what would be the consequences of such a development? How do we exonerate ourselves from culpability, and worse still, how do we even hope to survive it? Mr. President, I was part of the second republic and we fell. Memories of that fall are a miserable litany of woes we suffered, escaping death only by God's supreme mercy. Then we were suspected to have stolen all of Nigeria's wealth. After several months in prison, some of us were freed to come back to life penniless and wretched. Many have gone to their early graves un-mourned because the public saw us all as renegades.

I am afraid we are drifting in the same direction again. In life, perception is reality and today, we are perceived in the worst light by an angry, scornful Nigerian Public for reasons which are absolutely unnecessary.

Mr. President, if I write in this vein, it is because I am deeply troubled and I can tell you that an overwhelming percentage of our party members feel the same way though many may never be able to say this to you for a variety of reasons.

But the back stops at your table and in my position, not only as Chairman but also as an old friend and loyal defender of your development programmes which I have never stopped defending, I dare to think that we can, either by omission or commission allow ourselves to crash and bring to early grief, this beautiful edifice called democracy.

On behalf of the peoples Democratic Party, I call on you to act now and bring any, and all criminal, even treasonable, activity to a halt. You and you alone, have the means. Do not hesitate. We do not have too much time to waste.

A.I. Ogbeh, OFR
National Chairman

cc: Vice President
Chairman, Board of Trustees
Speaker, House of Representatives

• • •

Letter from Nigerian President Olusegun Obasanjo to Chief Audo Ogbeh, People's Democratic Party National Chairman (reproduced from http://www.dawodu.com/obas26.htm [accessed May 19, 2005]).

December 12, 2004

I am amused and not surprised by your letter of December 6, 2004 because after playing hide and seek games over a period of time, you have finally, at least in writing, decided to unmask and show your true colour.

Having made this introductory point, let us go over systematically and, in some detail, through the whole episode of the Anambra saga. I must add that I have expressed sadness and condemned the wanton destruction of properties that took place in Anambra recently.

When it turned out that, Governor Mbadinuju was an unmitigated failure in Anambra, as PDP governor in our first term, I made it clear to you that I would not go to Anambra to campaign if Governor Mbadinuju was being sponsored as PDP gubernatorial candidate in spite of his calamitous failure. You did not tell me that you were sending a discrete investigation team to Anambra to find out the situation on the ground.

You never said yes or no but I determined that, in good conscience, I could not go to Anambra to campaign for support and seek endorsement for Governor Mbadinuju.

About six weeks later, you came to report to me that you have sent two people discretely to ascertain on the ground whether people wanted Mbadinuju or not and you had received report that 66 2/3 of the people of Anambra did not want Mbadinuju.

For me, what we knew about Mbadinuju in terms of failure to pay salaries in some cases for over 7 months which led to school children not being able to take the WASCE did not need any discrete investigation.

However, your discrete investigation convinced you that I was right and you brought Mbadinuju to me, for you and I to tell him that he could not be a gubernatorial candidate of the PDP in Anambra.

You rightly, I believe, requested that I should work with you to give him a soft landing and we agreed to make him an ambassador after the election and we even agreed on which mission abroad, subject to our success in the elections.

Mbadinuju asked for a letter from me and I refused because I said that my word was my bond but that you were free to write him one. A few weeks after that meeting, Mbadinuju decamped from our party to the AD and sought election as governor of Anambra on the platform of the AD.

When the members of our party started jostling for nomination, as normal with me, I refused to endorse a candidate; it is only after the primaries that the party's candidate becomes my own candidate.

And in the case of Anambra, if I had wanted to support anybody at all, it would have been Jerry Ugokwe because he was one man I knew but, of course, I was consistent on my policy. And when Ngige emerged as the candidate of the PDP from the primaries, he was brought to be introduced to me and, of course, he became not only the party's candidate but also mine.

After enquiries about the situation in Anambra and about Ngige himself, I made a point to him that he should go and reconcile himself with his father with whom he was not on talking terms as I believed it was an abomination for an African son to be in a state of enmity with his father to the point of absolute non-communication. I advised Ngige to reconcile with his father and the rest of his family and he reported to me that he did.

The election took place and Ngige was declared the winner. I congratulated him along with other victorious candidates. Realizing that Ngige would need some assistance to help him through the teething problem of his administration, I invited him to consider having a non-partisan honourary committee of elders of the state and he agreed.

I talked to Igwe Nwokedi, Chief Mbasulike Amechi and the Anglican Bishop of Awka to get two more people with them to act as such honourary non-partisan advisory committee of elders for the governor.

For them to maintain their independence, I said that any transportation or administrative funds that they might require would be provided from the presidency rather than the state.

After two months, Igwe Nwokedi, who was supposed to be the chairman, reported that the governor was impossible to advise or to work with and that was the end of that effort. Mr. Chairman, I reported that effort to you.

When on one occasion, Chris Uba came to report that things appeared to be going wrong between him and the governor in the presence of Chief Amechi, I asked the latter to go and sort it out for them in his capacity as an elder of the state and veteran politician. I requested Chief Amechi to report back to me. The truth is that as far as Anambra was concerned, I considered it my duty to work with all stakeholders in the area of avoiding conflict and on that ground I promised to act on any report or advice from Chief Mbasulike Amechi.

I never had warning that things were going sour in the state any more until I was in Maputo, Mozambique on July 9, 2003 when I received report that the governor had resigned. I did what normally I do not do except in an emergency by using government facility for strictly non-governmental purpose. I instructed that an airplane from the presidential fleet be made available to a team to rush to Anambra to investigate what was happening. That team went on Friday morning while I was still in Mozambique and returned on Friday evening. You will recall that the team reported to you and I that what was happening in Anambra required urgent party action to resolve it as a family affair.

A Senate Panel that followed in the same vein re-opened something similar. Mr. Chairman, the following Sunday, you received and opened a brown envelope in my residence in Abuja that contained three different letters of resignation and a video of announcement of resignation of Governor Ngige. You were as shocked as I was and you promised to do something about it that night. You left with copies of the documents and the next thing you did after that was to insinuate that Ngige's problems were caused by me.

Unfortunately, as in many other instances, you failed to do what you should have done as the chief executive of the party and rather prefer to insult me not only as the President of the nation but also as the leader of the party which you seem never to recognize or acknowledge. From that point on, I only did my job as a President by investigating.

What the police did or did not do and dishing out punishment to be confirmed by the Police Service Commission which in its own report asked for a complete investigation of the matter. That investigation was carried out by the Attorney General and his report was acted upon. After that, I deliberately remained aloof about political events in Anambra except whatever may affect security and loss of life and property.

I, in fact, asked both Ngige and Chris Uba never to come to my office or to my residence and you know this. As far as I could remember, a childhood friend of yours came with you to discuss the issue of Anambra between you and I on one occasion.

Soon after, I briefed the party caucus in detail on my role, on what I saw and did and the party caucus endorsed every action that had been taken by the executive arm of government in respect with Anambra. A few months later, two members of your Working Committee—Olisa Metu (an Ex-Officio member) and Farouk (the youth leader)—came to appeal to me to specially intervene in reconciling Ngige and Chris Uba, I refused initially because I believed it was really the responsibility of the party. But since you had shirked your responsibility as party chairman, I conceded and asked the two members of the NWC to bring Ngige and Chris Uba to me. That was the only time, after several months, that I allowed them to enter my residence.

I was shocked that a man in the position of aspirant or one elected as governor could actually resign on three different occasions in writing and on one occasion, the resignation was on videotape. I, also, was of the opinion that for Ngige to have allowed that to happen, there must have been some extra-legal motivation. There has been accusation and counter-accusation as reasons for such ungainly behaviour. When the two of them came to see me, the two young men who had brokered the opportunity for Ngige and Chris Uba to see me wanted to leave. I refused and insisted that they had to be at the meeting because I wanted them as witnesses.

After almost two hours of talk, we dismissed hoping that fences would be mended and reconciliation would be fully established. They left and waited on the corridors for a while. Olisa Metu came back and requested that I should meet with Ngige and Chris Uba alone without witnesses for them to feel free to unwind.

Again, I did and that was when I got the real shock of my life when Chris Uba looked Ngige straight in the face and said, "You know you did not win the election" and Ngige answered "Yes, I know I did not win." Chris Uba went further to say to Ngige, "You don't know in detail how it was done." I was horrified and told both of them to leave my residence.

This incident was reported to you because although constitutionally, Ngige had been declared winner, for me and, I believe, for you there remains a moral burden and dilemma both as leaders in Nigeria and leaders of our party.

You did not consider it important enough to do anything or talk about it. I told Ngige that the only way I could live with this moral dilemma since he had been constitutionally declared as governor is that I will continue to deal with him in his capacity as the governor of a State in Nigeria purely and strictly on formal basis either until he runs out his term, he decides to follow the path of honour or until any competent authority declares otherwise. That remains my position to date.

That notwithstanding, immediately after the Court of Appeal overturned Justice Nnaji's order, the Police promptly obeyed. That is what rule of law is all about.

Furthermore, based on all that I had heard, I told Chris Uba and Ngige that their case was like the case of two armed robbers that conspired to loot a house and after bringing out the loot, one decided to do the other in and the issue of fair play even among robbers became a factor. The two robbers must be condemned for robbery in the first instance and the greedy one must be specially pointed out for condemnation to do justice among the robbers. To me, the determination of the greedy one is also a problem, maybe they are both equally greedy. Justice, fairness and equity are always the basis of peace and harmony in any human organisation or relationship. Anambra issue is essentially a human organizational and human relationship issue.

I was on a tour of five countries in five days going from the UK through Finland and Sweden with a stop-over in Libya to Tanzania last November when the recent issue of violence broke out. The Inspector General of Police who claimed that the crowd was overwhelming for the police strength was instructed to double the number of mobile police unit by bringing additional men and women from the adjoining states. He did so and he reported that 19 looters and destroyers were arrested and charged to court with some vehicles seized. NTA coverage of that unfortunate incidents is not the issue, wars are watched like theatrical plays in the contemporary world. The issue is whether or not the police performed or did not perform their duties.

Mr. Chairman, obviously you do not expect me to do less than I have done. I even went out to do more because since you failed to either resolve the political issues that are intra-party matters and they have been spread to engulf the entire state or decisively punish any offender, I decided in consultation with Governor Ngige, to set up a fact-finding and reconciliation committee under the Governor of Ebonyi State to put an end to the violence, create a conducive atmosphere for the Governor to return to his station and to ensure permanent peace, security through reconciliation of the known warring party members—Chris Ngige and Chris Uba—and their supporters. And this was after I had a meeting with both the PDP state chairman and the governor. Since the Governor of Ebonyi, whom I have asked to keep you fully posted on his findings and progress of his committee has not yet reported to me, and since I have taken every necessary step to ensure a resolution of the political problem in Anambra which you have failed to confront, I consider your letter opportunistic, and only a smokescreen and I believe I should answer it in some reasonable detail as I have done. I also took every reasonable step to beef up security to deal with the situation.

On Tuesday, December 7, 2004, after the party meeting on the crisis in Kogi State, you told me that you had written me a letter on threat to Ngige's life and you indicated to me, which you did not do in the letter, that one Honourable Chuma Nzeribe was the culprit. As I will not dilly-dally on an issue of security, even before I received your letter, I directed the Director-General of the State Security Service to look into the matter. It may interest you that almost on daily basis letters are received in my office of people alleging that other people want to assassinate them. All such allegations are forwarded to security people for investigation. None has been substantiated yet. But we will not take any issue of security lightly no matter who claims to be in danger.

And contrary to your belief and insinuation, just today, December 9, the governor of Anambra came to me to seek my opinion and advice on whether or not to constitute a commission of enquiry into what happened in the state. I did not hesitate to advise and encourage him to do so in order that all the facts would be exposed and verifiable truth established rather than trading in rumours.

Let me end on this note: whatever may be your reason for the ambivalent disposition and handling of the party problem in Anambra like you have done in other places and the ulterior motive for your letter, if and when in my capacity as President of Nigeria duty calls on me to act, I will not shirk my responsibility and we will at the end of the day be at the bar of the public both at the party level and national level. Let me also say that it is, indeed, unfortunate that you make so many unnecessary and unwarranted insinuations in your letter about our great country. I have taken judicial note of the ominous comparisons you made between a government in which you participated that was overthrown in a coup d'etat and this present administration.

I wonder if that is your wish since you may not now go out penniless. But whatever agenda you may be working at God is always in charge and in control. Warped perception must be differentiated from reality.

Perception created and manipulated for a sinister purpose cannot be reality. The greatest danger to any country is putting truth out of favour; extolling evils of lies, deceit, treachery, disloyalty, unpatriotism, corruption and unconstitutionally. That is my greatest fear for Nigeria and it should be yours and that of any right-thinking Nigerian. Not too long ago, I challenged you to think beyond the ordinary, the expected and the self, I still put that challenge on the table.

Let it be on record that I do believe that I have invested the totality of my life in what I may call "Enterprise Nigeria" and if it means that in the process of repositioning our dear country for sustainable greatness, what is dearest to me would have to be sacrificed, I will in good conscience, not hesitate to do so.

And if that will enhance Nigeria's development, it is a sacrifice that I will be glad to make. I have reached a stage in life that I have passed the state of being intimidated or being flattered.

I can stand before God and man and in clear conscience to defend every measure that I have taken everywhere in Nigeria since I became the President and will continue to act without fear or favour or inducement.

And it does not matter to me what is sponsored in the Nigerian media, in particular, the print media. I believe that our vindication will come through the truth, which is the only thing that can uplift a nation and make an honest man and a sincere believer in God free.

May I crave your indulgence to copy this letter to all those to whom your letter to me was copied. In addition, I am copying the President of the Senate, the number three man in the present hierarchy of this government and a party leader in his own right, whom you deliberately left out of the distribution list of your letter for reason best known to you. One thing I will never stop doing is praying for Nigeria in general and Anambra in particular.

May God continue to bless and prosper Nigeria. In spite of the malevolence of some Nigerians, Nigeria is moving to the cruising level and cruising speed. That is the work of God and what all Nigerians and friends of Nigeria should do is to join hands in hastening the work of God in Nigeria at this juncture.

May God help us to help ourselves. I wish you well.

Signed President Olusegun Obasanjo

cc: Vice-President Atiku Abubakar;
President of the Senate, Chief Adolphus Wabara;
the Speaker of the House of Representatives, Alhaji Aminu Bello Masari; and the Chairman of the Board of Trustees of PDP, Chief Anthony Anenih.

Notes

INTRODUCTION

1. For exceptions, see, for example, Parry (1986), Yang (1989, 1994), Gupta (1995), and Yan (1996). French anthropologists Giorgio Blundo and Jean-Pierre Olivier de Sardan have undertaken the most systematic anthropological studies of corruption that I am aware of, with most of their findings published in French. See, for example, Blundo and Olivier de Sardan (2001a, 2001b), and Blundo (2000, 2001a, 2001b, 2001c, 2003).

CHAPTER 1

1. For examples of media coverage, see "Halliburton's $2.4 Million Bribe Revisited," *Vanguard* (Lagos), February 3, 2004; Simon Romero, "Halliburton Seeks Distance between Itself and Inquiry," *New York Times*, June 14, 2004, C9; Simon Romero, "Halliburton Severs Link with 2 over Nigeria Inquiry," *New York Times*, June 19, 2004, C1; Hector Igbikiowubo, "Two More Enron Executives Charged in Nigerian Energy Deal," *Vanguard* (Lagos), October 21, 2003; Laurel Brubaker Calkins, "Six Accused over Enron Sham Sale," *National Post's Financial Post and FP Investing* (Toronto), September 22, 2004, 11.

2. Examples of anti-419 and humorous 419 Web sites can be found at http://www.419fraud.com/index.htm, http://home.rica.net/alphae/419coal/fighters.htm, and http://www.scamorama.com.

CHAPTER 2

1. The building of fences in Nigeria could itself be the subject of an interesting article. Few contracts are more coveted (except perhaps, on a larger scale, the repair of roads) because few contracts are more frivolous. Apparently, building fences is highly profitable; one can charge high amounts and do the job for little. While I was a Fulbright Fellow in 1996, the governing council at Abia State University voted to spend fourteen million naira to build a fence around the entire campus—rather than invest in books, laboratories, dormitories, and so on, all of which were in short supply or falling apart. By all accounts, building the fence was an obvious attempt to create a contract that would enrich those who awarded it. The university fence, like so many others, was justified based on concerns about security—though in this case, it was unclear whether security meant keeping the students in or others out.

2. I copied this version of this widely circulating joke from a Web site aimed at the Nigerian diaspora: http://www.motherlandnigeria.com/humor.html.

CHAPTER 3

1. The jokes about NGOs attest to the fact that Nigeria shares with the development industry a keen fondness for acronyms. I know of no two domains where there are more of them than in international development documents and official Nigerian publications. Indeed, it is surely no coincidence that as successive Nigerian governments learned to construct their legitimacy around the promises of development, they adopted the discursive practices of the development industry. But as is so often the case, Nigerians have outdone the originators.

2. On one of our last stops, I discovered that one of Mrs. Egwu's other endeavors was the construction of a small factory to make these "appropriate technology" clay bricks.

CHAPTER 4

1. Obasanjo had been a military head of state in the 1970s, and prior to 1999 had been the only military ruler to hand over power to a civilian government.

2. Many parts of Igboland did not have a precolonial tradition of chiefship, much less kingship. But the British imposed a more hierarchical political structure in parts of Nigeria that lacked such traditions as part of the colonial strategy of indirect rule (Afigbo 1972). Contemporary disputes over local "traditional" leadership in Igboland frequently have their roots in this colonial legacy.

3. For examples, see "Observers Point to Blatant Fraud in Nigerian Elections," *Deutsche Press-Agentur*, April 22, 2003; Glenn MacKenzie, "Obasanjo Wins Reelection but Nigerian Opposition Rejects the Results," Associated Press, April 22, 2003.

4. For detailed accounts of the Anambra crisis in the Nigerian press, see, for example, "Anarchy in Anambra," *Vanguard* (Lagos), July 11, 2003; "Story of the (Un)successful 'Coup,'" *Daily Champion* (Lagos), July 12, 2003; "Battle for the Soul of Anambra," *This Day* (Lagos), July 14, 2003; "Anambra Coup: The Real Issues," *Vanguard* (Nigeria), July 17, 2003; "The Trouble with Anambra," *This Day* (Lagos), July 17, 2003.

5. Traditional shrines are feared in the sense that it is believed that the deities to which these shrines are dedicated have the capacity to see the truth behind human appearances, and that they can also affect people's destiny. In the context of an oath sworn at a shrine, it is thought that a violation of such an oath will result in some sort of calamity—for example, an illness, an accident, or death. Fears about these shrines are exacerbated by the suspicion that they can be manipulated for evil purposes, and specifically that shrine priests can be paid to use their connections with the supernatural for malevolent objectives. In Nigerian parlance, the shrines, or at least their priests, can be 419, appearing to serve a positive function, but really operating nefariously. Media reports and popular rumors suggested that Governor Ngige had been forced to swear his oath of loyalty to Uba at a well-known shrine in the community of Okija. About a year after the initial crisis involv-

ing Ngige and Uba in Anambra State, a scandal erupted over the Okija shrines, illustrating the connections between corruption, social morality, and the idiom of the occult. I examine the case in chapter 5.

6. For accounts of the November 2004 mayhem in Anambra, see Anyaochukwu Agbo, "Day of the Jackals," *Tell* (Lagos), November 22, 2004, 16–23; Chris Ajaero, "The Plot That Failed," *Newswatch* (Lagos), November 29, 2004, 13–27.

7. See Dulue Mbachu and Glenn McKenzie, "Nigerian Leader Declares State of Emergency in Violence-Torn State amid Reports of New Attacks," Associated Press, May 18, 2004; "Obasanjo Declares State of Emergency in Plateau," *Vanguard* (Lagos), May 19, 2004.

8. Chief Audu Ogbeh's letter to President Obasanjo about the Anambra crisis and President Obasanjo's reply were published in many Nigerian newspapers. I retrieved the letters via the Internet at http://www.dawodu.com/ogbeh1.htm and http://www.dawodu.com/obas26.htm.

CHAPTER 5

1. The rise of some forms of Pentecostalism in Nigeria is closely related to popular desires for economic success as well as growing tensions between individualistic aspirations and group-oriented obligations to kin and communities of origin. In the wake of the Owerri riots, Pentecostalism served as a platform for the expression of popular discontent over inequality and the attainment of fast wealth through magic means. At the same time, some Pentecostal churches were accused of participating in satanic rituals to produce such wealth. I take up the relationship between discontents about corruption and the growing popularity of Pentecostalism and other evangelical sects in chapter 7. Similar phenomena have been addressed by Marshall (1991), Marshall-Fratani (1998), and Meyer (1995, 1998).

2. A principal goal of this chapter is to unpack what Nigerians mean when they speak of fast wealth, relating vernacular Nigerian ideas about the magic origins of such riches to an analysis of popular discontents about corruption. For introductory purposes, it is sufficient to reiterate that postcolonial political and economic systems in Nigeria have created tremendous opportunities for the accumulation of great wealth over a short period of time, through rents associated with the oil industry (Graf 1988; Panter-Brick 1978; Watts 1992) and other more criminal enterprises (Apter 1999; Bayart 1999). While corruption creates many opportunities for the rapid accumulation of wealth, the idioms of magic and witchcraft provide ordinary people a means to interpret and criticize these seemingly unfathomable riches.

3. When Nigerians talk about spraying money they refer to a widely practiced custom whereby individuals show support or admiration for others by placing bills on the bodies (usually the foreheads) of recipients. Money is typically sprayed on a bride and groom as they dance following a marriage ceremony, on the children of a dead elder as they parade with the elder's picture following a burial, and on all kinds of performers (musicians, comedians, public speakers, and so on) when their performance is appreciated. Prior to attending wedding and burial ceremonies, elite Nigerians make a point of stopping at the bank to acquire crisp new

banknotes because they produce the most dramatic effect. There are even street-corner entrepreneurs whose business is to sell new notes to those without the time to wait at the bank. On the way to a wedding one can stop and buy new notes. For example, one might pay eleven hundred naira in old notes to purchase a thousand in crisp twenty naira notes. The act of spraying itself has become a performance, and those who do the spraying are often drawing public attention to themselves as much as to those they are supporting. The dance of the sprayer is watched and admired, but most important, the quantity and denomination of the bills pasted to the foreheads of the sprayee are closely monitored. People who spray large sums of money are roundly applauded by the crowd—although as the criticisms of 419 men illustrate, such ostentation is resented even as it is admired.

4. The allegations of human-meat pepper soup found at the Pentecostal church and more than a dozen bodies dug up at the Otokoto Hotel are just a few examples of the exaggerated rumors that flourished in the wake of the Owerri riots. The meaning and significance of these rumors is something I will examine in detail below.

5. It is important to note that the beheaded child, eventually identified as Anthony Ikechukwu Okonkwo, became something of a symbol of inequality as well. He came from a poor family, and on the day he went missing he had been out hawking boiled peanuts for his guardians.

6. A house Aneke built for his mother-in-law was torched during the riots. The initial popular account I heard said that Aneke's house in Owerri was built for a girlfriend, rather than his mother-in-law. Building a house for one's mother-in-law, even if much of the money is looted from the government, fits much more closely with Nigerian standards of moral behavior than building a house for a lover. The former is a fulfillment of kinship obligations, while the latter is a purely selfish aggrandizement. It is surely not coincidental that popular accounts mentioned that the house was for Aneke's girlfriend rather than for his mother-in-law.

7. Okada, the popular name for motorcycle taxis in Nigeria, is itself an example of the kind of self-conscious (and playful) popular critiques of inequality that are so common in Nigerian discourse. Okada was the name of Nigeria's first (and for a time, largest) private airline. Only the elite could afford to travel on Okada Airlines.

8. As in much of Africa, burials, in addition to being rituals that mourn death and celebrate the life of the deceased, are cultural performances in which social ties are reinforced and social status is enacted. There are few moments in everyday life in southeastern Nigeria where so much of a person's reputation is at stake as in the burial of one's parent (Smith 2004a). Thus, "kidnapping" a rich industrialist's father's corpse for ransom is similarly as reasonable (from a criminal's point of view) and horrifying (from a victim's point of view) as kidnapping a child.

9. In 2000, I saw an advertisement on U.S. television for an online investment firm in which a man is shown on an operating table in a hospital because he has "money coming out the wazoo." In other words, he has done so well through his Internet stock trading that he has money coming out of his ass. Far from this being portrayed as a problem, the commercial suggests that there is nothing one would like more in this world than to have money coming out the ass. The juxtaposition of this commercial with Nigerian stories about money emanating from human

orifices offers an interesting contrast with regard to the means through which it is possible to achieve wealth in the two societies and the moralities about individual acquisition that result.

CHAPTER 6

1. I had a difficult time uncovering the origin of the name "the Bakassi Boys." The Bakassi peninsula is a geographic area between Nigeria and Cameroon that has been the object of a long dispute over sovereignty. Most people I asked could not explain why an Aba-based Igbo vigilante group would bear the name of a region that is distinctly non-Igbo. A few people told me that the name Bakassi connoted armed combat and a readiness to fight, projecting onto the Bakassi Boys a military prowess. The most compelling explanation for the name, however, came from a police report reproduced in a Nigerian weekly magazine, in which the original patron of the Bakassi Boys, the president of the traders' association, was questioned about the group. He said that the shoe market from which the vigilante group first emerged was newly located, and "situated at the boundary to Osisioma Local Government Area and Aba North Local Government Area which most time cause conflict between the two local government mentioned above hence the name Bakassi" (Police report 2001, 28). In other words, the Bakassi Boys got their name from the market from which they originally emerged, which got its name from a local border dispute. Johannes Harnischfeger (2003) asserts that the Bakassi Boys were named for a section of the market that was swampy like the Bakassi peninsula. I find this explanation for the derivation less convincing.

CHAPTER 7

1. One must be careful not to overemphasize the effect of democracy in increasing freedom of the press or liberating political discourse in Nigeria. On the one hand, both the Nigerian press and Nigerian popular discourse remained energetic throughout military rule, even during the height of the Abacha regime, during which newspapers were routinely raided, journalists detained, and political opponents silenced through a variety of means, including assassination. On the other hand, even since the new democratic dispensation, the government has sometimes interfered with press freedoms, and vocal political opposition is still perceived to carry risks. Nonetheless, both the press (especially the print media—radio and television have, until recently, been largely government controlled) and popular political discourse are remarkably vibrant.

2. Several Nigerian friends have advised me that it is a good strategy to look for an okada driver with gray hair. These men, my friends say, are more likely to have their own families and will therefore be less reckless than the younger drivers. Nigerians on the back of motorcycle taxis are in a constant battle with their chauffeurs to get them to slow down and be more careful.

3. As revivalist discourse about Biafra has surged in the wake of the transition to civilian rule, so too has the openness with which ordinary Igbos discuss their memories of the war, regardless of their positions regarding MASSOB's secessionist agenda (Smith 2005).

References

Abrahams, Ray. 1996. Vigilantism: Order and disorder on the frontiers of the state. In *Inside and outside the law: Anthropological studies of authority and ambiguity*, ed. Olivia Harris. New York: Routledge.

———. 1998. *Vigilant citizens: Vigilantism and the state.* Cambridge, UK: Polity Press.

Achebe, Chinua. 1983. *The trouble with Nigeria.* Oxford: Heinemann.

Adekeye, Fola. 2002. Killers on campus. *Newswatch* (Lagos), July 29.

Afigbo, Adiele E. 1972. *The warrant chiefs: Indirect rule in southeastern Nigeria, 1891–1929.* New York: Humanities Press.

Agbaje, Adigun, and Jinmi Adisa. 1988. Political education and public policy in Nigeria: The War against Indiscipline (WAI). *Journal of Commonwealth and Comparative Politics* 6, no. 1:22–37.

Agbo, Anyaochukwu. 2004. Day of the jackals. *Tell* (Lagos), November 22.

Ajaero, Chris. 2004. The plot that failed. *Newswatch* (Lagos), November 29.

Akani, Christian U. 2002. *Corruption in Nigeria: The Niger Delta experience.* Enugu, Nigeria: Fourth Dimension.

Akor, Ambrose. 1996. Owerri: Through fire, brimstone, and ritual killing. *Guardian* (Lagos), September 29.

Aku, Ali. 2003. *Anti-corruption crusade in Nigeria: The challenging of ICPC in national cleansing.* Abuja, Nigeria: ICPC.

Alaezi, O. 1999. *Ibos: Hebrew exiles from Israel.* Aba, Nigeria: Onzy Publications.

Amnesty International. 2002. *Thousands of summary executions by state-endorsed vigilante groups in south and southeast Nigeria.* http://web.amnesty.org/web/content.nsf/pages/gbr_nigeria_ (accessed May 20, 2002).

Anambra coup: The real issues. 2003. *Vanguard* (Lagos), July 17.

Anarchy in Anambra. 2003. *Vanguard* (Lagos), July 11.

Anderson, David. 2002. Vigilantes, violence, and the politics of public order in Kenya. *African Affairs* 101:531–55.

Anyaehie, Rowland. 1997. Eze Onu Egwunwoke now a refugee at the Imo State Government House. *Rising Sun* (Umuahia), March 17–24, 7.

Appadurai, Arjun. 1996. *Modernity at large: Cultural dimensions of globalization.* Minneapolis: University of Minnesota Press.

Apter, Andrew. 1999. IBB = 419: Nigerian democracy and the politics of illusion. In *Civil society and the political imagination in Africa: Critical perspectives*, ed. John Comaroff and Jean Comaroff. Chicago: University of Chicago Press.

———. 2005. *The Pan-African nation: Oil and the spectacle of culture in Nigeria.* Chicago: University of Chicago Press.

Ardener, Edward. 1970. Witchcraft, economics, and the continuity of belief. In *Witchcraft confessions and accusations*, ed. Mary Douglas. London: Travistock.

Argenti, Nicolas. 1998. Air youth: Performance, violence, and the state in Cameroon. *Journal of the Royal Anthropological Institute* 4, no 4:753–82.

Auslander, Mark. 1993. "Open the wombs!" The symbolic politics of modern Ngoni witchfinding. In *Modernity and its malcontents: Ritual and power in post-colonial Africa*, ed. Jean Comaroff and John Comaroff. Chicago: University of Chicago Press.

Bakassi Boys in Anambra State, 2000. *Comet* (Lagos), June 29, 1.

Baker, Bruce. 2002a. Living with non-state policing in South Africa: The issues and dilemmas. *Journal of Modern African Studies* 40, no 1:29–53.

———. 2002b. When the Bakassi Boys came: Eastern Nigeria confronts vigilantism. *Journal of Contemporary African Studies* 20, no. 2:223–44.

Banjo, Lanre. 2004. *A year after riggings*. http://www.nigeriaworld.com/ (accessed December 31).

Barber, Karin. 1982. Popular reactions to the petro-naira. *Journal of Modern African Studies* 20, no. 3:431–50.

———. 1987. Popular arts in Africa. *African Studies Review* 30, no. 3:1–78.

———. 1995. Money, self-realization, and the person in Yoruba texts. In *Money matters: Instability, values, and social payments in the modern history of West African communities*, ed. Jane Guyer. Portsmouth, NH: Heinemann.

Bastian, Misty. 1996. Married in the water: Spirit kin and other afflictions of modernity. *Journal of Religion in Africa* 26:1–19.

———. 2001. Vulture men, campus cultists, and teenaged witches. In *Magical interpretations, material realities: Modernity, witchcraft, and the occult in postcolonial Africa*, ed. Henrietta Moore and Todd Sanders. New York: Routledge.

———. 2003. "Diabolic realities": Narratives of conspiracy, transparency, and "ritual murder" in the Nigerian popular print and electronic media. In *Transparency and conspiracy: Ethnographies of suspicion in the new world order*, ed. Harry West and Todd Sanders. Durham, NC: Duke University Press.

Battle for the soul of Anambra. 2003. *This Day* (Lagos), July 14.

Bayart, Jean-François. 1993. *The state in Africa: The politics of the belly*. London: Longman.

———. 1999. The "social capital" of the felonious state or the ruses of political intelligence. In *The criminalization of the African state*, by Jean-François Bayart, Stephen Ellis, and Béatrice Hibou. Bloomington: Indiana University Press.

———. 2000. Africa in the world: A history of extraversion. *African Affairs* 99:217–67.

Bayart, Jean-François, Stephen Ellis, and Béatrice Hibou. 1999. *The criminalization of the state in Africa*. Bloomington: Indiana University Press.

Berry, Sara. 1985. *Fathers work for their sons: Accumulation, mobility, and class formation in an extended Yorùbá community*. Berkeley: University of California Press.

———. 1989. Social institutions and access to resources. *Africa* 59:41–55.

Bledsoe, Caroline. 1980. *Women and marriage in Kpelle society*. Stanford, CA: Stanford University Press.

Blundo, Giorgio, ed. 2000. *Monnayer les pouvoirs. Espaces, mécanismes et représentations de la corruption*. Paris: Presses Universitaires de France.

Blundo, Giorgio. 2001a. La corruption comme mode de gouvernance locale: Trois décennies de décentralisation au Sénégal. *Afrique Contemporaine* 199, no. 3e:106–18.

———. 2001b. "Dessus de table": La corruption dans la passation des marchés publics locaux au Sénégal. *Politique Africaine* 83:79–97.

———. 2001c. Négocier l'etat au quotidien: Intermédiaires, courtiers et rabatteurs dans les interstices de l'administration Sénégalaise. *Autrepart* 20:75–90.

———. 2003. Décrire le caché. Autour du cas de la corruption. *Pratiques de la description*, ed. Giorgio Blundo and Jean-Pierre Olivier de Sardan. Paris: Éditions de l'EHESS.

Blundo, Giorgio, and Jean-Pierre Olivier de Sardan. 2001a. La corruption quotidienne en Afrique de l'Ouest. *Politique Africaine* 83:8–37.

———. 2001b. Sémiologie populaire de la corruption. *Politique Africaine* 83: 98–114.

Brieger, W. R., P. E. Osamor, K. K. Salami, O. Oladepo, and S. A. Otusanya. 2004. Interactions between patent medicine vendors and customers in urban and rural Nigeria. *Health Policy and Planning* 19, no. 3:177–82.

Buchanan, Jim, and Alex Grant. 2001. Investigating and prosecuting Nigerian fraud. *United States Attorneys' Bulletin*, 39–47.

Buckley, Anthony D. 1985. *Yoruba medicine*. Oxford: Oxford University Press.

Calkins, Laurel Brubaker. 2004. Six accused over Enron sham sale. *National Post's Financial Post and FP Investing*, September 22.

Casanova, José. 2001. Religion, the new millennium, and globalization. *Sociology of Religion* 62:415–41.

Chabal, Patrick, and Jean-Pascal Daloz. 1999. *Africa works: Disorder as political instrument*. Bloomington: Indiana University Press.

Chukwurah, Henry, and Akin Alofetekun. 1996. Ritual murder spreads. *National Concord* (Lagos), November 25, 1.

Coleman, Simon. 2000. *The globalisation of charismatic Christianity: Spreading the gospel of prosperity*. Cambridge: Cambridge University Press.

Comaroff, Jean, and John Comaroff, eds. 1993. *Modernity and its malcontents: Ritual and power in postcolonial Africa*. Chicago: University of Chicago Press.

Comaroff, Jean, and John Comaroff. 1999a. Occult economies and the violence of abstraction: Notes from the South African postcolony. *American Ethnologist* 26, no. 2:279–303.

———. 2001. *Millennial capitalism and the culture of neoliberalism*. Durham, NC: Duke University Press.

Comaroff, John, and Jean Comaroff. 1999b. Introd. to *Civil society and the political imagination in Africa*, ed. John Comaroff and Jean Comaroff. Chicago: University of Chicago Press.

Cornwall, Andrea. 2002. Spending power: Love, money, and the reconfiguration of gender relations in Ado-Odo, southwestern Nigeria. *American Ethnologist* 29, no. 4:963–80.

Coronil, Fernando. 1997. *The magical state: Nature, money, and modernity in Venezuela*. Chicago: University of Chicago Press.

Corten, Andre, and Ruth Marshall-Fratani, eds. 2001. *Between Babel and Pentecost: Transnational Pentecostalism in Africa and Latin America*. Bloomington: Indiana University Press.

Curfew imposed on Owerri. 1996. *Daily Times* (Lagos), September 27, 1.

d'Azevedo, Warren. 1962. Common principles and variant kinship structures among the Gola of western Liberia. *American Anthropologist* 64, no. 3:404–20.

de Waal, Alexander. 1997. *Famine crimes: Politics and the disaster relief industry in Africa*. Bloomington: Indiana University Press.

Diamond, Larry Jay, Anthony H. M. Kirk-Greene, and Oyeleye Oyediran. 1997. *Transition without end: Nigerian politics and civil society under Babangida*. Boulder, CO: Lynne Rienner Publishers.

Dicklitch, Susan. 1998. *The elusive promise of NGOs in Africa: Lessons from Uganda*. New York: St. Martin's Press.

Edelson, Eve. 2003. The 419 scam: Information warfare on the spam front and a proposal for local filtering. *Computers and Security* 22, no. 5:392–402.

Edike, Tony. (2000a). Anambra residents restive over FG order on Bakassi Boys. *Vanguard* (Lagos), July 29.

———. 2000b. Bakassi Boys in Anambra State. *Vanguard* (Lagos), June 30.

Ehirim, Chuks. 1996. Ritual killings: Onitsha on fire. *Tempo* (Lagos), December 5.

Ekeh, Peter. 1975. Colonialism and the two publics in Africa: A theoretical statement. *Comparative Journal of Society and History* 17, no. 1:91–112.

Emelumba, Mbadiwe. 1996. Ekeanyanwu and Dutroux. *National Post* (Lagos), October 7–13, 1.

Emerole, Jonathan. 1996. Abure "exposes" Otokoto. *Statesman* (Owerri), October 16, 1.

Escobar, Arturo. 1995. *Encountering development: The making and unmaking of the Third World*. Princeton, NJ: Princeton University Press.

Eze, James. 2004. Okija: Those who fed fat on the shrine. *Sun* (Lagos), August 14.

Ezeh, P. J. 2002. Corruption and deviant behaviour in Nigeria: An anthropological perspective. In *Corruption in Nigeria: Critical perspectives*, ed. C.O.T. Ugwu. Nsukka, Nigeria: Chuka Educational Publishers.

Ferguson, James. 1990. *The anti-politics machine: "Development," depoliticization, and bureaucratic power in Lesotho*. New York: Cambridge University Press.

FG asks police to flush Bakassi Boys. 2000. *Vanguard* (Lagos), July 27.

Fisiy, Cyprian, and Peter Geschiere. 1991. Sorcery, witchcraft, and accumulation: Regional variations in south and west Cameroon. *Critique of Anthropology* 11, no. 3:251–78.

Forrest, Tom. 1993. *Politics and economic development in Nigeria*. Boulder, CO: Westview Press.

Fortes, Meyer. 1978. Parenthood, marriage, and fertility in West Africa. *Journal of Development Studies* 14, no. 4:121–48.

Geschiere, Peter. 1997. *Modernity of witchcraft: Politics and the occult in postcolonial Africa*. Charlottesville: University of Virginia Press.

Geschiere, Peter, and Josef Gugler. 1998. The urban-rural connection: Changing issues of belonging and identification. *Africa* 68, no. 3:309–19.

Geschiere, Peter, and Francis Nyamnjoh. 1998. Witchcraft as an issue in the "politics of belonging": Democratization and urban migrants' involvement with the home village. *African Studies Review* 41, no. 3:69–91.

Gifford, Paul. 1987. "Africa shall be saved": An appraisal of Reinhardt Bonnke's Pan-African crusade. *Journal of Religion in Africa* 27, no. 1:63–92.

———. 1998. *African Christianity: Its public role.* London: Hurst.

———. 2004. *Ghana's new Christianity: Pentecostalism in a globalizing economy.* Bloomington: Indiana University Press.

Gore, Charles, and David Pratten. 2003. The politics of plunder: The rhetorics of order and disorder in southern Nigeria. *African Affairs* 102, no. 407:211–40.

Graf, William. 1988. *The Nigerian state: Political economy, state class and political system in the post-colonial era.* London: Heinemann.

Gugler, Josef. 2002. The son of the hawk does not remain abroad: The urban-rural connection in Africa. *African Studies Review* 45, no. 1:21–41.

Gupta, Akhil. 1995. Blurred boundaries: The discourse of corruption, the culture of politics, and the imagined state. *American Ethnologist* 22, no. 3:375–402.

Guyer, Jane. 1993. Wealth in people and self-realization in Equatorial Africa. *Man* 28, no. 2:243–65.

———. 1995. Wealth in people, wealth in knowledge: Introduction. *Journal of African History* 36, no. 1:83–90.

——— 2004. *Marginal gains: Monetary transactions in Atlantic Africa.* Chicago: University of Chicago Press.

Haller, Dieter, and Cris Shore, eds. 2005. *Corruption: Anthropological perspectives.* London: Pluto.

Halliburton's 42.4 million bribe revisited. 2004. *Vanguard* (Lagos), February 3.

Halttunen, Karen. 1982. *Confidence men and painted women: A study of middle-class culture in America, 1830–1870.* New Haven, CT: Yale University Press.

Hancock, Graham. 1989. *Lords of poverty: The power, prestige, and corruption of the international aid business.* New York: Atlantic Monthly Press.

Hannerz, Ulf. 1996. *Transnational connections: Culture, people, places.* New York: Routledge.

Harnischfeger, Johannes. 2003. The Bakassi Boys: Fighting crime in Nigeria. *Journal of Modern African Studies* 41, no. 1:23–49.

Hart, Benedict. 1996. Aneke hits back at Onuegwu Nwoke. *National Post* (Lagos), November 24–December 1, 3.

Haynes, Jonathan. 2000. *Nigerian video films.* Athens: Ohio University Center for International Studies.

Haysom, Nicholas. 1990. Vigilantism and the policing of South African townships: Manufacturing violent stability. In *Towards justice? Crime and state control in South Africa,* ed. Desirée Hansson and Dirk van Zyl Smit. Cape Town: Oxford University Press.

Heidenheimer, Arnold, ed. 1970. *Political corruption: Readings in comparative analysis.* New York: Holt, Reinhart and Winston.

Henderson, Richard. 1972. *The king in every man: Evolutionary trends in Onitsha Ibo society and culture.* New Haven, CT: Yale University Press.

Hibou, Béatrice. 1999. The "social capital" of the state as an agent of deception or the ruses of economic intelligence. In *The criminalization of the African state,* by Jean-François Bayart, Stephen Ellis, and Béatrice Hibou. Bloomington: Indiana University Press.

Hudock, Ann. 1999. *NGOs and civil society: Democracy by proxy?* Cambridge, UK: Polity Press.

Human Rights Watch. 2002. The Bakassi Boys: The legitimization of murder and torture. New York: Human Rights Watch.

———. 2003. The O'odua People's Congress: Fighting violence with violence. New York: Human Rights Watch.

Ibrahim, Jibrin. 2004. The first lady syndrome and the marginalisation of women from power: Opportunities or compromises for gender equality. *Feminist Africa* 3. http://www.femistafrica.org/03–2004/jibrin.html.

Igbikiowubo, Hector. 2003. Two more Enron executives charged in Nigerian energy deal. *Vanguard* (Lagos), October 21.

Ikelegbe, Augustine. 2001. The perverse manifestation of civil society: Evidence from Nigeria. *Journal of Modern African Studies* 39, no. 1:1–24.

Imo State Government. 1997. *Government white paper on the report of the judicial commission of inquiry into the disturbances of 24–25 September 1996 in Owerri.* Owerri: Office of the Secretary of the State Government.

Jeganathan, Pradeep. 2004. Checkpoint: Anthropology, identity, and the state. In *Anthropology in the margins of the state,* ed. Veena Das and Deborah Poole. Santa Fe, NM: School of American Research Press.

Jimmy, E. O., E. Achelonu, and S. Orji. 2000. Antimalarials dispensing pattern by patent medicine dealers in rural settlements in Nigeria. *Public Health* 114, no. 4:282–85.

Joseph, Richard. 1987. *Democracy and prebendal politics in Nigeria: The rise and fall of the second republic.* Cambridge: Cambridge University Press.

Karl, Terry Lynn. 1997. *The paradox of plenty: Oil booms and petro-states.* Berkeley: University of California Press.

Kirk-Greene, Anthony H. M., and Douglas Rimmer. 1981. *Nigeria since 1970: A political and economic outline.* New York: Africana.

Kleinberg, Remonda Bensabat, and Janine A. Clark. 2000. *Economic liberalization, democratization, and civil society in the developing world.* New York: St. Martin's Press.

Klitgaard, Robert. 1990. *Tropical gangsters.* New York: Basic Books.

Lame, Ibrahim, and Femi Adekunle. 2001. *Fighting corruption and organized crime in Nigeria: Challenges for the new millennium.* Ibadan, Nigeria: Spectrum Books.

Letter to the editor. 2004. *Newswatch* (Lagos), November 8, 4.

Lewis, Oscar. 1959. *Five families: Mexican case studies in the culture of poverty.* New York: Basic Books.

Lucas, Emma. 2000. We decide, they decide for us: Popular participation as an issue in two Nigerian women's development programmes. *Africa Development* 25, nos. 1–2:75–97.

Maduemesi, Uche. 1996. Roots of ritual killers: Across the land, innocent civilians are being killed and their parts "harvested" for ritual sacrifice. *Tell* (Lagos), October 14, 18–21.

Maier, Karl. 2000. *This house has fallen: Nigeria in crisis.* Boulder, CO: Westview Press.

Mama, Amina. 1995. Feminism or femocracy: State feminism and democratisation in Nigeria. *Africa Development* 20, no. 1:37–58.

———. 1998. Khaki in the family: Gender discourses and militarism in Nigeria. *African Studies Review* 41, no. 2:1–18.

Mamdani, Mahmood. 1996. *Citizen and subject: Contemporary Africa and the legacy of late colonialism.* Princeton, NJ: Princeton University Press.

Marshall, Ruth. 1991. Power in the name of Jesus. *Review of African Political Economy* 52:21–38.

———. 1995. "God is not a democrat": Pentecostalism and democratisation in Nigeria. In *The Christian churches and the democratisation of Africa,* ed. Paul Gifford. New York: Brill.

Marshall-Fratani, Ruth. 1998. Mediating the global and the local in Nigerian Pentecostalism. *Journal of Religion in Africa* 38, no. 3:278–313.

———. 2001. Prosperite miraculeuse: Les pasteurs Pentecostistes et l'argent de dieu au Nigeria. *Politique Africaine* 82:24–44.

Mbachu, Dulue, and Glenn McKenzie. 2004. Nigerian leader declares state of emergency in violence-torn state amid reports of new attacks. Associated Press, May 18.

Mbembe, Achille. 1992. Notes from the postcolony. *Africa* 62, no. 1:3–38.

———. 2001. *On the postcolony.* Berkeley: University of California Press.

McCall, John. 2004. Juju and justice at the movies: Vigilantes in Nigerian popular videos. *African Studies Review* 47, no. 3:51–67.

MacKenzie, Glenn. 2003. Obasanjo wins re-election but Nigerian opposition rejects the results. Associated Press, April 22.

Meyer, Birgit. 1995. "Delivered from the powers of darkness": Confessions of satanic riches in Christian Ghana. *Africa* 65, no. 2:236–55.

———. 1998. The power of money: Politics, occult forces, and Pentecostalism in Ghana. *African Studies Review* 41, no. 3:15–37.

———. 2004. Christianity in Africa: From African independent to Pentecostal-charismatic churches. *Annual Review of Anthropology* 33:447–74.

Middleton, John, and Edward H. Winter, eds. 1963. *Witchcraft and sorcery in East Africa.* London: Routledge Paul.

Mudimbe, V. Y. 1988. *The invention of Africa: Gnosis, philosophy, and the order of knowledge.* Bloomington: Indiana University Press.

———. 1992. *The surreptitious speech: Présence Africaine and the politics of otherness, 1947–1987.* Chicago: University of Chicago Press.

National Democratic Institute. 2003. *Statement of the National Democratic Institute international observer delegation to Nigeria's April 19 presidential and gubernatorial elections,* Abuja, April 21.

National Population Commission (Nigeria) and ORC Macro. 2004. *Nigeria demographic and health survey 2003.* Calverton, MD: National Population Commission and ORC National Macro.

Nelson, Charles. 1996. PAT 101: Principles of patronage. *Issue: A Journal of Opinion* 24, no. 1:45–51.

Nwachi, Lindsay. 1996. Dr. Amamasi "punished" by kidnappers for refusing the stealing of Iwuanyanwu father's corpse? *Rising Sun* (Umuahia), October 21–28, 6.

Nwakanma, Obi. 2005. The Igbo: Living in the belly of the whale. *Vanguard* (Lagos), February 6.

Nwakanma, Obi, and Sam Onwuemedo. 1996. The day Owerri bled. *Sunday Vanguard* (Lagos), September 29, 20.

Nye, Joseph. 1967. Corruption and political development: A cost-benefit analysis. *American Political Science Review* 56, no. 1:417–27.

Obibi, Collins. 1996. Behind the eruptions in Owerri. *Guardian* (Lagos), October 4, 11.

Obasanjo declares state of emergency in Plateau. 2004. *Vanguard* (Lagos), May 19.

Observers point to blatant fraud in Nigerian elections. 2003. *Deutsche Press-Agentur.* April 22.

Ofou, Felix. 1996. Another severed head found in Imo. *Punch* (Lagos), November 1, 1.

Ohakah, Chibisi. 1996. Ritual killers on the prowl. *Champion* (Lagos), December 7, 14.

Ojuwale, Olu. 2004. The patrons of Okija shrine. *Newswatch* (Lagos), October 11, 14–20.

Okonta, Ike, and Oronto Douglas. 2001. *Where vultures feast: Shell, human rights, and oil in the Niger Delta.* San Francisco: Sierra Club Books.

Olivier de Sardan, Jean-Pierre. 1999. A moral economy of corruption in Africa? *Journal of Modern African Studies* 37, no. 1:25–52.

Olivier de Sardan, Jean-Pierre. 2005. *Anthropology and development: Understanding contemporary social change.* London: Zed.

Ononuju, E. 1996. *Igbos: A missing tribe in Israel.* Aba, Nigeria: Emancipation Books.

Onwubiko, Emmanuel. 2000. Obasanjo forgives NAU students, okays Bakassi Boys. *Guardian* (Lagos), August 28.

Oriji, John. 2003. The ivory tower and its descent to the "dark ages": A study of the epidemics of cultism in southern Nigerian universities. Paper presented at the annual meeting of the African Studies Association, Boston, October 30.

Osaghae, Eghosa E. 1998. *Crippled giant: Nigeria since independence.* Bloomington: Indiana University Press.

Othman, Shehu. 1984. Classes, crises, and coup: The demise of the Shagari regime. *African Affairs* 83, no. 333:441–61.

Our justice system has failed us. 2004. *Insider Weekly* (Lagos), August 26, 22–24.

Panter-Brick, Keith, ed. 1978. *Soldiers and oil: The political transformation of Nigeria.* Totowa, NJ: Cass.

Parry, Jonathan. 1986. The gift, the Indian gift, and the "Indian gift." *Man* 21, no. 3:453–73.

The police report on the Umuahia murders. 2001. *Insider Weekly* (Lagos). July 16, 18–28.

Pratten, David. 2000. From secret societies to vigilantes: Identity, justice, and development among the Annang of southeastern Nigeria. PhD diss., University of London.

Price, Robert 1974. Politics and culture in contemporary Ghana: The big-man small-boy syndrome. *Journal of African Studies* 1, no. 2:173–204.

Rebhorn, Wayne A. 1988. *Foxes and lions: Machiavelli's confidence men*. Ithaca, NY: Cornell University Press.

Reno, William. 1993. Old brigades, money bags, new breeds, and the ironies of reform in Nigeria. *Canadian Journal of African Studies* 27, no. 1:66–87.

The result of our sit-at-home. 2005. http://www.biafraland.com/August_26_2004.htm (accessed March 9).

Robbins, Joel. 2004. The globalization of Pentecostal Christianity. *Annual Review of Anthropology* 33:117–43.

Romero, Simon. 2004a. Halliburton severs link with 2 over Nigeria inquiry. *New York Times*, June 19.

———. 2004b. Halliburton seeks distance between itself and inquiry. *New York Times*, June 14.

Said, Edward. 1978. *Orientalism*. New York: Pantheon Books.

Scandal rocks Winners Chapel. 2004. *Newswatch* (Lagos), July 19.

Shack, William, and Eliot Skinner, eds. 1979. *Strangers in African societies*. Berkeley: University of California Press.

Shaw, Rosalind. 1997. The production of witchcraft/witchcraft as production: Memory, modernity, and the slave trade in Sierra Leone. *American Ethnologist* 24, no. 4:856–76.

Sissener, Tone Kristin. 2001. *Anthropological perspectives on corruption*. Chr. Michelsen Institute, http://www.cmi.no/publications/publication.cfm?pubid=910 (accessed January 22, 2005).

Skinner, Elliot. 1963. Strangers in West African societies. *Africa* 33, no. 4:307–20.

Smith, Daniel Jordan. 2000. "These girls today *na war-o*": Premarital sexuality and modern identity in southeastern Nigeria. *Africa Today* 47, nos. 3–4:98–120.

———. 2001a. "The arrow of God": Pentecostalism, inequality, and the supernatural in southeastern Nigeria. *Africa* 71, no. 4:587–613.

———. 2001b. Kinship and corruption in Nigeria. *Ethnos* 66, no. 3:344–64.

———. 2001c. Romance, parenthood, and gender in a modern African society. *Ethnology* 40, no. 2:129–51.

———. 2002. "Man no be wood": Gender and extramarital sex in contemporary southeastern Nigeria. *Ahfad Journal* 19, no. 2:4–23.

———. 2003. Patronage, per diems, and "the workshop mentality": The practice of family planning programs in southeastern Nigeria. *World Development* 31, no. 4:703–15.

———. 2004a. Burials and belonging in Nigeria: Rural-urban relations and social inequality in a contemporary African ritual. *American Anthropologist* 106, no. 3:569–79.

———. 2004b. Contradictions in Nigeria's fertility transition: The burdens and benefits of having people. *Population and Development Review* 30, no. 2:221–38.

———. 2004c. HIV/AIDS in Nigeria: The challenges of a national epidemic. In *Crafting the new Nigeria: Confronting the challenges*, ed. Robert Rotberg. Boulder, CO: Lynne Rienner.

———. 2005. Legacies of Biafra: Marriage, "home people," and human reproduction among the Igbo of Nigeria. *Africa* 75, no. 1:30–45.

Smith, M. G. 1964. Historical and cultural conditions of political corruption among the Hausa. *Comparative Studies in History and Society* 6, no. 2:164–94.

Smith, Russell, Michael Holmes, and Philip Kaufmann. 1999. Nigerian advance fee fraud, no. 121. In *Trends and issues in crime and criminal justice.* Canberra: Australian Institute of Criminology.

Story of the (un)successful "coup." 2003. *Daily Champion* (Lagos), July 12.

Taussig, Michael. 1997. *The magic of the state.* New York: Routledge.

Tignor, Robert. 1993. Political corruption in Nigeria before independence. *Journal of Modern African Studies* 31, no. 2:175–202.

The trouble with Anambra. 2003. *This Day* (Lagos), July 17.

Two hundred male organs found in a goat belly at Otokoto's house. 1996. *Rising Sun* (Umuahia), November 11–18, 3.

2004: The year of Biafra identity. 2005. http://www.biafraland.com/2004.htm (accessed March 9).

Uchendu, Victor. 1965. *The Igbo of southeast Nigeria.* Fort Worth, TX: Holt, Rinehart and Winston.

Udegbe, Clement. 1996. Owerri mayhem and state security. *This Day* (Lagos), October 23.

Ugwu, C.O.T., ed. 2002. *Corruption in Nigeria: Critical perspectives.* Nsukka, Nigeria: Chuka Educational Publishers.

UNAIDS. 2004. *2004 report on the global AIDS epidemic.* Geneva: UNAIDS.

United Nations International Children's Emergency Fund. 2004. *The state of the world's children, 2005.* New York: UNICEF.

Uvin, Peter. 1998. *Aiding violence: The development enterprise in Rwanda.* West Hartford, CT: Kumarian Press.

Wall, L. Lewis. 1988. *Hausa medicine: Illness and well-being in a West African culture.* Durham, NC: Duke University Press.

Watts, Michael. 1984. State, oil, and accumulation: From boom to bust. *Society and Space* 2:402–28.

———. 1992. The shock of modernity: Petroleum, protest, and fast capitalism in an industrializing society. In *Reworking modernity: Capitalism and symbolic discontent,* ed. Allan Pred and Michael Watts. New Brunswick, NJ: Rutgers University Press.

———. 1994. Oil as money: The devil's excrement and the spectacle of black gold. In *Money, power, and space,* ed. Stuart Corbridge, Nigel Thrift, and Ron Martin. Oxford: Blackwell.

Werner, Cynthia. 2000. Gifts, bribes, and development in post-Soviet Kazakhstan. *Human Organization* 59, no 1:11–22.

White, Luise. 1997. The traffic in heads: Bodies, borders, and the articulation of regional histories. *Journal of Southern African Studies* 23, no. 2:325–38.

Wolf, Eric R. 1982. *Europe and the people without history.* Berkeley: University of California Press.

Yan, Yunxiang. 1996. *The flow of gifts: Reciprocity and social networks in a Chinese village.* Stanford, CA: Stanford University Press.

Yang, Mayfair Mei-Hui. 1989. The gift economy and state power in China. *Comparative Studies in History and Society* 31, no. 1:24–54.

———. 1994. *Gifts, favors, and banquets: The art of social relationships in China.* Ithaca, NY: Cornell University Press.

Index